Internetworking

Multimedia

Internetworking
Multimedia

JON CROWCROFT, MARK HANDLEY and IAN WAKEMAN

Morgan Kaufmann Publishers
San Francisco, California

UK   Taylor & Francis, 11 New Fetter Lane, London EC4P 4EE
USA Morgan Kaufmann Publishers, 340 Pine Street, Sixth Floor, San Francisco, CA 94104-3205

Taylor & Francis is an imprint of the Taylor & Francis Group

British Library Cataloguing in Publication Data
A catalogue record for this book is available from the British Library.
ISBN 0-7484-0808-8 (cased) Not for sale in the USA and Canada
      0-7484-0807-X (pbk) Not for sale in the USA and Canada

Library of Congress Cataloging-in-Publication Data is available for this book
ISBN 1-55860-584-3 (pbk) For sale in the USA and Canada only

Taylor & Francis cover design by Youngs
Morgan Kaufmann cover design by Ross Carron Design. Cover photograph © 1999 PhotoDisc, Inc.
Typeset in Times 10/12pt by Santype International Ltd, Salisbury, Wiltshire
Printed and bound by T.J. International Ltd, Padstow, Cornwall
Cover printed by Flexiprint, Lancing, West Sussex

Contents

Figures

Tables

Preface

This book is about multimedia communication using the Internet. We wrote this book for (at least) three reasons. Firstly, we use the Internet to communicate and have done so for many years. Increasingly, we find ourselves using it as a replacement for the telephone, for conferencing and for delivering classes and seminars to remote participants. We think that this is the way that communication will be achieved in general for a wide variety of applications in the future, and feel that this view is worth reading about. Secondly, we work in education and teach students about the principles behind communication and multimedia, and we want to share the ideas and explanations with a broader readership than just the students who read our notes. Finally, we are all involved in researching and developing Internet protocols and mechanisms to improve multimedia communication applications and services, and want to explain the state of the art and trends to a wider audience.

The book's intended readership is users, working engineers and students at the Masters level who are both studying and implementing multimedia in the Internet. We assume familiarity with the standard Internet protocols and with communication and computer science at the general level of recent high-school or first-year university courses.

ROADMAP, OUTLINE AND ORGANISATION

The book is organised in ten chapters which are broadly categorised into three parts. The first part comprises Chapters 1–4 and is about technology: we cover media data types; network technology especially looking at so-called real time support; multicast routing support for interactive multimedia; coding and compression. Part Two consists of three chapters (5–7) and is about middleware: we discuss transport protocols and the important concept of application layer framing; we look at multimedia session creation, advertisement, invitation and so on; we look at conference control architectures. Part Three also comprises three chapters (8–10) and is about applications and application support: we look at the applications themselves (audio, video, shared authoring/viewing of documents and so on); lastly, we discuss media-on-demand; we describe the security requirements and mechanisms for providing solutions to problems.

Each chapter in this book starts with an introduction which explains what the chapter covers, then has a roadmap which explains how the material in the chapter fits together, and ends with a summary which captures what has been explained in the chapter.

This is a very fast-moving area. We have attempted to be as accurate as possible, but this book is out of date even before we write it. The standards, the code and the applications themselves are, as always, the best source of information.

ACKNOWLEDGEMENTS

Thanks first to Paul White, Stuart Clayman and Saleem Bhatti for permission to use their material in Chapters 2, 4 and 9. Thanks to the IETF's Audio and Video WG, the MMusic WG, the IAB's End2end Research Group, the Integrated and Differentiated Services and RSVP WGs, and to UCL and the (D)ARPA, and the EC MICE projects. Thanks to Craig Partridge at BBN, Khalid Sayood of the University of Nebraska–Lincoln, Deborah Estrin of USC, Tony Ballardie, Joc Chappell, Rex P. Tseng, and especially Syngen Brown for copious feedback on the last draft. Thanks to Petri Aukia for some LaTeX help.

Thanks to Rachel Brazear and Tony Moore for editorial work and cover designs.

Thanks to Andrew Carrick for encouragement and editorial help on two previous books.

We must acknowledge a broad debt to Van Jacobson, lately of the Lawrence Berkeley Network Laboratory, for his pioneering work, upon which is based a large part of what we describe in this book.

Thanks finally to Dave Clark at MIT for generous feedback, and to Jennifer Mann of MK for editorial assistance.

PART ONE

Technology

CHAPTER ONE

Introduction:
A Brief History of Real Time

1.1 INTRODUCTION

This book is about interactive multimedia in the Internet. We are used to conventional multimedia in everyday life through the telephone and television, through hi-fi/CDs and through video cameras and VCRs. A great deal of effort in the telecommunications research world has been aimed at trying to mimic these technologies in the digital telephony world. However, the work in Internet-based multimedia has gone a great deal further in flexibility and usability of services owing to its emphasis on computer-based solutions. Applications can be more intelligent, and can be integrated with each other making them more usable and more efficient. A simple example of this is the use of shared whiteboards during voice conferences, with visual indications of who is speaking and who is drawing. Another example is the idea of customisable call handling in Internet telephony ('if I am talking to the boss, and the caller is my employee, forward their call to my assistant, otherwise hand them to my answerphone avatar'). The only limit here is the imagination of the application creator.

The Internet was developed originally to support data communications between computers, but the definition of *data* has a habit of broadening, just as computers have a habit of becoming more flexible. The processing and storage capacity of computers has increased exponentially; so has the size and capacity of the Internet. All have now reached the point where we can capture, compress, store, decompress, replay, send and receive digital audio and video almost as easily as files of text.

From early research experiments in the late 1970s and early 1980s, through to the deployment of the late 1980s and early 1990s, multimedia has grown as a presence in the network. Interactive multimedia, whether for media-on-demand from World Wide Web servers or between users in multimedia conferencing systems, is becoming quite pervasive.

The Internet has undergone a number of enhancements to make this possible, as have its protocols. There is also a huge investment in middleware – software systems to enable more complex applications to be built quickly and effectively for distributed computing. Then there is a surprising variety of applications, not just conferencing or video-on-demand, but also image dissemination, games, multi-player multimedia VR, and so on.

In this book, we describe the technologies and systems that make this possible. Unlike previous books about multimedia and networking, which are descriptive, we attempt to prescribe the approach that has emerged in the Internet Engineering Task Force, or IETF. This is the group that carries out standards development for Internet protocols, services and applications. There are working groups on audio/video transport, multimedia conference control, integrated and differentiated services and resource reservation (to name but a few).

We believe that the model that has evolved in this environment is more scalable and flexible, and caters for more heterogeneity than alternative models, and is thus more suited to deployment for the public at large. It is also a very good model for how to develop multimedia distributed systems in general for many purposes; moreover, it is also fun.

1.2 ROADMAP

The roadmap for this chapter is best captured in Figure 1.1. The diagram shows the Internet protocols that are concerned with the format and delivery of multimedia content. The chapter is mostly a microcosm of the book, which means that it covers these protocols largely in a *bottom-up* approach, starting with delivery of packets in the Internet, and ending with a description of some multimedia application protocols. In between, we take a look at content description, at network service models, and at middleware for creation, transport, control and retrieval of multimedia.

1.3 CONTENT AND DELIVERY

There are two aspects to Internet multimedia: the content, and the delivery. This chapter is an introduction to these two topics, of which the rest of this book is a detailed discussion. The oft-cited convergence of computing and communications

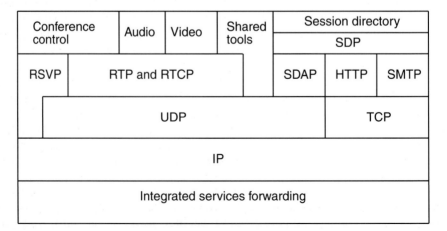

Figure 1.1 The Internet multimedia protocol stack.

is particularly important because of the convergence of multimedia and computing at the same time. There are three dominant multimedia applications in the world today which appear to be separate but are in many ways likely to merge as a result of the Internet, namely telephony, television and the World Wide Web. In fact, the main reason that the merge is likely is that it enables the development and deployment of a far wider set of intelligent and easy to use services to the paying public more quickly and cost effectively than any pre-existing technological approach.

The open model of the Internet means that services can be delivered to the right users, while the costs associated with delivering them unnecessarily to some of the wrong users can also be avoided. The low entry cost means that services can emerge that would normally not be considered viable (virtual community web TV for example, where a community may be widely dispersed, for example a set of speakers of a given language throughout the world).

1.4 FROM LETTERS AND NUMBERS TO SOUND AND VISION

Throughout the past four decades computers have been restricted to dealing with two main types of data – words and numbers, text and arithmetic processing – through word processing and spreadsheets etc. Codes for numbers (binary, BCD, fixed point, IEEE floating point and so on), are fairly well standardised. Codes for text (ASCII, EBCDIC, but also fonts, Kangi, ppt and so on) are also reasonably well understood. Higher-level 'codes' – links, indexes, references and so on – are the subject of such standards as the ubiquitous hypertext markup language, HTML.

Now computers, disks and networks are fast enough to process, store and transmit audio, video and computer-generated visualisation material as well as text and graphics and data: hence the multimedia revolution.

One fact about multimedia that cannot be overstated is that it is big – like space in the *Hitchhiker's Guide to the Universe*, it is much bigger than you can imagine. Of course, we are not talking about the hype here, we are talking about the storage transmission and processing requirements.

To paraphrase Maurice Zapp, from David Lodge's novel *A Small World*: 'Every encoding is a decoding'. The idea behind this glib quote is that each time we invent a new way of representing and transmitting information, we also have to teach ourselves to receive and comprehend that new type of representation. In the rest of this section, we take a look at some aspects of representation that need to be understood with regard to multimedia.

Numbers and letters have standard encodings: ASCII and IEEE floating point are the most widespread now (at least for common English language text processing, and for numeric programming). In the past there has been a plethora of other encodings, even for simple Roman alphabet text. As multilingual support has become common, we have seen a brief increase in the number of encodings; then, as the problems become better understood, a standard set of character sets is emerging. Digital multimedia encodings in the form of audio and video are still at a very early stage in terms of standards, and there are many, partly because of the range of possible processing, storage and transmission performance capacities available on computers and networks, where some systems are right at the limits of their abilities to do any useful work at all.

Each new medium needs to be coded and we need to have common representations for objects in the medium; there are many choices. For example, speech can be coded as a sequence of samples, a sequence of phonemes, a string of text with a voice synthesiser setting, and so on, requiring more or less intelligence or processing at the sender and receiver, and providing more or less structural information (and as a result, typically allowing more compression). Similarly, video can be coded as a sequence of bitmaps, or else can be broken down into some description of scenes, objects within scenes, motion of objects and so on.

The codings now involve possible relationships with time and between different media. When we read a block of text, it is usually up to the reader to choose how quickly to read it. *Hypertext* to some extent breaks this rule, at least by relating text non-linearly with other text. When we listen to speech or have a conversation with another autonomous being, we do not control the rate of arrival of information so obviously. When we combine media, sound and vision, for example, we typically expect the combined media on a recording (or seen remotely) to maintain the temporal relationship that they had at source. This is what really defines data as being *multimedia*. *Hypermedia* is multimedia that is arranged with non-linear relations between subsequences.

Compression, and hierarchical encoding are also needed. Multimedia data are typically much more bulky than text or numerical data. A typical simple-minded sampled audio sequence might take 8 kBps. This compares badly with 8 kB of text: assume we had 10 characters per word, then this would constitute 800 words, and might take a quick speaker a minute to read aloud. In other words, speech requires at least two orders of magnitude more bytes than text. Video is far worse still, although clearly, comparisons are more difficult since the value of typical information content is quite different.

All of this means that we need to consider compression techniques, to save storage and transmission capacity. Luckily, much audio and video is redundant (contains in effect repeated or less useful data) and is often far more amenable to compression than text.

Metalanguages (codes for codings) are required. Typically, while we are still evolving a wide range of codings and compression techniques, we need protocols for exchange of media between different systems. We also need protocols to relate the different media (for synchronisation and for hypermedia).

Next, let us look at some audio and video input forms and digital encodings.

1.5 ANALOGUE AND DIGITAL

Audio and video all start life in the 'analogue domain'. (Domain is used in this context just to mean before or after some particular conversion). It is important to understand the basic requirements of the media in time and space. The analogue domain is usually best understood in terms of the range of frequencies in use for a particular quality. For sound, this means how low and high a note or sound is allowed. For video, this translates into the number of distinguishable colours. For video, we also have to consider the frame rate. Video is similar to film in that it consists of a number of discrete frames. You may recall seeing old films which were shot at a lower frame rate than is used nowadays, and flicker is visible. To refine this point further, we should distinguish between the rate at which a scene is sampled and the rate at which a frame on a screen is displayed. For many moving image systems, these may be different. For example, films may show the same frame more than once to reduce flicker. Although cathode ray tubes have significant persistence, video systems may refresh different parts of the screen at different rates – *interlacing* is used in many systems where alternate lines of the screen are refreshed in alternate cycles. This is motivated by the possible reduction in bandwidth, in both the analogue and digital domains.

Both sound and image can be broken down at any instant into a set of basic frequencies. This is the 'waveform'. We can record all of the frequencies present at any one time, or we can choose to record only the 'important' ones. If we choose to record less than all frequencies, we get less 'fidelity' in our recording, so that the playback is less like the original. However, the less we record, the less tape/recording media we need.

Audio and video start as waves, a sequence of compression and rarefaction of air, or the fluctuation of an electric and magnetic field, with time. Waves need to be captured, by some device, and then sampled digitally. Typically, a 'sample-and-hold' technique is used: an electromechanical or light-sensitive device responds to the sound or light and produces an analogue electrical signal. This can be averaged over a sample period by providing some discrete clock signal and an averaging circuit. The value during this sample period can then be converted to a digital value of a given accuracy ('quantised').

We can do this sampling 'perfectly' by sampling twice as often digitally as the highest analogue frequency, or we can take advantage of human frailty and reduce the quality by decreasing the sample frequency (the clock rate above) and/or the quantisation (number of bits used per sample).

1.5.1 What is bandwidth?

The term 'bandwidth' is used by electrical engineers to refer to the frequency range of an analogue signal. Often, especially in the Internet community, the term is used loosely to refer to channel capacity, or the bit rate of a link. Note that because of sampling, quantisation and compression, the bit rate needed for a given bandwidth analogue signal is potentially many times (orders of magnitude even) less than the perfect sample signal requirement would imply.

Analogue audio for humans is roughly in the range 50 Hz to 20 kHz. Human speech is intelligible, typically even when restricted to the range 1–3 kHz, and the telephone networks have taken advantage of this since very early days by providing only limited quality lines. This has meant that they can use low quality speakers and microphones in the handset – the quality is similar to AM radio.

It is not entirely a coincidence, therefore, that the copper wires used for transmission in the telephone system were principally chosen for the ability to carry a baseband signal that could convey speech ('toll') quality audio.

In most systems, luckily, telephone wires are over-engineered. They are capable of carrying a signal at up to 16 times the 'bandwidth' of that used by pure analogue phones from the home to the exchange over one kilometre, and 300 times this bandwidth up to 100 metres. For the moment, though, the 'last mile' or customer subscriber-loop circuits have boxes at the ends that limit this to what is guaranteed for ordinary audio telephony, while the rest of the frequencies are used for engineering work.

Video signals, on the other hand, occupy a much wider frequency range. Analogue TV, which defined for about 60 years the input, output and transmission standards, has several different standards, but is typically amplitude modulated on a 3.58 MHz carrier. The signal that is conveyed on this is a sequence of 'scanlines', each making up a screen. The scanline is in essence a sample of the brightness and colours across a horizontal line as detected in the camera, and as used to control the electron gun in the TV monitor.

In the CCIR 601 standard, a digital version of this is defined, which makes use of two samples of 8 bits each of colour (chrominance) and one of brightness (luminance) at 13.5 MHz. The resulting data rate is around 166 Mbps.

It is not entirely a coincidence that old cable TV networks are capable of transmitting these data rates; however, modern hybrid fibre-coax networks are intended to carry a much larger number of compressed digital channels.

The purpose of talking about the media encoding and channel capacity requirements is to show the relationship between particular media and the transmission technology associated with them. The two largest networks in the world in terms of terminals are the telephone network and the TV network. Each addresses a particular capacity and pattern of communication. If a data network such as the Internet is to carry these media, and if the 'terminals' or workstations and microcomputers of the Internet are to be able to capture, store, transmit, receive and display such media, then the network and end systems have to deal with these types of data one way or another. If we compress the data, and decompress at a receiver, then the rate/capacity is still required outside of the compressed *domain*, and the compression/decompression engines need to be able to cope with this, even though they may spare the network (or storage device).

The word 'encoding' is often used as a noun as well as a verb when talking about multimedia. Nowadays, there is a vast range of encodings in use or development. There are a variety of reasons for this: codes for audio and video depend on the quality of audio or video required. A very simple example of this is the difference between digital audio for ISDN telephones (64 kbps PCM, see Chapter 4, section 4.6.5) and for CD (1.4 Mbps 16 bit, etc.);[1] another reason for the range of encodings is that some encodings include linkages to other media for reasons of synchronisation (for example between voice and lips); yet another reason is to provide future proofing against any new media (holograms?); finally, because of the range of performance of different computers, it may be necessary to have a 'metaprotocol' to negotiate what is used between encoder and decoder. This permits programs to encode a stream of media according to whatever is convenient to them, while a decoder can then decode it according to its capabilities. For example, some HDTV (high definition television) standards are actually a superset of current standard TV encodings so that a 'rougher' picture can be extracted by existing TV receivers from new HDTV transmissions (or from playing back new HDTV videotapes). This principle is quite general.

1.6 PROTOCOLS

Protocols are the rules needed for communication. In human and computer communication, standard protocols eliminate confusion and time wasted misunderstanding each other. In computer communication, protocols comprise three main components: interfaces, which define the rules for *using* a protocol, and provide a service to the software that uses the interface; packet formats, which define the syntax for the exchange of messages between local and remote systems; and procedures, which define the *operational* rules concerning which packets can be exchanged when.

Communication systems are built up out of multiple *layered* protocols. The concept of *layering* is twofold. Firstly, common services can be built in all devices or subsystems, and specialised services built out of these for those devices or subsystems that need them. Secondly, the details of operation of local, or technology-specific features of a protocol can be hidden by one layer from the layer above it.

In this book, we illustrate these different aspects protocols in several different ways. When we want to show the layering of protocols, we make use of a *stack* diagram, such as Figure 1.1. When we want to show the operational rules of a protocol, we sometimes use a *time-sequence diagram* such as Figure 1.3, which portrays a particular instance of exchange of packets. In some places, we document the layout of the packets themselves, to show what control functions are conveyed in each transmission, reception or exchange.

In the rest of this chapter we introduce these aspects of the Internet multimedia protocols as well as the more subtle question of performance. Later chapters cover these aspects in more detail. First of all, we look at names, addresses and routes.

1.6.1 Names, addresses and routes

The user is usually very aware of the names of objects in the Internet. We frequently see reference to Web sites and pages (for example, `http://www.cs.ucl.ac.uk/staff/jon`) which incorporate domain name system names for a system or service in the network. A name in effect tells the user *what something is*.

Names are useful to human users for this very reason, but are unwieldy and inefficient for computer systems. Typically, they are *mapped* into addresses, using a directory or nameservice. Addresses then tell a piece of software (or the network operator or manager) *where something is*. Each host in the network has a unique address of (currently) 32 bits (128 bits in IP version 6). More accurately, each interface on each host in the Internet has a unique address which is made up of two components, as shown in Table 1.1.

Table 1.1 The structured Internet address.

Host part; Network part

All Internet protocol (IP) packets carry both a source and a destination address. Typically, the network part is indicated by applying a mask of some number of bits to the address, leaving the bits for the host part. Common divisions are 24 bits for network and 8 bits for host, and 16 bits for network part and 16 for the host part.

The network part of the destination address is used by routers to index routing tables to figure out *where a packet must be delivered to*. In fact, a 'longest match' lookup of the prefix or network part must be done which can be difficult to optimise. Recent work (Brodnik *et al.*, 1997) has achieved very good lookup times and table sizes.

All packets in the Internet protocol layer carry these addresses so that they can be delivered to the right destination and so that we can determine where they came from. As we look at other layers in the Internet multimedia protocol stack, we will see what other control information is carried in packets to carry out additional functions.

1.6.2   Internet multimedia protocols

The overall protocol architecture that makes up the capability to deliver multimedia over what was originally a pure data network is surprisingly not so very different from the original Internet architecture.

The protocol stacks for Internet multimedia are show in Figure 1.1 above. Most of the protocols are not deeply layered, unlike many other protocol stacks, but rather are used alongside each other to produce a complete session. It is possible to use multimedia applications over the Internet without some (or all) of the additional protocols (for example, omission of RSVP or omission of session description protocol (SDP), and so on) depending on the performance or functionality required. Later chapters will show how each new protocol adds value to the basic IP packet delivery model.

In the next section, we discuss the underlying unicast and multicast delivery model, which must be added within the IP layer to give maximum benefit to the network.

Packet switched data networking adds value to circuit switched networks by sharing the capacity amongst multiple users in time. The data stream from each user is broken into chunks to form packets, which require only capacity when each packet is being sent. The capacity required is thus the sum of the average bandwidth, rather than the total peak bandwidth. This 'statistical multiplexing gain' comes at the expense of having sometimes to queue packets for access to the transmission channel.

The statistical multiplexing gain is quite large for traditional bursty data applications such as Web access. For multimedia traffic, this gain is harder to achieve (depending on the compression algorithms used, as discussed in later chapters, it can even become even harder) and yet we can get a *spatial* gain in use of the network by using group communication carefully. A simple way to send data to multiple recipients is to send it multiple times from the source. Such 'multiple unicasts' make very poor use of the links near the sender, and potentially incur a lot of delay before a single transmission is completed. The Internet offers a mechanism to avoid these overheads called *IP multicast*.

Multicast is essential in the context of Internet technologies that may replace television (streaming services, as discussed in Chapter 9), but it is also highly relevant in telephony services, especially in the business community: it is extremely common for one telephone call to spawn another – the ability to teleconference is not widespread in the traditional plain old telephone system (POTS) except at some commercial cost or in a restricted subset of telephones. The Internet ability to provide this service is quite powerful.

We discuss some of the limitations of multicast as a service in Chapter 3. Some of the problems that vendors have had in supporting large-scale multicast as well as service guarantees in router products have prompted the design of a new generation of routers coming onto the market as we write. Similarly, the understanding of service guarantees and multicast has been slow to diffuse into the commercial Internet service provider community until recently, but this is changing rapidly.

1.7 INTERNET SERVICE MODELS

Traditionally, the Internet has provided best-effort delivery of datagram traffic from senders to receivers. No guarantees are made regarding when or if a datagram will be delivered to a receiver. However, datagrams are normally dropped only when a router exceeds a queue size limit owing to congestion. The best-effort Internet service model does not assume first-in-first-out (FIFO, also known as first-come-first-served) queuing, although many routers have implemented this. The effect is to provide rather unfair distribution of resources.

With best-effort service, if a link is not congested then queues will not build at routers, datagrams will not be discarded in routers, and delays will consist of serialisation delays at each hop plus propagation delays. With sufficiently fast link speeds, serialisation delays are insignificant compared with propagation delays. However, if a link is congested, with best-effort service queuing delays will start to influence end-to-end delays, and packets will start to be lost as queue size limits are exceeded.

1.7.1 Non-best-effort service

Real time Internet traffic is defined as datagrams that are delay sensitive. 'Real time' is an oft-misused term, and we are guilty here too. In process control systems, telemetry monitoring and so on, real time really refers to systems with drop-dead deadlines, after which information is irretrievably lost, or catastrophic consequences ensue if deadlines are missed. In multimedia systems, while we might have *data* with real time delivery requirements, we are at liberty to lose it without necessarily losing much *information*. We are also at liberty to relax schedules for delivery, since humans are tolerant creatures compared with machines. It could be argued that all datagrams are delay sensitive to some extent, but for these purposes we refer only to datagrams where exceeding an end-to-end delay bound of a few hundred milliseconds renders the datagrams useless for the purpose for which they were intended. For the purposes of this definition, transmission control protocol (TCP) traffic is normally considered not to be real time traffic, although there may be exceptions to this rule.

On congested links, best-effort service queuing delays will adversely affect real time traffic. This does not mean that best-effort service cannot support real time traffic, merely that congested best-effort links seriously degrade the service provided. For such congested links, a better-than-best-effort service is desirable.

To achieve this, the service model of the routers can be modified. At a minimum, FIFO queuing can be replaced by packet forwarding strategies that discriminate different 'flows' of traffic. The idea of a flow is very general. A flow might consist of 'all marketing site Web traffic', or 'all file server traffic to and from teller machines' or 'all traffic from the CEO's laptop wherever it is'. On the other hand, a flow might consist of a particular sequence of packets from an application in a particular machine to a peer application in another particular machine between specific times of a specific day.

Flows are typically identifiable in the Internet by the tuple (source machine, destination machine, source port, destination port, protocol), any of which could be 'any' (wildcarded). In the multicast case, the destination is the group, and can be used to provide efficient aggregation.

Flow identification is called classification, and a class (which can contain one or more flows) has an associated service model applied. This can default to best effort.

Through network management, we can imagine establishing classes of long-lived flows – enterprise networks ('intranets') often enforce traffic policies that distinguish priorities which can be used to discriminate in favour of more important traffic in the event of overload (though in an underloaded network, the effect of such policies will be invisible, and may incur no load or work in routers). The router service model to provide such classes with different treatment can be as simple as a priority queuing system, or it can be more elaborate.

Although best-effort services can support real time traffic, classifying real time traffic separately from non-real time traffic and giving real time traffic priority treatment ensures that real time traffic sees minimum delays. Non-real time TCP traffic tends to be elastic in its bandwidth requirements, and will then tend to fill any remaining bandwidth.

We could imagine a future Internet with sufficient capacity to carry all of the world's telephony traffic. Since this is a relatively modest capacity requirement, it might be simpler to establish POTS (plain old telephone system) as a static class which is given some fraction of the capacity overall, and then no individual call need be given an allocation (i.e. we would no longer need the call set-up/tear-down that was needed in the legacy POTS which was present only because of under-provisioning of trunks and to allow the trunk exchanges the option of call blocking). The vision is of a network that is engineered with capacity for all of the average load sources to send all the time.

1.7.2   Reservations

For flows that may take a significant fraction of the network (i.e. are 'special') , we need a more dynamic way of establishing these classifications. In the short term, this applies to any multimedia calls since the Internet is largely under-provisioned at time of writing.

The resource reservation protocol, RSVP, is being standardised for just this purpose. It provides flow identification and classification. Hosts and applications are modified to speak RSVP client language, and routers speak RSVP.

Since most traffic requiring reservations is delivered to groups (for example, TV), it is natural for the receiver to make the request for a reservation for a flow. This has the added advantage that different receivers can make heterogeneous requests for capacity from the same source. Again the routers conspire to deliver the right flows to the right locations. RSVP accommodates the wildcarding noted above. This is discussed in more detail in Chapter 2, section 2.10.

1.7.3   Admission control

If a network is provisioned such that it has excess capacity for all the real time flows using it, a simple priority classification ensures that real time traffic is minimally delayed. However, if a network is insufficiently provisioned for the traffic in a real time traffic class, then real time traffic will be queued, and delays and packet loss will result. Thus, in an under-provisioned network either all real time flows will suffer or some of them must be given priority.

RSVP provides a mechanism by which an admission control request can be made, and if sufficient capacity remains in the requested traffic class, then a reservation for that capacity can be put in place.

If insufficient capacity remains, the admission request will be refused, but the traffic will still be forwarded with the default service for that traffic's traffic class. In many cases, even an admission request that failed at one or more routers can still supply acceptable quality as it may have succeeded in installing a reservation in all the routers that were suffering congestion. This is because other reservations may not be fully utilising their reserved capacity.

1.7.4   Accounting

If a reservation involves setting aside resources for a flow, this will tie up resources so that other reservations may not succeed, and depending on whether the flow fills the reservation, other traffic is prevented from using the network. Clearly, some negative feedback is required in order to prevent pointless reservations from denying service to other users. This feedback is typically in the form of billing. For real time non-best-effort traffic that is not reserved, this negative feedback is provided in the form of loss owing to congestion of a traffic class, and it is not clear that usage-based billing is required.

Billing requires that the user making the reservation is properly authenticated so that the correct user can be charged. Billing for reservations introduces a level of complexity to the Internet that has not typically been experienced with non-reserved traffic, and requires network providers to have reciprocal usage-based billing arrangements for traffic carried between them. It also requires mechanisms whereby some fraction of the bill for a link reservation can be charged to each of the downstream multicast receivers.

Recent work on charging (Kelly, 1994) has proposed quite simple models of billing associated with multimedia traffic. A generalised model for pricing bursty connections (or flows in our context) was proposed in Kelly (1996):

$$aV + bT + c$$

where V is the traffic volume at the minimum requested rate (can be zero) and T is the time at the average (measured) rate. The parameters a, b and c depend on the tariffing scheme, for example peak rate or IP subscriber's line rate, plus equipment rental. A minimum rate (for example MCR or controlled load) gives a volume-related charge (constant also factors in providers' dimensioning) and a mean rate (for example for variable bit rate or guaranteed) gives a time-related charge. Mixes are allowed.

Delay bound can be simply a boolean in the QoS API, which is easily implemented as the ToS delay preference bit in IP header; in most cases, this just selects a priority queue, although sometimes it selects a terrestrial over satellite route.

For multimedia applications, which will probably initially use a service that approximates to a lightly loaded network, we get a charge model similar to that of the TCP, which may be surprising, but it has lots of nice practical properties: for example, a typical network that permits 'premium service' TCP and Internet telephony might implement the interface for the user as a single bit to select between normal TCP service (MCR==0), and controlled load TCP as well as telephony.

The option for how to bill could be based on measured volume over time (the interval of a round trip time (RTT) is probably reasonable for both telephony and TCP-based traffic), or might simply relate to the fact that most domestic users access the net over a dial-up link, so the time-related charge could be folded in there trivially, and the volume-related charge based on measured mean rate – conveniently, the access line polices the peak rate trivially, since it is typically a modem plus telephone line or digital ISDN line, with a fixed line speed anyhow. This is discussed further in Chapter 2.

1.8 MULTICAST IN THE INTERNET

IP unicast packets are transmitted with a source and destination address, which enable routers to find a path from sender to receiver. IP *multicast* packets are transmitted with a source and group address, which extend this functionality to provide delivery to a set of receivers.

IP multicast enables efficient many-to-many datagram distribution. It is one of the basic building blocks of the Internet multimedia architecture. For most conferencing purposes, for example, unicast is viewed as being a special case of multicast routing. It adds functionality to the Internet so that it can provide services resembling those in television broadcast networks, as well as those in CB radio networks and other, as yet unforeseen, communication patterns.

1.8.1 The multicast model

Multicasting is the ability of the network to efficiently deliver information to multiple recipients. An analogy here is with TV and radio broadcasting. The electromagnetic spectrum (ether) is divided into frequencies which are allocated by some authority to TV and radio stations. These frequencies are then advertised in TV and radio listings magazines and so forth. Users then tune into these frequencies by turning a dial on their set. If they have a smart set (or a TV and VCR with separate tuners) they can receive multiple stations.

The multicast packet delivery model, illustrated in Figure 1.2, is similar to broadcast, but superior. A multicast capable host computer (or host for short) on the Internet that runs an application which receives multicast simply joins a set of receivers on the Net, identified by a group address. How does an application choose a multicast address to use?

In the absence of any other information, we can bootstrap a multicast application by using well known multicast addresses. Routing (unicast and multicast) and Internet group management protocols (IGMPs) can do just that. However, this is not the best way to manage applications of which there is more than one instance at any one time.

For these, we need a mechanism for allocating group addresses dynamically, and a directory service which can hold these allocations together with some key (session information for example – see Chapter 6), so that users can look up the address associated with the application. The address allocation and directory functions should be distributed to scale well.

Address allocation schemes should avoid clashes, hence some kind of hash function suggests itself. Furthermore, both the address allocation system and the directory service can take advantage of the baseline multicast mechanism by advertising sessions through multicast messages on a well known address, and using this to inform other directory servers to remove clashes and inform applications of the allocation. This is discussed in much more detail in Chapter 7.

Group addresses are an extension of the Internet addressing scheme to provide dynamically assigned addresses for a set of interfaces with a single identifier. Some people argue that since it is not identifying a location, but is a key for looking

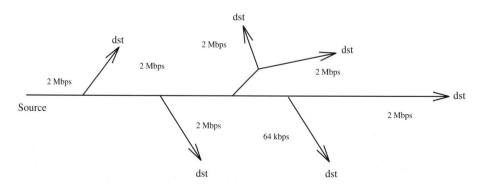

Figure 1.2 The Internet multicast model.

up routing entries, it is really a name, not an address. However, since it is taken from a new section of the same identifier space as normal Internet protocol addresses, the word *address* has stuck.

As a side-effect of a host computer joining an IP multicast group, two things happen:

1   The host reprograms its network interface to receive packets to the additional group address that is being used for this multicast.

2   The host informs all nearby routers of the fact that there is (at least) one recipient for packets to that multicast address.

Groups are distinguished by having separate multicast addresses (just as unique hosts are distinguished by having unique unicast addresses). Multicast address assignment is generally dynamic (although some addresses are set aside for well known groups), and under the control of collections of the users. This is in contrast to frequency assignment in the electromagnetic spectrum, where the bandwidth (in the sense of number of different possible frequencies) is a scarce resource compared with the number of multicast Internet addresses. In the radio and TV world, frequencies are assigned under global and national treaties and laws. In the Internet, there are some tools for multicast address management, which we will look at in Chapter 7.

A host computer does not have to be in a multicast group to be able to send to it. Anyone, anywhere can send a packet at any time to any group (in the time-honoured Internet style). Hosts can take part in multiple multicast sessions. It is up to the receiving applications to be able to deal with multiple receptions. For example, if you receive audio from multiple audio sessions, do you want to mix them and then play them out (to the confusion of the user) or let the applications allow the user to choose? Of course, if you are receiving audio from multiple sources sending to the same session, the user probably does want to hear them. If you receive multiple video sessions, do you want to display the video in multiple windows, or let the user choose one or more sessions? There are two separate questions here, one of network capacity and the other of addressing. Since Internet addresses are used for each packet, there is no virtual circuit or long-term association, so it is possible to flood a receiver with traffic just by knowing their address and having more capacity near a source than at the sink. With multicast, a receiver can 'pull down' more traffic than they may be able to handle by joining multiple groups (or even single groups that are being sent to by faster sources than the receiver has upstream capacity for).

The routers in the Internet (the sorting offices or switching matrix glue that link everything together) that are capable of multicast use the location of groups or of senders to determine the delivery tree that is used to get packets from the source to the set of receivers. This tree is usually quite optimal in terms of the number of links that packets traverse. Packets are also not transmitted multiple times on the same link anywhere, they are copied only at appropriate points. We shall look at styles of delivery trees a bit more in Chapter 3. For now, imagine sending a memo to a group of people but only having to print one copy at source. Then as the memo arrives at various sorting offices, if there are any local recipients, the sorting office puts the memo in the copier and delivers it to those recipients, saving on shipping a huge bag of copies from the original sender to all the sorting offices, but at some cost of copying along the way instead.

This model of packet delivery has had a profound effect on the way that application programmers have learned to construct multicasting programs. The tasks of figuring out who is in a conference, whether they are ready to receive or not, whether a user has the right to speak, and so forth, are all moved to a completely separate level of the system because of this model. In other words, the multicast model is policy-free in terms of call set-up, floor control, membership control, activity, session information and so on. The separate functions of membership, activity and conference control are discussed in detail in Chapter 7.

This is in direct contrast to existing models of conferencing. For example, in audio telephony, the receiver(s) must have their telephones on-hook. Particular callers must call them, one at a time, and add recipients to a conference call. Even if a telephone bridge is used, the bridge needs to call each of the participants, and all of their calls typically go via the bridge. There is more discussion of this model of group communication at the lower levels in Chapter 3. People have come to use Internet multicast conferences in two styles:

1 The TV broadcast model is where a seminar or meeting is simply disseminated for anyone to see or hear.

2 The CB radio style is where users chat interactively and openly, coming in and out of a virtual meeting-place as and when they like.

The addition of security and privacy features has also led to closed, more formally structured use which we look at in Chapter 10. The popularity of this technology is indicated to some extent by the growth in the number of sites attached to the Internet that provide global multicast access.

It is instructive to think about alternative ways that group communication might be supported in a network. For example, we might put a list of addresses in a packet of information we wish to send to a list of recipients. This would work so long as the group was fixed and reasonably small, but would quickly become unmanageable for groups in the hundreds or thousands, which we already find in use in the Internet. An alternative might be to employ a central distribution server where we send everything, and it fans it out to all the recipients. This would fly in the face of the entire Internet design philosophy, since it would be a central site, subject to failure and performance problems. Instead, Internet multicast distributes both the group control and the data distribution tasks into the network.

Finally, then, routers forwarding packets with multicast destinations use the group address, or the source address together with the information distributed through the group management protocols (as we will see in Chapter 3) to determine where to forward packets to.

1.8.2   A brief history of trees

In Chapter 3, we discuss multicast routing topologies at great length. Here we give a brief overview of the evolution of multicast to date. Originally, the multicast routing was based on the thesis work of Steve Deering (Deering, 1988a) and comprises two parts:

1   *Tunnels*: These are used to glue together Internet sites which have multicast-capable routers but are separated by routers that do not support multicast, thus forming a virtual topology on top of the underlying Internet unicast routing. This has proved invaluable in this (and other) work in terms of deploying new versions of the routing. This has given rise to the term *Mbone*, short for multicast backbone, which is the name for the virtual glue of routers that interconnect islands of native IP multicast via tunnels through non-multicast-capable sections of the Internet.

2   *Distance vector multicast routing protocol (DVMRP) routing*: This is the actual routing protocol, which is a natural extension to the age-old routing information protocol, using the paths that are calculated to get from a set of sources D to a particular destination, S for unicast, as a way to get multicast from S to D.

DVMRP employs a scheme called pruning to eliminate branches from the network that do not contain members of a group whenever a source starts sending. As the Internet multicast capability has grown (in early 1998 it had several thousand sites, where a site might be a research laboratory or university campus, in 22 countries), there have been many groups that are small, and sparse. This has meant that the amount of routing control overhead from pruning traffic (and multicast traffic delivered unnecessarily to sites without members before they are pruned) has caused people to rethink the routing scheme. Several alternatives have emerged:

MOSPF (multicast extensions to the unicast routing scheme OSPF, open shortest path first) allows aggregation of traffic and groups and also permits paths to be chosen based on different types of service (ToS).

CBT (core-based trees) is based on a manager placing a core or centre router appropriately in the network by calculating where the place is that all routing traffic would go through if we formed a minimal spanning tree from the centre to all groups. This is a tricky calculation and takes smart heuristics. It results in lower link usage than DVMRP and does not need pruning, but it can increase the delays in paths between users, which may be critical for some kinds of multimedia interactions.

PIM (protocol independent multicast) is based on a mix of the ideas from CBT and DVMRP, and relies on the underlying unicast routing to calculate its paths. It is also capable therefore of exploiting underlying policies concerning routes, including potentially, ToS selection of paths.

The two extremes of multicast tree topology are explained at great length in Chapter 3, and for a quick preview, take a look at Figure 3.2 there. At the time of writing, there is a great deal of research and development in the area of multicast routing, and it remains to be seen what the main scheme will be. However, the power of the basic original IP multicast model is in no doubt.

1.9 TRANSPORT PROTOCOLS

So-called real time delivery of traffic requires little in the way of transport protocol. In particular, real time traffic that is sent over more than trivial distances is not retransmittable. In fact, a number of facets of an end-to-end protocol need to be redesigned or refined including:

1 *Separate flows for each media stream*: With packet multimedia data there is no need for the different media comprising a session to be carried in the same packets. In fact it simplifies receivers if different media streams are carried in separate flows (i.e. separate transport ports and/or separate multicast groups). This also allows the different media to be given different quality of service (QoS), for example, under congestion, a router might preferentially drop video packets over audio packets. In addition, some sites may not wish to receive all the media flows, for example a site with a slow access link may be able to participate in a session using only audio and a whiteboard whereas other sites in the same session may also send and receive video.

2 *Receiver adaptation*: Best-effort traffic is delayed by queues in routers between the sender and the receivers. Even reserved priority traffic may see small transient queues in routers, and so packets comprising a flow will be delayed for different times. Such delay variance is known as jitter.
   Real time applications such as audio and video need to be able to buffer real time data at the receiver for sufficient time to remove the jitter added by the network and to recover the original timing relationships between the media data. In order to know how long to buffer for, each packet must carry a timestamp which gives the time at the sender when the data were captured. Note that for audio and video data timing recovery it is not necessary to know the absolute time at which the data were captured at the sender, only the time relative to the other data packets.

3 *Synchronisation*: As audio and video flows will receive differing jitter and possibly differing quality of service, audio and video that were grabbed at the same time at the sender may not arrive at the receiver at the same time. At the receiver, each flow will need a play-out buffer to remove network jitter. Interflow synchronisation can be performed by adapting these play-out buffers so that samples/frames that originated at the same time are played out at the same time. This requires that the times that different flows from the same sender were captured are available at the receivers.

1.9.1 The real time transport protocol, RTP

The Internet transport protocol for real time flows is RTP (Schulzrinne *et al.*, 1996). This provides a standard format packet header which gives media-specific timestamp data, as well as payload format information and sequence numbering amongst other things. RTP is normally carried using UDP. It does not provide or require any connection set-up, nor does it provide any enhanced reliability over UDP. For RTP to provide a useful media flow, there must be sufficient capacity in the relevant traffic class to accommodate the traffic. How this capacity is ensured is independent of RTP.

RTP media timestamps units are flow specific – they are in units that are appropriate to the media flow. For example, 8 kHz sampled PCM encoded audio has a timestamp clock rate of 8 kHz. This means that interflow synchronisation is not possible from the RTP timestamps alone.

Every original RTP source is identified by a source identifier, and this source identity is carried in every packet. RTP allows flows from several sources to be mixed in gateways to provide a single resulting flow. When this happens, each mixed packet contains the source identities of all the contributing sources.

Each RTP flow is supplemented by real time control protocol (RTCP) packets. There are a number of different RTCP packet types. RTCP packets provide the relationship between the real time clock at a sender and the RTP media timestamps, and provide textual information to identify a sender in a session from the source identity. This is described in more detail in Chapter 5.

1.10 MULTIMEDIA SESSIONS

The idea of a session is closely aligned with the idea of a human activity. A session is a collection of communication exchanges which together make up a single overall identifiable task. For example, a conversation, or the viewing of a single 'program', or a collaborative meeting.

Multimedia sessions come in many shapes and sizes, but there are really only two models for session control: lightweight sessions and tightly coupled conferencing.

Lightweight sessions are multicast-based multimedia conferences that lack explicit session membership and explicit conference control mechanisms. Typically, a lightweight session consists of a number of many-to-many media streams supported using RTP and RTCP using IP multicast.

The concept of lightweight sessions is explored in more detail in the introduction to Part Two which follows Chapter 4.

The rendezvous mechanism for lightweight sessions is a multicast-based session directory. This distributes session descriptions (Handley and Jacobson, 1996) to all the potential session participants. These session descriptions provide an advertisement that the session will exist, and also provide sufficient information including multicast addresses, ports, media formats and session times so that a receiver of the session description can join the session. As dynamic multicast address allocation can be optimised by knowing which addresses are in use at which times, the session directory is an appropriate agent to perform multicast address allocation.

Tightly coupled conferences may also be multicast based and use RTP and RTCP, but in addition they have an explicit conference membership mechanism and may have an explicit conference control mechanism that provides facilities such as floor control.

Such conferences may be initiated either by invitation (the 'conference' calls a user), or by user initiation (the user calls the 'conference'). In the latter case, the rendezvous mechanism can be handled by the same session directory that handles lightweight sessions, with the addition of a description of the contact mechanism to be used to join the conference to the description of the session. In the former case, a call-up mechanism is required which can be combined with the explicit conference membership mechanism.

No standard mechanism currently exists to perform either the conference membership mechanism or the 'dial-up' mechanism in the Internet, and the many proprietary conferencing systems available all implement this in different ways. At the time of writing, it seems likely that a protocol based on the ITU's T.124 recommendation will be derived for Internet usage.

For both models, a rendezvous mechanism is needed. Note that the conference control model is orthogonal to issues of quality of service and network resource reservation.

1.11 CONFERENCE MEMBERSHIP AND RECEPTION FEEDBACK

IP multicast allows sources to send to a multicast group without being a receiver of that group. However, for many conferencing purposes it is useful to know who is listening to the conference and whether the media flows are reaching receivers properly. Performing both these tasks accurately restricts the scaling of the conference. IP multicast means that no one knows the precise membership of a conference at a specific time, and this information cannot be discovered, as to try to do so would cause an implosion of messages, many of which would be lost. This is not to say that we cannot know the bounds of a conference membership, a subset of whom might be present at any time – this can be done using encryption and restricted distribution of encryption keys, of which more in Chapter 10. Instead, RTCP provides approximate membership information through periodic multicast of session messages which, in addition to information about the recipient, also give information about the reception quality at that receiver. RTCP session messages are restricted in rate, so that as a conference grows, the rate of session messages remains constant and each receiver reports less often. A member of the conference can never know exactly who is present at a particular time from RTCP reports, but does have a good approximation of the conference membership.

Reception quality information is intended primarily for debugging purposes, as debugging of IP multicast problems is a difficult task. However, it is possible to use reception quality information for rate-adaptive senders, although it is not clear whether this information is sufficiently timely to be able to adapt fast enough to transient congestion. However, it is certainly sufficient for providing adaptation to a 'share' of the current capacity.

The principal reason that it is hard to use this approach for general congestion avoidance is the fact that feedback messages are necessarily delayed and each receiver reports at a rate which is only inversely proportional to the membership of the conference (otherwise the network is flooded with these reports). While this means that the larger and more densely the receiver population permeates the network, the more places are sampled periodically: for modestly sized groups, this may mean that network conditions as perceived by a source are quite out of date. Some other aspects of RTCP reports are discussed in Chapter 8.

1.12 SECURITY

Security is more socially critical in multimedia communication than in traditional data communication. Intrusion or disclosure of person-to-person communication is more keenly felt than of 'mere' data.

Unicast and multicast multimedia communication require some additional techniques for protection against these and a variety of other security attacks. For example, there is a temptation to believe that multicast is inherently less private than unicast communication since the traffic visits so many more places in the network. In fact, this is not the case except with broadcast and prune-type multicast routing protocols DVMRP. However, IP multicast does make it simple for a host to anonymously join a multicast group and receive traffic destined for that group without the other senders' and receivers' knowledge. If the application requirement is to communicate between some set of users, then strict privacy can in any case be enforced only through adequate end-to-end encryption.

RTP specifies a standard way to encrypt RTP and RTCP packets using private key encryption schemes such as DES (National Institute of Standards and Technology, 1988). It also specifies a standard mechanism to manipulate plain text keys using MD5 (Rivest, 1992) so that the resulting bit string can be used as a DES key. This allows simple out-of-band mechanisms such as privacy-enhanced mail to be used for encryption key exchange.

1.12.1   Authentication and key distribution

Key distribution is closely tied to authentication. Conference or session directory keys can be securely distributed using public key cryptography on a one-to-one basis (by email, a directory service, or by an explicit conference set-up mechanism), but this is only as good as the certification mechanism used to certify that a key given by a user is the correct public key for that user. Such certification mechanisms X.509 are not specific to conferencing, and no standard mechanism is currently in use for conferencing purposes other than privacy enhanced mail PEM (Linn, 1993).

Even without privacy requirements, strong authentication of a user is required if making a network reservation results in usage-based billing.

1.12.2   Encrypted session announcements

Session directories can make encrypted session announcements using private key encryption and carry the encryption keys to be used for each of the conference media streams in the session. While this does not solve the key distribution problem, it does allow a single conference to be announced more than once to more than one key-group, where each group holds a different session directory key, so that the two groups can be brought together into a single conference without having to know each other's keys. This is discussed in detail in Chapter 10.

1.13 APPLICATIONS OTHER THAN AUDIO AND VIDEO

A variety of other applications have been developed other than audio and video ones. There are some public domain application examples that we will use to illustrate the direction in which applications appear to be evolving to accompany multimedia applications.

Image multicast (imm) is an image dissemination program from the University of Hawaii; Whiteboard (wb) is a shared whiteboard from the Lawrence Berkeley Laboratory (LBL); and network text editor (nte) is a shared text editor from UCL and ISI. These are discussed in detail in Chapter 8. The basic design principle used for them is an idea from Jacobson at LBL, called lightweight sessions, and nte services, discussed in Chapter 8 to illustrate this idea further. We can see an example of the creation of a lightweight session in Figure 1.3.

Figure 1.3 shows the time sequence involved in setting up a lightweight session between two sites. In this case, site A creates a session advertisement and some time later starts sending a media stream even though there may be no receiver at that time. Some time later, site B joins the session and starts to receive the traffic. At

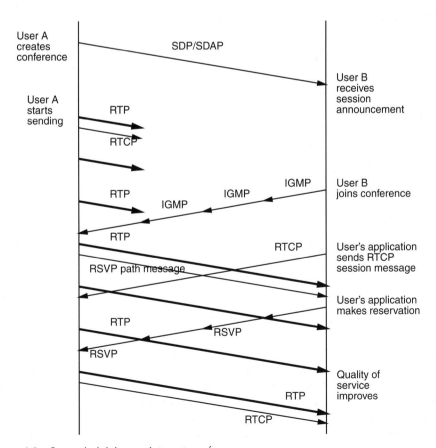

Figure 1.3 Stages in joining an Internet conference.

the earliest opportunity site B also makes an RSVP reservation to ensure that the flow quality is satisfactory. This is discussed throughout the book, and particularly in the introductions to Parts Two and Three.

1.14 SUMMARY

In this chapter we have given an overview of the components that go towards making multimedia on the Internet feasible and flexible. We have looked at media capture and encoding, at network models for transmission, and at some of the basic ideas in the area of service models for such transmission, as well as co-ordination of these delivery services.

As well as sending and receiving multimedia traffic from end systems, the network must somehow or other provide some minimal performance guarantees to give the quality required by the end user. Within this minimum, there may be variation in network performance (throughput, delay, loss and so on) which is accommodated by adaption in end systems.

As well as supporting communication, there must be mechanisms to *prevent* unwanted communication, and also to prevent attacks on desired communication.

At a higher level, there have to be mechanisms for humans to create, advertise and discover the existence of multimedia sessions, and to be able to find which are the relevant applications for a given session.

Finally, there are data communication tools that allow users to co-ordinate sessions consisting of multiple media tools running on multiple systems, to allow seamless communication which transcends traditional telephony, television and data communications.

Note

1 The IEC 958 standard specifies the digital interface as carrying up to 20 bits per channel, at 32 kHz, 44.1 kHz or 48 kHz.

CHAPTER TWO

Network Service Models

2.1 INTRODUCTION

In this chapter we take a look at the network service models for supporting multimedia traffic. We look at mechanisms to provide varying levels of assurance about performance in terms of delay, throughput and loss, and standards and protocols for implementing these mechanisms.

2.2 ROADMAP

Figure 2.1 illustrates the components of the user and network that must interact to provide a network service. In this chapter we cover the way that the Internet provides some of these components and how they can be fitted together to make a given service model that a user requires.

2.3 SHARING AND CARING

The Internet was once intended to support multiple types of service (Leiner *et al.*, 1985), but this intent was lost in the mists of time as its most basic, *best-effort* service model became hugely successful throughout the 1990s. This service model is the contract, or perhaps in the Internet case, the lack of contract that exists between the network provided and its users.

A good analogy for a service model is that of a transportation system: we do not expect the roads to take us to a destination, we expect them to allow us to drive there, but we do expect a train or a plane to take us to a destination. These represent different levels of service guarantees. We can take the analogy further if we add that we have no expectation from the existence of roads about journey times, but we have an expectation from the existence of timetables for our train journey times. Thus we can see that a service model refers both to the interface and to the performance that a system gives us. In this sense, it is more subtle and rich than most contracts.

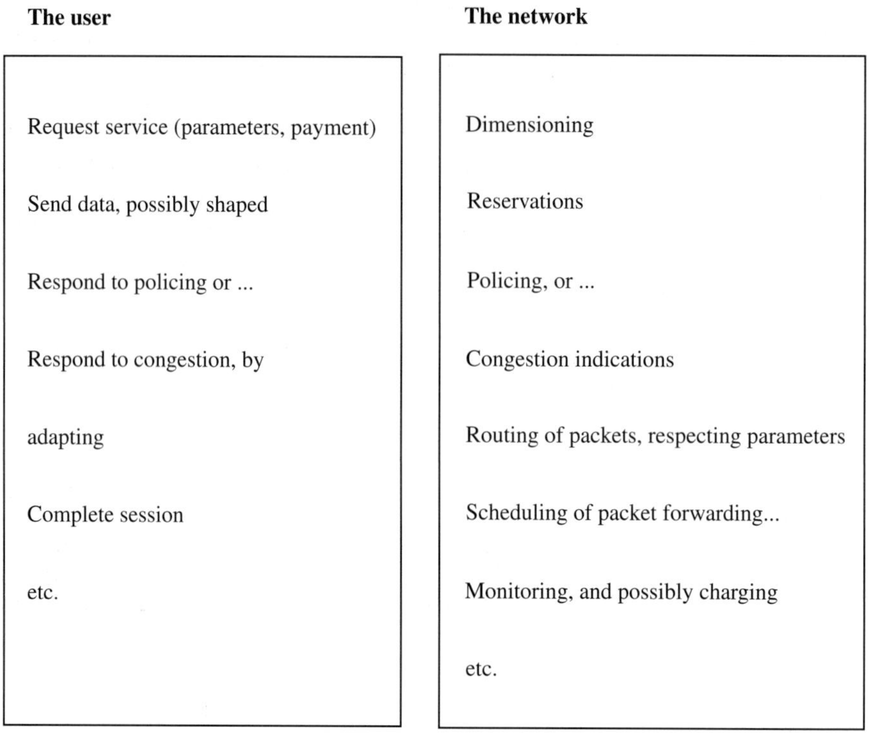

The user   **The network**

Request service (parameters, payment)
Send data, possibly shaped
Respond to policing or ...
Respond to congestion, by
adapting
Complete session
etc.

Dimensioning
Reservations
Policing, or ...
Congestion indications
Routing of packets, respecting parameters
Scheduling of packet forwarding...
Monitoring, and possibly charging
etc.

Figure 2.1 Roadmap of user and network service interface.

In networks that are able to carry a range of different types of traffic from different applications, this contract is usually expressed in terms of a set of performance measures. In Table 2.1 we illustrate a range of models used for service specification.

The most detailed way of expressing performance is through quality of service (QoS) parameters (these might be more properly understood if they were called quantity of service parameters). Quality of service typically defines which parameter(s) in a set are relevant to a particular service contract and then defines valid ranges of values for those parameters. Going back to our transport analogy, a train ticket might allow one person to travel, or it might allow a car on the train with all its passengers, or it might be a season ticket. Then the ticket may specify a particular seat on a particular train with a particular journey time, at the most specific.

Table 2.1 Service contract models.

Contract model	Specification
Model	What it defines
Type of service (ToS)	High or low values of throughput, delay, loss
Class of service	Several externally specified service models, selected by class parameter
Quality of service (QoS)	Exact service selected inline by specific signalling

In its simplest form, one might express the applications in terms of whether each end was a human or a computer, and whether the medium was data, audio or video. For example, a file transfer is of data between two computers, whilst remote terminal access requires moving data between a computer and a human, and an audio conference requires you to move audio between two or more humans and so forth. The difference between human and computer reception lies in two places: the way human perception of sound and vision cannot be told to wait – there is a minimum rate for delivering continuous media (hence its name); the way people interact – there is a maximum delay between utterance and comprehension above which natural conversation becomes impossible. Of course, there are computer-to-computer networked applications that require delay bounds (for example, telemetry or process control), but multimedia typically is delivered to or between humans, and that is what this book is concentrating on.

The Internet has had no basic, widely implemented way of expressing these rate and delay parameters, qualitatively or quantitatively. This is because the very fundamental way that one accesses the Internet to convey anything from source to destination(s) is without warning. In essence, any computer connected to the Internet may attempt to communicate with any other computer(s) at any moment.

This is in direct contrast to traditional telecommunications networks used for example for telephony. The plain old telephone network requires users to do three things:

1   The sender and recipient must have an account with one or more service providers.

2   A receiver must have put their telephone on hook first.

3   A sender places a call.

These requirements have the consequence that the telephone network gets warnings that a customer is about to use it (and the network has the opportunity to say no), and that once the network has said yes, neither the sender nor the receiver can use up any more network resources (unless they have another line; but that is just like there being another user).

This means that the telephone network can be provisioned (dimensioned is another term used for this) reasonably easily for the expected number of calls at any time. Each call represents a fixed resource commitment. An unexpectedly high number of attempted calls (say on a popular holiday) can simply result in some calls being blocked (not getting through owing to lack of internal resources). The relevant parameters for designing a telephone network are shown in Table 2.2.

These parameters allow one to design a network for a given call blocking probability. In essence, for a given level of user expectation (or dissatisfaction), it is possible to cost out a given infrastructure.

Call blocking is just another manifestation of congestion or overload, except that the degradation of service is to the users who get none, rather than to users who have already established access to the network. Some telephony systems actually suffer from overload during high call rates (flash call overload, for example during television dial-in programmes) and use an adaptive 'call gapping' procedure to reduce the rate of progression of call control itself.

Table 2.2 Parameters for telephone network load.

Parameter	Description
Call frequency	How often a given user places a call
Call holding time	How long a call lasts
Call locality	The probability that a call is local or long distance

Table 2.3 Congestion manifestation.

Service type	Description
Elastic (Internet based)	Congestion leads to lower rate or quality
Brittle (Circuit based)	Congestion leads to call blocking

Another type of network beloved of telecommunications companies is what is called the leased line. This makes an even stronger commitment in terms of resource (and assumes an even stronger requirement for this guarantee) between the network and the user in that this is a service that is in place from when it is installed as opposed to when the call is placed. In other words, the opportunity to say no is not there after the lease has been signed. A form of congestion exists for leased line networks which is that the provider may not be able to deploy a line fast enough for a given consumer; this is an extreme example of call blocking.

The Internet model is commonly referred to as a best-effort service. Each request to send is honoured by the network as best it can. This works for communication of data between computers (usually) since the receiver can always wait for data that is late, and the sender can usually resend any data that is lost or distorted in transmission, however long it takes to discover this loss. This ability to cope with variable delivery rates and delays is often termed *elasticity*. If you picture the communications pipe between sender and recipient as a tube made of elastic carrying some liquid, then the delay and decrease in delivery rate is just like what happens if you stretch the tube – it gets longer and thinner. The difference between Internet-based and circuit-based networks is illustrated in Table 2.3. This is extensively discussed in section 5.3 in Chapter 5.

The problems with using this type of technology to convey audio and video are twofold: that if the sender and receiver are humans, they cannot tolerate arbitrary delays; if the rate at which video and audio arrive is too low, the signal becomes incomprehensible. Using the elastic pipe analogy, if a fire engine was trying to put out a fire with such a water pipe, whenever it got stretched too much, the water would arrive too little and too late. We illustrate the range of service requirements for some example application usage in terms of the time or space between accesses to successive units of data in Figure 2.2.

2.3.1 User expectation and service models

The service model that a network provides has a profound effect on users' expectations. For example, users of the modern telephone network expect that their telephone call will rarely be blocked (i.e. not get through), and furthermore that

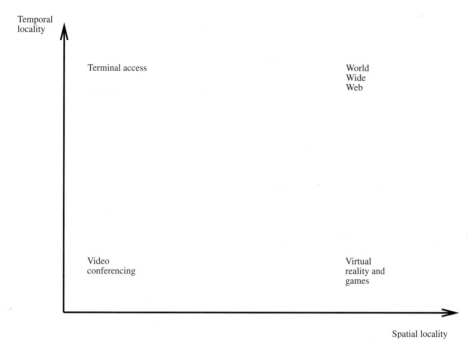

Figure 2.2 Locales in space and time.

when they get through to the intended recipient, that the call will practically never be dropped unexpectedly except by the receiver hanging up. In contrast, mobile telephone service levels are actually acceptable to users even though call dropout and blocking are both frequent occurrences in today's service provision. In other words, it is important to consider users' expectations and also the added value of an overall network (who can reach whom, when and where) when considering quality of service requirements.

By contrast, today's typical Internet user expects always to be able to start an application, but that the quality of communication has no guarantee and can vary from almost no throughput and very high delays right through to perfect communication, with no apparent correlation between the behaviour and their own actions.

This lack of expectation of quality has led to user acceptance of quite low quality audio and video communication, both in base level and in high variation of media quality and delay. This acceptance would seem quite surprising when compared with early experiments with video-over-phone type networks, but is not so surprising given existing Internet users' previous experience of the highly variable performance of traditional Internet data (non-multimedia) applications.

2.4 SERVICE SCHEDULES AND QUEUES

The performance of a communications path through a number of links is made up of contributions from many places. The raw throughput of each link in the path (the capacity) comes from the technology used, as does the error rate due to noise.

The delay for a given path is made of two main contributions: propagation time, and store and forward time in routers and switches, bridges, hubs and so on along the way. For fixed wire terrestrial networks, the propagation time is unalterable, so that the main thing that can be changed is the store and forward time at the interconnect devices. This is just like the time spent in a car journey waiting at traffic lights. In a road system without lights or toll roads, all cars are treated the same – the model is 'first-come-first-served' or 'first-in-first-out'. The best-effort service in the Internet is the same.

For some users, to change this service involves recognising their traffic and giving it different treatment in the queue. In a lightly loaded network, just as on a lightly loaded road, there is typically no queue. Having said that, it might not do for someone to arrive early – this is captured in the notion of 'work conservation' in some systems – indeed, in digital telephone networks it is enforced by a queue discipline which separates all traffic from other traffic and gives each call its own schedule, usually through time division multiplexing.

In the Internet, none of the future integrated services that are described in this chapter do this. Instead what they do is simply allow higher-quality traffic to work *ahead* of lower-quality traffic. Thus the notion is that to permit quality of service for some users, the others (at least at busy times) must get less share.

There are quite a few different proposed queuing systems to do this – the baseline for comparison is called *fair queuing*, which is in essence a round-robin scheduler for each source–destination pair currently using a route through this particular router. Fair queuing can be extended to include a notion of weight (i.e. systematic unfairness, perhaps associated with importance or money). Other mechanisms include approximations to fair queuing (for example, stochastic fair queuing).

A given device can implement several different queuing mechanisms, and sort packets into the appropriate queue based on some notion of packet classification, so that we can retain best-effort service while supporting better effort for some users (albeit at the cost of lower share for best effort).

2.5 EVOLUTION OF THE INTERNET SERVICE MODEL

Traditionally, the best-effort Internet has provided the worst possible service: packets are forwarded by routers solely on the basis that there is any known route, irrespective of traffic conditions along that route. Routers that are overloaded discard packets, typically dropping packets at the tail of the queue of those awaiting to depart along their way.

Other types of digital network have been built, most notably, for wide public access, the digital telephone network, with user access based on the narrowband integrated services digital network (ISDN) architecture. This is, in fact, the fixed-effort ISDN, which gives you a constant data rate from source to sink, irrespective of whether you have something ready to send at any moment or not (or whether you have something that needs to be sent at the offered rates).

More recently, we have seen the evolution of both of these network architectures towards more flexible support for multiple service categories. Multiservice IP and broadband ISDN, provided by ATM, are both being redesigned from the ground up to cater for actual perceived multimedia application requirements.

To this end, the notion of traffic classes, each of which has a range of parameters (usually known as quality of service parameters even though they are quantitative) have been designed. In the ITU and ATM forum, these are called bearer service classes, and in the IP integrated services Internet work, they are flow classes.

2.5.1 Classification and admission

A class is supported typically by some queuing discipline being applied especially to a particular flow of traffic. This may be something that is set up by network manager, programmed into a router, or might be requested by a user (or a site or between one network and another) via some so-called signalling protocol.

In the Internet, the signalling protocol has to provide not only the traffic flow category, and the parameters, but also a way for a router to recognise the packets belonging to the flow, since there is no 'virtual circuit' or 'flow identifier' in current Internet protocol packets. Of course, IP version 6 (IPv6) will change this, if and when it sees deployment.

This 'classification' is simply based on a set of packet fields that remain constant for a flow: for example, UDP and TCP port numbers (or any other transport-level protocol demultiplexing field), IP-level transport protocol identifier, together with a source and destination IP host (interface) addresses, serve to uniquely identify a flow for FTP, Web and most Mbone applications.

To create this classification dynamically, and to set up the right mapping from it into the right queues in routers along a path, the Internet community has devised RSVP, the resource reservation protocol.

When a service request is made, the network has a chance to do something it cannot do in the normal IP router case: it can *decide in advance* whether it can support the request or not, and has the option to deny access (or at least to deny guarantees of service) to a flow. This is known as an admission test. It depends on the user knowing their own traffic patterns, which is not always possible (though for many applications, the programmer may have calibrated them, and wired in these parameters). Where not possible, the network may simply monitor, and carry out 'measurement-based admission'.

Parameters for quality of service typically include average and peak values for throughput, delay and errors; in practice, these may be expressed as burstiness, end-to-end delay, jitter, and a worst-case error (or residual packet loss) rate.

The debate has raged for many years over which parameter set is necessary and sufficient for Internet (computer) based multimedia. When a sender can adapt a send rate dynamically to perceived conditions, and a receiver can adapt to measured conditions (as well as interpolate, extrapolate for loss, excessive delay and so on), more flexibility is possible in these parameters than traditionally provided.

For example, delay adaptation at a receiver can be simply achieved so that as long as the average rate of traffic is accommodated across the network, the peak rate is buffered, and delay variance caused by bursts at peak rate or by other traffic (depending on the queuing disciplines used in intermediate nodes) does not incur more than some peak delay bound, then a smooth play-out of media is quite simple.

In fact, a combination of an adaptive play-out buffer and interpolation can tolerate a modest percentage of packets arriving too late. Furthermore, one can devise coding schemes that permit high loss tolerance, which means that they can co-exist with highly bursty traffic with either a more heavily loaded network (i.e. more delay variance caused by more bursts), or less well policed or shaped queues in the intermediate systems. This is discussed in greater detail in Chapter 5.

2.5.2   Integrated services model

The Internet is not a static set of services and protocols, and there has been a great deal of effort since 1990 to add a broader range of services to the Internet model. The Integrated Services working group (Braden *et al.*, 1994) of the IETF has now defined five classes of service which should satisfy the vast majority of future applications (although the scheme is extensible, so that future applications which need new services are not excluded).

The current five classes of service are:

1 *Best-effort*: This is the traditional service model of the Internet, as described above, typically implemented through FIFO queuing in routers.

2 *Fair*: This is an enhancement of the traditional model, where there are no extra requests from the users, but the routers attempt to partition network resources in some fair share sense. This is typically implemented using a random drop approach to overload, possibly combined with some simple round-robin serving of different sources.

3 *Controlled load*: This is an attempt to provide a guarantee that a network appears to the user as if there is little other traffic – it makes no other guarantees. It is really a way of limiting the traffic admitted to the network so that the performance perceived is as if the network were over-engineered for those that are admitted.

4 *Predictive or controlled delay*: This is where the delay distribution that a particular flow perceives is controlled. This requires the source (or a group where it is applied collectively to all sources sending to a group) to make some pre-statement to the routers that a particular throughput is required. This may be rejected.

5 *Guaranteed*: This is where the delay perceived by a particular source or to a group is bounded within some absolute limit. This may entail both an admission test as with class 3, and a more expensive forwarding queuing system.

The separation of these service classes is important, since the billing model of the network is related to the service model. For example, elastic services such as those we have traditionally used in the Internet do not require a usage charge for traffic which gets no guarantees. However, when an application needs, or asks for, guarantees, there is a requirement to present some feedback to prevent everyone idly asking for the maximum guarantee (so that the network can make an informed decision). This feedback can most easily be provided by billing, although some researchers assert that it is necessary only to incur a charge when the network would be unable to meet all the current requests, rather than whenever people make a request. This is analogous with billing people for road use during congested periods and not at other times, and billing people with larger cars in an attempt to adjust the demand.

This aspect of the Internet is relevant to considerations of video conferencing, since it may well be that large parts of the Internet will not permit such applications until either reservation or billing, or both, are in place as new technology.

2.5.3 Differentiated services

Differentiated services have emerged in the Internet arena as a class of service approach to providing better than best-effort quality, in contrast to integrated services which uses the more stringent, and complex, quality of service approach.

In essence the observation is that through pricing and understanding of user requirements we can control, and users can accept a limited repertoire of quality of service parameters which can be defined as *profiles* for particular application usage types. These have detailed specifications, but since they are only added at the rate at which new usage patterns and new applications are devised, there is no need to signal the parameters explicitly. Instead the parameters are programmed into routers, and a class of service is selected by subscription or by marking using class of service bits in the differentiated services byte present in every packet in the IPv4 and IPv6 packet headers. Other functions are still present (described in detail later in this chapter) but are simplified and invoked less frequently. There is great enthusiasm for this approach at present.

2.6 RESOURCE RESERVATION PROTOCOL (RSVP)

The protocol that has been devised to establish a reservation in the network for particular flow classes is called the resource reservation protocol, or RSVP (Zhang *et al.*, 1993). It might be more accurate to describe it as a dual function protocol that serves to install knowledge about classes of traffic in the network (a filter specification) as well as what particular type or quality of service these flows will need (a flow specification). This separation is important, as the filter specification can be reused in a number of ways. The simplest way that the filter specification is reusable is the fact that it can refer to a flow received by an application, rather than to one that is sent. This means that a sender can send video at a rate convenient to them, but that receivers can select the sub-band rates that are most convenient to each of them. This receiver-based reservation is quite different from the telephony model of how to do things, and fits well with the multicast model described in some detail in the next chapter – it is a bit like the way people can choose what size TV screen they have independent of the TV transmitted signal (or choose whether the TV is colour or monochrome, or has mono or stereo audio). The second way that the filter generalises the idea of a reservation is that it can include a wildcard so that it can refer to groups of sources. For example, in an audio conference, there is no necessity to set aside resources for all the audio feeds at once, since humans are typically capable of organising themselves in a conversation so that there is only one person speaking at any time. Hence, sources will ask for reservations that are only marginally more than a unicast audio reservation for a multiway audio conference. Flow specifications are cast in terms of the class of service, combined with the quantitative parameters as needed. For example, a mean rate combined with a burstiness (also known as leaky bucket parameters by analogy with a water bucket with a given volume and size of leak) suffice to characterise many applications. Future versions of the Internet protocol will incorporate tags (known as flow identifiers) which may make the classification of packets by newer routers a more efficient task. Again, the flow identifier has been designed with possible future bearer networks such as ATM in mind. Thus it is 24 bits in size, just as the VCI/VPI field is in ATM used for roughly the same function.

2.7 SERVICE CLASSES AND ASSURANCE

RSVP	IETF proposed standard RFC 2205
ISSLL	IETF work in progress.
IPv6	IETF last call

As explained in Chapter 1, there are a variety of proposed service classes in the integrated services Internet, ranging from best effort, through controlled load, to guaranteed service. Associated with these are two functions:

1 *Admission control decision*: whether traffic can be supported with the current network resources.

2 *The policing action*: monitoring of a flow may determine that it exceeds either what has been asked for or what can be supported, or both.

Admission control can also be viewed as 'refusal control' or call or reservation blocking. Thus for best effort there is no admission test, and policing consists simply of packet dropping. There is currently much debate about exactly what packet-dropping policy is fair to a set of competing best-effort flows under overload conditions. It is the case that FIFO (or 'drop tail') is not fair to flows which adapt, based on monitored successful rates of packets per RTT (for example, TCP) with different RTTs. Other schemes such as random early detection routing (see Floyd and Jacobson, 1993a) promise better fairness, and even help discern deliberate attempts to gain an unfair share.

For services with guaranteed performance, we would in general expect a network to be designed to admit more calls than it denies, even when there is a broad range of services available. Most users will use the average service, after all. However, the average service may be something that changes over time. It may also be the case that the user has no means to tell (at least easily) exactly what parameters should be set to what values. In fact, measurements of actual parameters show that they vary rather more, and in a more long-term correlated way than had previously been expected. A consequence of this has been that people have proposed 'measurement-based admission control'. This is basically an extension of the Internet philosophy of sending a packet and 'just seeing' if there is enough capacity.

However, we still need some way for the sender to indicate that *some* level of guarantee is needed. It has been suggested that this indication could take a very simple form: a price plus a delay sensitivity. This is still a research topic.

2.8 DETAILED ANALYSIS OF THE INTEGRATED SERVICES

In response to the growing demand for an integrated services Internet, the Internet Engineering Task Force (IETF, n.d.) set up an Integrated Services (intserv) working group (n.d.; see also Braden *et al.*, 1994) which has since defined several service classes that if supported by the routers traversed by a data flow can provide the data flow with certain QoS commitments. By contrast, best-effort traffic entering a router will receive no such service commitment and will have to make do with whatever resources are available. The level of QoS provided by these enhanced QoS classes is programmable on a per-flow basis according to requests from the end applications. These requests can be passed to the routers by network management procedures or, more commonly, using a reservation protocol such as RSVP which is described in section 2.6. The requests dictate the level of resources (for example bandwidth, buffer space) that must be reserved along with the transmission scheduling behaviour that must be installed in the routers to provide the desired end-to-end QoS commitment for the data flow. A data flow identifies the set of packets to receive special QoS. It is defined by a 'session' identified by a generalised port specification, as in Table 2.4, comprising the IP address, transport layer protocol type and port number of the destination along with a list of specific senders to that session that are entitled to receive the special QoS. Each sender is identified by source address and port number, while its protocol type must be the same as that for the session. The concept of an IP address for unicast and multicast was outlined in Chapter 1.

In determining the resource allocations necessary to satisfy a request, the router needs to take account of the QoS support provided by the link layer in the data forwarding path. Furthermore, in the case of a QoS-active link layer such as ATM or certain types of LAN the router is responsible for negotiations with the link layer to ensure that the link layer installs appropriate QoS support should the request be accepted. This mapping to link layer QoS is medium-dependent and the mechanisms for doing so are currently being defined by the Integrated Services over Specific Link Layers (ISSLL) working group of the IETF (n.d.). In the case of a QoS-passive link layer such as a leased line, the mapping to the link layer QoS is trivial since transmission capacity is handled entirely by the router's packet scheduler.

Each router must apply admission control to requests to ensure that they are accepted only if sufficient local resources are available. In making this check, admission control must consider information supplied by end applications regarding the traffic envelope that their data flow will fall within. One of the parameters in the traffic envelope that must be supplied is the maximum datagram size of the data flow, and should this be greater than the MTU of the link then admission control will reject the request since the integrated services models rely on the assumption that datagrams receiving an enhanced QoS class are never fragmented. Think of the packet arrival process as having a pattern like a waveform. The envelope is its typical shape.

Table 2.4 Session for reservation.

Destination address; Source address; Destination port; Source port; IP protocol (UDP or TCP)

Once an appropriate reservation has been installed in each router along the path, the data flow can expect to receive an end-to-end QoS commitment provided no path changes or router failures occur during the lifetime of the flow, and provided the data flow conforms to the traffic envelope supplied in the request. Owing to refresh timers used by RSVP, a flow may recover its QoS commitment without taking any special action. With the advent of QoS-aware routing, it may be that there is not even a gap in the perceived provision of the service contract.

Service-specific policing and traffic reshaping actions as described in sections 2.9.1 and 2.9.2 will be employed within the network to ensure that non-conforming data flows do not affect the QoS commitments for behaving data flows. The IETF has considered various QoS classes (for example, Baker *et al.*, 1996; Heinanen, 1996; Shenker *et al.*, 1996b, Wroclawski, 1996a) although to date only two of these, guaranteed service (Shenker *et al.*, 1996b) and controlled-load service (Wroclawski, 1996a), have been formally specified for use with RSVP (see Wroclawski, 1996b). First, we will look at the simpler of these services, namely controlled load.

2.9 HOST FUNCTIONS

RSVP use with integrated services	IETF proposed standard RFC 2210
Controlled load	IETF proposed standard RFC 2211
Guaranteed service	IETF proposed standard RFC 2212

2.9.1 Controlled-load service

Controlled-load service (Wroclawski, 1996a) provides approximately the same quality of service under heavy loads as under light loads. A description of the traffic characteristics (the Tspec, described in section 2.9.2) for the flow desiring controlled-load service must be submitted to the router as for the case of guaranteed service although it is not necessary to include the peak rate parameter. If the flow is accepted for controlled-load service then the router makes a commitment to offer the flow a service equivalent to that seen by a best-effort flow on a lightly loaded network. The important difference from the traditional Internet best-effort service is that the controlled-load flow does not noticeably deteriorate as the network load increases. This will be true regardless of the level of load increase. By contrast, a best-effort flow would experience progressively worse service (higher delay and, sooner or later, loss) as the network load increased. The controlled-load service is intended for those classes of applications that can tolerate a certain amount of loss and delay provided they are kept to a reasonable level. Examples of applications in this category include adaptive real time applications. Controlled load has some fairly simple implementations, in terms of the queuing systems in routers. It also functions adequately for the existing Mbone applications, which can adapt to the modest (small) scale end-to-end delay and variations and jitter that it may introduce, through the use of adaptive play-out buffering (Hardman *et al.*, 1995). It is not suited to applications that require very low latency (for example, distributed VR systems and so forth).

One possible example of the use of the controlled-load service is that of Mbone applications, over a private intranet, where traffic conditions and global policies can be managed such that a statistical throughput guarantee is enough, and propagation delays will be low enough that, for most users, interactive software based multimedia conferencing tools will perform adequately. A more interesting example might be the provision of SNA or DEC LAT tunnelling across a public Internet service provider's backbone network. SNA and DEC LAT are both somewhat delay sensitive owing to their detailed protocol operations, although not as much as some real-time systems are. However, using the same Internet path to carry them with arbitrary interference from other applications' flows would not work well (or at all).

Next we discuss the service provided where the user requires some commitment to a delay guarantee, namely the guaranteed service.

2.9.2 Guaranteed service

Guaranteed Service (Shenker *et al.*, 1996b) provides an assured level of bandwidth, with a firm end-to-end delay bound and no queuing loss for conforming packets of a data flow. It is intended for applications with stringent real-time delivery requirements such as certain audio and video applications that have fixed play-out buffers and are intolerant of any datagram arriving after their playback time. Guaranteed service really addresses the support of 'legacy' applications that expect a delivery model similar to traditional telecommunications circuits.

Each router characterises the guaranteed service for a specific flow by allocating a bandwidth, R, and buffer space, B, that the flow may consume. This is done by approximating the 'fluid model' of service (Parekh and Gallagher, 1993, 1996) so that the flow in effect sees a dedicated wire of bandwidth R between source and receiver.

In a perfect fluid model, a flow conforming to a token bucket of rate r and depth b will have its delay bounded by b/R provided $R \geqslant r$. To allow for deviations from this perfect fluid model in the router's approximation, two error terms, C and D are introduced. Among other things the router's approximation must take account of the medium-dependent behaviour of the link layer of the data forwarding path. These errors arise from the finite packet sizes that are being dealt with. For example, any packet may experience an excess delay as it is forwarded owing to the size of the packets in the same queue and to inaccuracies in scheduling from packets (of a possibly different size) in other queues bound for the output link. These terms are derived for weighted fair queuing schedulers in Parekh's seminal work (see Parekh and Gallagher, 1993, 1996). Consequently the delay bound now becomes $b/R + C/R + D$. However, with guaranteed service a limit is imposed on the peak rate, p, of the flow which results in a reduction of the delay bound.

In addition, the packetisation effect of the flow needs to be taken into account by considering the maximum packet size, M. While the Internet protocol permits, in principle, a wide range of packet sizes, in practice the range supported makes stating this upper limit practical and realistic. These additional factors result in a more precise bound on the end-to-end queuing delay as follows.

The composed terms, Ctot and Dtot represent the summation of the C and D error terms respectively for each router along the end-to-end data path. In the case $p > R \geqslant r$, there are three delay terms, made from the contributions of the burst

Table 2.5 Tspec and Rspec for guaranteed service.

Tspec parameters		Rspec parameters	
p	peak rate of flow (bytes/second)	R	bandwidth, i.e. service rate (bytes/second)
b	bucket depth (bytes)	S	Slack term (ms) (see section 2.10.6)
r	token bucket rate (bytes/second)		
m	minimum policed unit (bytes)		
M	maximum datagram size (bytes)		

of packets, b (the bucket depth), sent at the peak rate p and serviced at the output link rate R, plus the sum over all hops, of errors introduced at each hop due to a packet-size-worth of fluid flow approximation, plus a third term, made up of cross-traffic scheduling approximation contributions. In the case $R \geqslant p \geqslant r$, the first term is absent, since the link rate is greater than the peak, so there are no packets queued from this flow itself. In order for a router to invoke guaranteed service for a specific data flow it needs to be informed of the traffic characteristics of the flow, Tspec, along with the reservation characteristics, Rspec. These are detailed in Table 2.5.

Furthermore, to enable the router to calculate sufficient local resources to guarantee a lossless service it requires the terms Csum and Dsum which represent the summation of the C and D error terms, respectively, for each router along the path since the last reshaping point.

Guaranteed service traffic must be policed at the network access points to ensure conformance to the Tspec, so that traffic does not interfere with other flows and cause them to miss their contract. We discuss this further below.

In addition to policing of data flows at the edge of the network, guaranteed service also requires reshaping of traffic to the token bucket of the reserved Tspec at certain points on the distribution tree. Any packets failing the reshaping are treated as best-effort and marked accordingly if such a facility is available. Reshaping must be applied at any point where it is possible for a data flow to exceed the reserved Tspec even when all senders associated with the data flow conform to their individual Tspecs.

Traffic conforming to a leaky bucket specification has still some degrees of freedom to take different shapes within the envelope. Shaping can improve both the way such traffic mixes and its buffering requirements. Such an occurrence is possible in the following two multicast cases (readers may care to reread this section after reading Chapter 3):

1 At branch points in the distribution tree where the reserved Tspecs of the outgoing branches are not the same: in this case the reserved Tspec of the incoming branch is given by the 'maximum' of the reserved Tspecs on each of the outgoing branches. Consequently some of the outgoing branches will have a reserved Tspec that is less than the reserved Tspec of the incoming branch, and so it is possible that in the absence of reshaping, traffic that conforms to the Tspec of the incoming branch might not conform when routed through to an outgoing branch with a smaller reserved Tspec. As a result, reshaping must be performed at each such outgoing branch to ensure that the traffic is within this smaller, reserved Tspec.

2   At merge points in the distribution tree for sources sharing the same reservation, the sum of the Tspecs relating to the incoming branches will be greater than the Tspec reserved on the outgoing branch. Consequently, when multiple incoming branches are each simultaneously active with traffic conforming to their respective Tspecs it is possible that when this traffic is merged onto the outgoing branch it will violate the reserved Tspec of the outgoing branch. Hence, reshaping to the reserved Tspec of the outgoing branch is necessary.

This reshaping will necessarily incur an additional delay (in essence, to smooth a collection of peaks over some troughs of traffic flow must entail slowing down early packets since one cannot speed up later packets).

When merging heterogeneous reservation requests from receivers onto the tree flowing from the same source, there is an additional problem known as the 'killer reservation' problem, which manifests itself in two ways. Firstly, a large reservation made subsequent to an existing smaller reservation may fail. If this is the case, a naive implementation will cause the entire reservation to fail. The solution to this is to introduce extra states into the reservation protocol such that subsequent failures do not break existing reservations. Secondly, a receiver may continually attempt to make a large reservation, retrying quickly after every failure. This may continually block a smaller reservation request that might otherwise succeed. Again, a merge point might keep state concerning recent failed reservations and favour new ones that are more likely to succeed over retries for ones that have recently failed.

There are a number of applications in the military and commercial worlds which have hard delay bound requirements. For example, the distributed interactive simulation program has a scenario with 100 000 participants in an online war game simulation, where the applications send messages to each other that represent events between objects in the real world. Participants should see progress (missiles hitting tanks) in an ordered and timely fashion. A somewhat different scenario, but with remarkably similar network guarantee requirements, is that of share dealer networks. Here, share price advertisements are multicast to the dealer terminals, with hard delay bounds on delivery delays (and rates), and delay bounds on the response times, since the price in the real world is varying, possibly very rapidly, and the requirement is that a bid to buy at a price does not encounter an offer to sell that is significantly out of date.

2.9.3   Policing and conformance

Routers implementing the controlled-load and guaranteed services must check for conformance of data flows to their appropriate reserved Tspecs. This is known as policing. Any non-conforming data flows must not be allowed to affect the QoS offered to conforming data flows or to affect unfairly the handling of best-effort traffic.

Within these constraints the router should attempt to forward as many of the packets of the non-conforming data flow as possible. This might be done by dividing the packets into conforming and non-conforming groups and forwarding the non-conforming group on a best-effort basis. Alternatively, the router may choose to degrade the QoS of all packets of a non-conforming data flow equally. The usual enforcement policy is to forward non-conforming packets as best-effort datagrams. There is some debate about actually making non-conforming packets lower effort than best effort since otherwise there is an incentive for users to send deliberately at higher rates than their Tspec would allow.

Action with regard to non-conforming datagrams can be configurable to allow for situations such as traffic-sharing where the preferred action might be to discard non-conforming datagrams. This configuration requirement also applies to reshaping. If and when a marking facility (for example, a bit in the IP header to indicate that a packet has exceeded its flow parameters) becomes available then these non-conforming datagrams should be marked to ensure that they are treated as best-effort datagrams at all subsequent routers.

An additional requirement for policing over that of meeting the global traffic contract is that there are possible consequences for pricing if excess traffic is not seen to receive a lesser service guarantee.

2.9.4   Integrated services on specific link technology

Assuming a backbone network is implemented as a set of routers connected together by point-to-point circuits, integrated services must be implemented by putting in place the appropriate queuing strategies in the routers. Typically, theory tells us that weighted fair queuing of IP packets (or hierarchical round-robin service) will provide at least a baseline for implementation. In fact, for controlled load, simple priority queuing schemes may suffice. There are a number of other service disciplines being researched.

Where routers are interconnected by other types of link, particularly shared media (LANs, satellite channels etc.), or switches, then the interconnect technology must be controlled as well. In the standards work, specifications are emerging for mapping the guaranteed service and controlled load to run over token ring, SMDS, frame relay, and a variety of transfer capabilities and QoS classes on switched ATM (asynchronous transfer mode) networks.

For non-deterministic (but popular) subnetworks such as Ethernet, the technology must be enhanced somehow. This is a matter for current development.

When an IP network is operated across ATM switches (i.e. hosts and routers are interconnected by ATM *clouds*), then there are interworking units that map RSVP requests into Q.2931 requests. On other types of link (for example, shared LANs), other techniques are used to provide the service guarantees.

These classes of traffic are roughly in line with those developed in the broadband integrated services digital networks standards communities (the ITU and ATM forum) for ATM networks. They define the equivalent services in terms of the bandwidth rather than delay model, but the intent is similar. UBR, ABR, VBR and CBR stand for unspecified, available, variable and constant bit rate services, respectively. ATM is seen in some quarters to be the multiple service network of the future. It is clear that it is able to convey roughly the same services as are being devised for IP, which should lead to the possibility of layering one service on the other fairly easily.

2.10 RESOURCE RESERVATION PROTOCOL (RSVP) REVISITED

The resource reservation protocol, RSVP (Braden *et al.*, 1996) was designed to enable the senders, receivers and routers of communication sessions (either multicast or unicast) to communicate with each other in order to set up the necessary router state to support the services described in sections 2.9.1 and 2.9.2. It is worth noting that RSVP is not the only IP reservation protocol that has been designed for this purpose. Others include ST-II (Delgrossi and Berger, 1995) and ST-II+ (Mitzel *et al.*, 1994) which incidentally contain some interesting architectural differences to RSVP such as the use of hard-state and sender-initiated reservations rather than soft-state and receiver-initiated reservations as in RSVP. With hard-state the network is responsible for reliably maintaining router state whereas with soft-state the responsibility is passed to the end systems which must generate periodic refreshes to prevent state timeout.

An earlier Internet signalling protocol, ST-II+ permits both sender and receiver-initiated reservations; ST-II permits sender-initiated reservations only. For further discussion of alternatives we refer the interested reader to Mitzel *et al.* (1994). However, in this book the only reservation protocol we consider in detail is RSVP since currently this has the most industry support.

RSVP is a novel signalling protocol in at least three ways:

1 It accommodates multicast, not just point-to-multipoint (one-to-many) reservations. To this end, the receiver-driven request model permits heterogeneity, in principle, and the filter mechanism allows for calls that reserve resources efficiently for the aggregate traffic flow (for example, for audio conferencing).

2 It uses soft state, which means that it is tolerant of temporary loss of function without entailing fate-sharing between the end systems and the network nodes. This means that QoS routing can be deployed separately (in more than one way).

3 RSVP is quite straightforward in packet format and operations, and so is relatively low cost in terms of implementation in end systems and routers. One thing that RSVP is not is a routing protocol. RSVP does not support QoS-dependent routing itself (in other words, such routing is independent of RSVP, and could precede or follow reservations).

RSVP identifies a communication session by the combination of destination address, transport layer protocol type and destination port number. It is important to note that each RSVP operation only applies to packets of a particular session and as such every RSVP message must include details of the session to which it applies.

Although RSVP is applicable to both unicast and multicast sessions we concentrate here on the more complicated multicast case.

RSVP is not a routing protocol, it is a signalling protocol; it is merely used to reserve resources along the existing route set up by whichever underlying routing protocol is in place. Figure 2.3 shows an example of RSVP for a multicast session involving one sender, S1, and three receivers, RCV1–RCV3.

The primary messages used by RSVP are the Path message which originates from the traffic sender and the Resv message which originates from the traffic receivers. The primary roles of the Path message are, firstly, to install reverse routing state

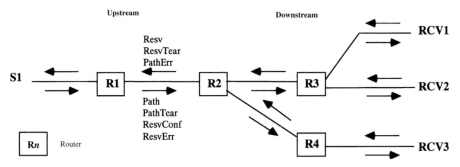

Figure 2.3   Direction of RSVP messages.

in each router along the path and, secondly, to provide receivers with information about the characteristics of the sender traffic and end-to-end path so that they can make appropriate reservation requests. The primary role of the Resv message is to carry reservation requests to the routers along the distribution tree between receivers and senders. Returning to Figure 2.3, as soon as S1 has data to send, it begins periodically forwarding RSVP Path messages to the next hop, R1 down the distribution tree. RSVP messages can be transported raw within IP datagrams using protocol number 46, although hosts without this raw I/O capability may first encapsulate the RSVP messages within a UDP header.

2.10.1   Reservation styles and merging

Associated with each reservation made at a router's interface is a Filterspec describing the packets to which the reservation applies along with an effective Flowspec. Both the Filterspec and effective Flowspec are obtained from a merging process applied to selected Resv messages arriving on the router's interface. The rules for merging are dependent upon the reservation 'style' of each Resv message as described below. In addition, the router calculates the Filterspec and Flowspec of Resv messages to be sent to the previous hop(s) upstream by applying style-dependent merging of stored reservation state. Any changes to stored reservation state that result in changes to the Resv messages to be sent upstream will cause an updated Resv message to be sent upstream immediately. Otherwise Resv messages are created based on stored reservation state and sent upstream periodically. As for Path state, all reservation state is stored in routers using soft-state and consequently relies on periodic refreshes via Resv messages to prevent state timeout. The periodic Resv message is necessary and sufficient to prevent reservation state timeout. If a router crashes, a Path message is necessary after reboot so that the Resv can rendezvous with it.

In addition, just as a PathTear message exists explicitly to tear down path state, a ResvTear message exists explicitly to tear down reservation state.

Currently three reservation styles are permissible as described below and illustrated in Figures 2.4–2.6 where the convention style (Filterspec{Flowspec}) is used to summarise the requests made by the Resv messages. It should be noted that the merging processes described below apply only to packets of the same session. (This is true of any RSVP process.) Also, merging can only occur between messages

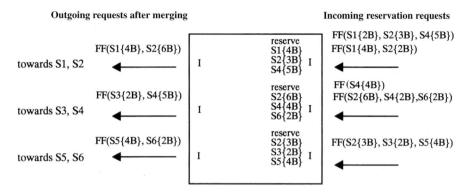

Figure 2.4 Fixed filter reservation example.

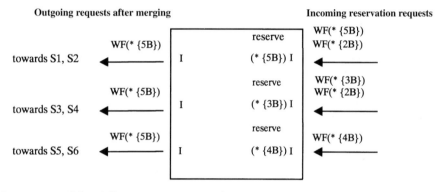

Figure 2.5 Wildcard filter reservation example.

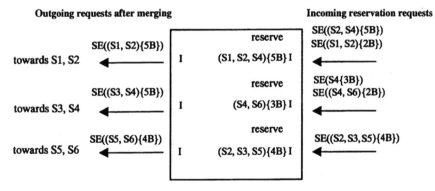

Figure 2.6 Shared explicit reservation example.

with the same reservation style. Details of the reservation style are as follows, where it is assumed that each interface I in Figures 2.4–2.6 is routable to each of the router's other interfaces.

- *Wildcard filter (WF) (shared reservation and wildcard sender selection)*: The Filterspec of each WF reservation installed at an interface is a wildcard and matches to any sender from upstream. The effective Flowspec installed is the maximum from all WF reservation requests received on that particular interface.

The Flowspec of each WF Resv message unicast to a previous hop upstream is given by the maximum Flowspec of all WF reservations installed in the router. More strictly speaking, only WF reservations whose 'scope' applies to the interface out of which the Resv message is sent are considered for this second merging process. Scope details are required for WF reservations on non-shared trees to prevent looping. Further details can be found in Braden *et al.* (1996).

- *Shared explicit (SE) (shared reservation and explicit sender selection)*: The Filterspec of each SE reservation installed at an interface contains a specific set of senders from upstream and is obtained by taking the union of the individual Filterspecs from each SE reservation request received on that interface. The effective Flowspec installed is the maximum from all SE reservation requests received on that particular interface. The Filterspec of an SE Resv message unicast out of an interface to a previous hop upstream is the union of all senders whose previous hop is via that interface and which are contained in the Filterspec of at least one SE reservation in the router.

SE and WF styles are useful for conferencing applications where only one sender is likely to be active at once, in which case reservation requests for, say, twice the sender bandwidth could be reserved in order to allow an amount of over-speaking. Although RSVP is unaware of which service (controlled-load or guaranteed) reservations refer to, RSVP is able to identify those points in the distribution tree that require reshaping in the event that the reservations are for guaranteed service as described in section 2.9.2. Consequently, at all such points, RSVP informs the traffic control mechanisms within the appropriate router accordingly although such action will only result in reshaping if the reservation is actually for guaranteed service.

2.10.2   Path messages

Each Path message includes the following information:

- Phop, the address of the last RSVP-capable node to forward this Path message. This address is updated at every RSVP-capable router along the path.
- The sender template, a filter specification identifying the sender. It contains the IP address of the sender and optionally the sender port (in the case of IPv6 a flow label may be used in place of the sender port).
- The sender Tspec defining the sender traffic characteristics.
- An optional Adspec containing OPWA information (see sections 2.10.4 and 2.10.5) which is updated at every RSVP-capable router along the path to attain end-to-end significance before being presented to receivers to enable them to calculate the level of resources that must be reserved to obtain a given end-to-end QoS.

2.10.3   Processing and propagation of Path messages

Each intermediate RSVP-capable router along the distribution tree intercepts Path messages and checks them for validity. If an error is detected then the router will drop the Path message and send a PathErr message upstream to inform the sender who can then take appropriate action.

Assuming the Path message is valid, the router does the following: update the path state entry for the sender identified by the sender template. If no path state exists, then create it. Path state includes the sender Tspec, the address, Phop of the previous hop upstream router and optionally an Adspec. The Phop address needs to be stored in order to route Resv messages in the reverse direction up the tree. The sender Tspec provides a ceiling to clip any inadvertently over-specified Tspecs subsequently received in Resv messages; set clean-up timer equal to clean-up timeout interval and restart timer. Associated with each path state entry is a clean-up timer, the expiration of which triggers deletion of the path state. Expiration of the timer will be prevented if a Path message for the entry is received at least once every clean-up timeout interval. This is the RSVP soft-state mechanism and ensures that state automatically times out if routing changes while subsequent Path messages install state along the new routing path. In this way the use of soft-state rather than hard-state helps to maintain much of the robustness of the initial Internet design concepts whereby all flow-related state was restricted to the end systems (Clark, 1988).

The router is also responsible for generating Path messages based on the stored path state and forwarding them down the routing tree making sure that for each outgoing interface the Adspec (see section 2.10.4) and Phop objects are updated accordingly. Path messages will be generated and forwarded whenever RSVP detects any changes to stored path state or is informed by the underlying routing protocol of a change in the set of outgoing interfaces in the data forwarding path. Otherwise a Path message for each specific path state entry is created and forwarded every refresh period timeout interval in order to refresh downstream path state. The refresh period timeout interval is several times smaller than the clean-up timeout interval so that occasional lost Path messages can be tolerated without triggering unnecessary deletion of path state. However, it is still a good idea to configure a minimum network bandwidth and router processing resources for RSVP messages to protect them from congestion losses.

Although all path state would eventually timeout in the absence of any refreshes via Path messages, RSVP includes an additional message, PathTear, to expedite the process. PathTear messages travel across the same path as Path messages and are used explicitly to tear down path state. PathTear messages are generated whenever a path state entry is deleted and so a PathTear message generated by a sender will result in deletion of all downstream path state for that sender. Typically, senders do this as soon as they leave the communications session. Also, deletion of any path state entry triggers deletion of any dependent reservation state (see above).

2.10.4 Adspec

The Adspec is an optional object descriptor that the sender may include in its generated Path messages in order to advertise to receivers the characteristics of the end-to-end communications path. This information can be used by receivers to determine the level of reservation required in order to achieve their desired end-to-end QoS.

The Adspec consists of a message header, a default general parameters part and at least one of the following: guaranteed service part, controlled-load service part. Omission of either the guaranteed or controlled-load service part is an indication to receivers that the omitted service is not available. This feature can be used in a multicast session to force all receivers to select the same service. At present, RSVP does not accommodate heterogeneity of services between receivers within a given multicast session although, within the same service model, the parameters may differ for receivers in the same session, so the core objective of supporting heterogeneity is mainly met.

Default general part

The default general parameters part includes the following fields which are updated at each RSVP-capable router along the path in order to present end-to-end values to the receivers.

- *Minimum path latency*: This is the sum of individual link latencies and represents the end-to-end latency in the absence of any queuing delay. In the case of guaranteed service, receivers can add this value to the bounded end-to-end queuing delay to obtain the overall bounded end-to-end delay.

- *Path bandwidth*: This parameter is the minimum of individual link bandwidths along the path.

- *Global break bit*: This bit is cleared when the Adspec is created by the sender. Encountering any routers that do not support RSVP will result in this bit being set to one in order to inform the receiver that the Adspec may be invalid.

- *Integrated services (IS) hop count*: This is incremented by one at every RSVP/IS-capable router along the path.

- *PathMTU*: This stands for path maximum transmission unit and is the minimum of MTUs of individual links along the path.

Correct functioning of IETF integrated services requires that packets of a data flow are never fragmented. It might be possible to devise a scheme to support QoS for fragmented traffic, but the key problem of how loss of fragment results in loss of overall datagram is hard to work around.

This also means that the value of M in the Tspec of a reservation request must never exceed the MTU of any link to which the reservation request applies to. MTU Discovery can be employed to avoid this.

A receiver can ensure that this requirement is met by setting the value of M in the Tspec of its reservation request to the minimum of the PathMTU values received in 'relevant' Path messages. The value of M in each generated reservation request may be further reduced on the way to each sender if merging of Resv messages occurs (see section 2.10.2). The minimum value of M from the Tspec of each Resv message received by the sender should then be used by the sending application as the upper limit on the size of packets to receive special QoS. In this way, fragmentation of these packets will never occur. In cases where the last hop to a sender is a shared medium LAN, the sender may receive Resv messages across the same interface from multiple next hop routers.

The specification (see Wroclawski, 1996b) recommends that the value of M in the sender Tspec, which has played no part in the above MTU negotiation process, should be set equal to the maximum packet size that the sender is capable of generating rather than what it is currently sending.

Guaranteed service part

The guaranteed service part of the Adspec includes the following fields which are updated at each RSVP-capable router along the path in order to present end-to-end values to the receivers.

- $Ctot$: End-to-end composed (as explained above, from the sum of each router/hop's estimate of the error) value for C.
- $Dtot$: End-to-end composed value for D.
- $CSum$: Composed value for C since last reshaping point.
- $DSum$: Composed value for D since last reshaping point (CSum and DSum values are used by reshaping processes at certain points along the distribution tree).
- *Guaranteed service break bit*: This bit is cleared when the Adspec is created by the sender. Encountering any routers that do support RSVP/IS but do *not* support guaranteed service will result in this bit being set to one in order to inform the receiver that the Adspec may be invalid and the service cannot be guaranteed.
- *Guaranteed service general parameters headers/values*: These are optional, but if any are included then each one overrides the corresponding value given in the default general parameters fragment as far as a receiver wishing to make a guaranteed service reservation is concerned. These override parameters could, for example, be added by routers along the path that have certain service-specific requirements. For example, a router may have been configured by network management so that guaranteed service reservations can take up only a certain amount, Bgs, of the outgoing link bandwidth. Consequently, if the default path bandwidth value in the Adspec to be sent out of this interface is greater than Bgs then a guaranteed service specific path bandwidth header and value equal to Bgs may be included in the Adspec. As for default general parameters, any service-specific general parameters must be updated at each RSVP hop.

Controlled-load part

The controlled-load service part of the Adspec includes the following fields which are updated at each RSVP-capable router along the path in order to present end-to-end values to the receivers.

- *Controlled-load service break bit*: This bit is cleared when the Adspec is created by the sender. Encountering any routers that do support RSVP/IS but do not support controlled-load will result in this bit being set to one in order to inform the receiver that the Adspec may be invalid and the service cannot be guaranteed.
- *Controlled-load service general parameters headers/values*: As for the guaranteed service fragment, override service-specific general parameters may be added to the controlled-load service fragment.

2.10.5 Making a reservation using one pass with advertising (OPWA)

One path with advertising (OPWA) refers to the reservation model for the case where the sender includes an Adspec in its Path messages to enable the receiver to determine the end-to-end service that will result from a given reservation request. If the sender omits the Adspec from its Path messages then the reservation model is referred to simply as one pass, in which case there is no easy way for the receiver to determine the resulting end-to-end service. The objective of this aspect of the RSVP reservation model, both for one pass and one pass with advertising is to minimise the latency (in terms of number of handshakes between senders and recipients) before a reservation is in place. Here we consider the OPWA case.

Let us assume that the sender omits the controlled-load service data fragment from the Adspec thereby restricting each receiver to reservation of guaranteed service only. Upon receiving Path messages the receiver extracts the following parameters from the sender Tspec: r, b, p, m. In addition, the following are extracted from the Adspec: minimum path latency, Ctot, Dtot, PathMTU, path bandwidth. These values are used to assess the two cases:

$$p > R \geqslant r \tag{2.1}$$

$$R \geqslant p \geqslant r \tag{2.2}$$

In a way similar to incremental route calculation, OPWA permits incremental accumulation of the delay for a reservation. The required bound on end-to-end queuing delay, Qdelreq is now calculated by subtracting the minimum path latency from the value of end-to-end delay required by the receiver's application. Typically, the receiver would then perform an initial check by evaluating equation (2.2) for R equal to the peak rate, p. If the resultant delay was greater than or equal to Qdelreq then equation (2.2) would be used for calculation of the minimum value of R necessary to satisfy Qdelreq. Otherwise equation (2.1) would be used for this purpose. This minimum value of R is then obtained by inserting Qdelreq into either equation (2.1) or (2.2) along with M (given by PathMTU), Ctot, Dtot, r, b, p, as appropriate. If the obtained value of R exceeds the path bandwidth value as obtained from the Adspec of the received Path message then it must be reduced accordingly. The receiver can now create a reservation specification, Rspec, comprising firstly the calculated value, R, of bandwidth to be reserved in each router, and secondly a slack term that is initialised to zero. In some cases, even with R set to the minimum permissible value of r, the resultant end-to-end queuing delay as given by equations (2.1) and (2.2) will still be less than Qdelreq, in which case the difference can be represented in a non-zero slack term. In addition, there are other scenarios explained in section 2.10.6 in which the slack term may not be initialised to zero. The Rspec can now be used in the creation of a Resv message which also includes the following:

- An indication of the reservation style which can be FF, SE or WF (see section 2.10.1).

- A filter specification, Filterspec (omitted for the case of WF reservation style). This is used to identify the sender(s) and the format is identical to that of the sender template in a Path message.

- A flow specification, Flowspec, comprising the Rspec and a traffic specification Tspec. Tspec is usually set equal to the sender Tspec except that M will be given by PathMTU obtained from the received Adspec.

- Optionally, a reservation confirm object, ResvConf, containing the IP address of the receiver. If present, this object indicates that the node accepting this reservation request at which propagation of the message up the distribution tree finishes should return a ResvConf message to the receiver to indicate that there is a high probability that the end-to-end reservation has been successfully installed.

In practice there are certain scenarios in which a ResvConf message might be received by a receiver only for the request to be rejected shortly afterwards.

The Resv message is now sent to the previous hop upstream as obtained from the stored path state. Upon reaching the next upstream router the Resv messages can be merged with other Resv messages arriving on the same interface according to certain rules as described earlier to obtain an effective Flowspec and Filterspec. The following action is then taken.

The effective Flowspec is passed to the traffic control module within the router which applies both admission control and policy control to determine whether the reservation can be accepted. Admission control is concerned solely with whether enough capacity exists to satisfy the request, while policy control also takes into account any additional factors that need to be considered (for example, certain policies may limit a user's reserved bandwidth even if spare bandwidth exists). If the reservation attempt is denied then any existing reservations are left unaltered and the router must send a ResvErr message downstream. If the reservation request is accepted then reservation state is set up in accordance with the effective Flowspec and Filterspec. In accepting the request it may be permissible to alter the Rspec associated with the reservation from (Rin, Sin) to (Rout, Sout) in accordance with the rules described earlier

The resultant reservation may then be merged with other reservations in accordance with the rules stated earlier to obtain a new Resv message that is sent to the next router upstream, the address of which is obtained from the stored path state.

2.10.6 Slack term

When a receiver generates an Rspec for a Resv message to be sent for a guaranteed service reservation request it must include a slack term, S (ms), as well as the amount of bandwidth, R, to be installed in each router along the path. The value of S represents the amount by which the end-to-end delay bound will be below the end-to-end delay required by the application, assuming each router along the path reserves R bandwidth according to the guaranteed service fluid approximation. Inclusion of a non-zero slack term offers the individual routers greater flexibility in making their local reservations. In certain circumstances this greater flexibility could increase the chance of an end-to-end reservation being successful. Some routers have deadline-based schedulers that decouple rate and delay guarantees. Such a scheduler may sometimes be unable to meet its deadline requirement for guaranteed service, in which case it might still be able to accept the reservation providing the slack term is at least as large as the excess delay. The excess delay would then be subtracted from the slack term before unicasting the Resv message to the previous hop upstream. Similarly, a rate-based scheduler might be able to admit a reservation request by reserving less than the requested bandwidth and unicasting the reduced reservation request to a previous hop upstream provided it could extract enough slack. Any router using available slack to reduce its reservation must conform to the rules in the following equation to ensure that the end-to-end delay bound remains satisfied:

$$\text{Sout} + \frac{b}{\text{Rout}} + \frac{\text{Ctoti}}{\text{Rout}} \leqslant \text{Sin} + \frac{b}{\text{Rin}} + \frac{\text{Ctoti}}{\text{Rin}} \qquad r \leqslant \text{Rout} \leqslant \text{Rin} \tag{3}$$

where:

Ctoti is the cumulative sum of the error terms, C, for all the routers that are upstream of, and including the current element, i.

(Rin, Sin) is the reservation request received by router i.

(Rout, Sout) is the modified reservation request unicast to the previous hop router upstream.

An example of how intelligent use of the slack term can increase the probability of an end-to-end reservation request being accepted is illustrated in Figures 2.7 and 2.8.

Suppose the token bucket rate (as defined earlier) of the data to be sent is 1.5 Mbps and the receiver has calculated from the Tspec and Adspec parameters in received Path messages so that the desired end-to-end delay can be achieved by a reservation of ($R = 2.5$ Mbps, $S = 0$) which is then requested in Figure 2.7. However, because R3 has only 2 Mbps of unused bandwidth and there is no slack available, the reservation is denied. In Figure 2.8, the reservation is increased to $R = 3$ Mbps and the amount by which such a reservation would be within the required delay bound is put in the slack term ($S > 0$). R5 and R6 reserve the requested 3 Mbps. R3

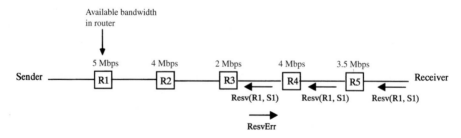

Figure 2.7   R1 = 2.5 Mbps, S1 = 0. Reservation request denied.

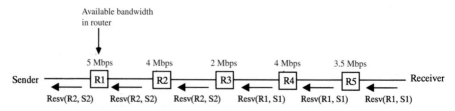

Figure 2.8   R1 = 3 Mbps, S1 > 0, R2 = 2 Mbps, S2 < S1. Reservation accepted.

can reserve only a value of 2 Mbps which, if used as the new reservation value in the propagated Resv message, will cause an increase in the end-to-end delay bound. R3 can calculate this increase, di, and if it is less than the value of the slack term S1 in the received Resv message then the request can be accepted and a reservation of 2 Mbps installed in R3. R3 will then set the Rspec in the Resv message to ($R = 2$ Mbps, $S2 = S1 - di$) before unicasting it to the next hop upstream which results in R2 and R1 also reserving 2 Mbps. The end-to-end delay bound of the reserved path is now no greater than that for a reservation of 2.5 Mbps in every router if that were possible.

2.11 QoS ROUTING

We wrote earlier that the only way to alter performance for a multimedia flow was by changing the schedule in a router or switch. However, there is another way, which is to select a different path. There are two problems with this. Firstly, alternate path routing is a complex problem, and few protocols currently support this on the basis of requests and current network conditions. Secondly, alternate paths are there for some reason, and that reason is usually that some other user is about to use them. Hence it may be a bad idea economically to make use of alternate paths that deviate very far from the best current obvious route. The jury is still out on this topic.

2.12 FUTURES

We have looked at the evolution of the Internet from a best-effort, FIFO, destination routed, unicast network, to a multiservice, QoS routed, multicast-capable system. We have seen that detailed progress has been made in that, if supported by the routers along an end-to-end data path, RSVP can permit end systems to request integrated services that provide end applications with enhanced QoS commitments over conventional best-effort delivery. RSVP can be used by end applications to select and invoke the appropriate class and QoS level. In addition, if the OPWA reservation model is used with RSVP then the requesting application is able to determine the resultant end-to-end QoS in advance of making the reservation. Without RSVP, a fallback service of best effort is still available from the unused capacity. In the near future, some research needs to be carried out in a number of areas:

1 Accounting and billing need to be integrated into the model in a scalable way.
2 Aggregation of non-specifically related reservations (or flows) would be useful – in the same way that ATM provides virtual paths as well as virtual circuits, we might like to build virtual private Internets using, for example, the address aggregation mechanism CIDR, to be used within a reservation. (The extension has been proposed in the RSVP working group to allow the generalised port to be accompanied by masks, in the same way that routing protocols distribute updates with masks.)
3 Authentication of users of RSVP is essential if we are to incur bills when we use it.
4 The usage accounting model must accommodate mirror servers in some way.

5   Some scheme to permit settlements or something akin to them will need to be evolved to allow deployment of RSVP and integrated services across paths that entail more than a single intranet or commercial Internet service provider.

6   Lastly, simply experience of using a multiservice network is needed to see which pieces of this complex system are used frequently, since it is not at all clear that the entire edifice is all either necessary or sufficient.

2.13   IP AND ATM

The two basic tasks of an intermediate node in a packet switched network are to forward packets, maintaining as far as economically possible, appropriate timing relationship between packets provided that they meet the service contract; and to deliver them along the appropriate route to the destination (Stevens, 1992).

The Internet (Postel, 1981a,b) has hitherto defined a simple service model that does not offer any definition of the timing model, and it has sufficed to provide a single FIFO queue in a router. In contrast, the path selection mechanisms in the Internet have been rich, typically permitting rapid deployment of new routers and rapid response to changes in traffic patterns. This has been achieved by making a hop-by-hop, packet-by-packet, routing lookup. Some people confuse this with a routing decision – in fact, the routing decision is made when a path computation is done, which is typically whenever new routing information is available to each node, and is a management task that often operates somewhat slower than the route lookup/forwarding decision. However, to give flexibility, IP packets all contain source and destination information, which permits a choice of route.

Recently, to add further services, the Internet Standards have been enhanced (White and Crowcroft, 1997) to provide a signalling protocol, and a family of service models based on the theory in Parekh and Gallagher (1993, 1996). This shows how a weighted fair queuing system can provide bounded delays for variable length packet *flows*, provided that the traffic is constrained by a leaky bucket, and that an admission test (for the appropriate leaky bucket specification) is carried out at the edge (or at each hop) of the path – this is known as a flow specification – and subsequent packets are matched to the admitted flow by classifying them based on the source, destination and transport-level ports (application-level multiplexing IDs) (Partridge, 1993). This is the integrated services Internet. There has been some doubt about whether it is possible to build routers fast enough to classify packets according to their flow-spec and to carry out a WFQ insertion.

In contrast to this, two other hybrid approaches to building a fast Internet have been proposed:

1   Frame relay or ATM switch fabric

2   Hybrid switch/router nodes

The first approach envisages a network provided (presumably) by telecommunications carriers made up of traditional virtual circuit based packet switches based around either frame relay (today) or ATM (tomorrow). Routers would operate between site networks and act as access devices. Here there is a clear division of slow-changing, backbone provisioning, and more rapidly changing edge networks – this is not terribly different from today's systems, although there could be more flexible access to differential services from the routers (for example, interaction between RSVP requests to routers, and router access via say Q.2931 to backbone QoS support).

The second approach is a more integrated approach, attempting to capitalise on the benefits of virtual circuits at one level, and on the flexibility advantages of dynamic IP routing at another. All nodes provide both functions in some manner. There are four main proposals for how to achieve this latter architecture.

The principal performance gain that is expected from all the proponents of these schemes is that the switch designers for ATM capitalise on the fixed-sized header, with the short VCI/VPI field, that permits simple tables for the lookup for forwarding, and the small fixed-sized cell, that permits low latency, and jitter, in combining bursty flows for forwarding. Sometimes, there is a mistaken claim that the queue insertion procedure could be faster than for integrated services IP. In fact, recent work by Zhang and colleagues (Bennett and Zhang, 1996; Zhang and Stephen, 1998) shows that this is not at all the case.

1   *CSR (cell switched router) – from Toshiba (and others)*: This approach simply uses normal IP routing for forwarding packets, but *shreds* them, so that the store-and-forwarding latency is much lower.

2   *Flow label – implemented in Ipsilon devices*: This is a smart technique for matching a flow of IP packets onto a virtual circuit, dynamically. In essence, flow characteristics are pre-programmed into a recogniser which opens VCs only for individual flows that are expected to persist long enough. Short flows are bundled onto a default VC.

3   *Tag switching – proposed by Cisco*: All routes from the routing table are used to generate tags, which are then used in the backbone to indicate a VC to follow.

4   *ARIS (aggregated route-based IP switching)*: All backbone egress points are used to generate tags which are used to bundle together like-minded flows onto a VC.

There are a number of problems with all these hybrid approaches, including: VC setup times; exhausting VCI/VPI tables; management complexity; difficulty supporting mobility; difficulty supporting multicast (many-to-many); possible lack of fault tolerance.

2.13.1   Mapping classes and QoS

The integrated services model has an initial deployment scenario of routers connected together by point-to-point links. In that situation, packet scheduling for service classes needs only to be deployed within the routers, to provide the service overall.

However, many parts of the Internet involve other interconnection technologies between routers. Two common, but extremely different situations are:

1   Routers interconnected via local area networks, such as ethernet, FDDI, 100 Mbps ethernet, 100VG, and so forth.

2   Routers interconnected by non-broadcast multiple access (NBMA) networks such as frame relay, SMDS and ATM – these are often referred to as switched *clouds*, typically because of the way that they are drawn on internetwork maps.

The Integrated Services over Specific Link Layers working group of the IETF has defined the mapping of some of the IP-level services onto services provided at the lower layer.

In some cases, the link layer as currently deployed cannot support the upper layer services with any reasonable guarantee, and so some enhancement is typically called for. One such case is the ethernet where the shared media access is so non-deterministic that an enhancement based on some form of distributed band-width manager is required to provide anything beyond best-effort IP service over an ethernet hop.

In the case of NBMA networks, particularly ATM, a much richer variety of services is available at the lower layer for IP to utilise. In fact, there are multiple possible mappings from the high-level IP service, to the proposed 'bearer service classes' of ATM – for example:

- Guaranteed service could be provided over CBR or rtVBR.
- Controlled load could be provided over CBR, rtVBR, nrtVBR or ABR.
- Best effort could be provided over CBR, rtVBR, nrtVBR, ABR or UBR.

This area is very active, and simplification will no doubt be sought and found by the market. In the next three subsections, we briefly describe the 'pure' IP approach.

2.13.2   Topology control

One of the principal reasons for the success of IP is the flexibility for addressing and routing. At the same time, this has led to problems. Stability of routing is reported to be getting worse, and there is some concern about the exhaustion of the global IPv4 address space. This is being solved by the introduction of IPv6, but the performance problems for route lookup might seem to be exacerbated by this. In fact, the work of Degermark and others at SICS (see Brodnik *et al.*, 1997) shows that it is feasible to construct a novel data structure that not only permits fast routing lookup, but which reduces the size of the routing table as well. In fact, the entire routing table of today's Internet can be fitted into the on-chip data cache of a common desktop processor (Pentium) and a lookup ('longest match prefix') computed in eight memory accesses in the worst case. The scaling complexity of the data structure is with the route depth, not with the size of the network, and so should not slow down much as we move to one billion end systems.

This is useful since it permits us to consider using IP addresses (and possibly fully generalised port specifications) as the key, the basis for deciding what to do with a packet as well as where to send it. This gives high degrees of flexibility (one can alter QoS mid flow, as well as route).

2.13.3   QoS control

QoS control requires some number of alternative queues, as well as some form of admission, policing and possibly shaping.

Assuming that admission and policing can be done on small numbers of flows at the 'edge' (ingress) of the network, then we can police (and shape) aggregate flows as they approach the core of the network (recent results from Guerin's group at T. J. Watson show that this in fact gets *higher* utilisation). Then the problem is that of the performance of queue insertion.

2.13.4 Queue insertion/lookup performance

Queue insertion for weighted fair queuing (WFQ) is typically a sort algorithm (actually, it depends on the interleave of the arrival processes – if they are loosely synchronised, then it is possible that one may only rarely have to do more than a few swaps).

Zhang's work shows that for CBR (guaranteed service in integrated service Internet terminology), a different queuing algorithm called worst-case fair weighted fair queuing achieves better delay jitter bounds, and yet can have $O(1)$ insertion time.

2.13.5 Conclusions on IP and ATM

It would appear that a purist IP architecture for all switching nodes in the Internet is both feasible and, for management reasons (and therefore cost), attractive. Because (and not despite) of the work done on QoS and scalable ATM switch design, it would seem that the exposure of ATM at any interface is completely unnecessary, except perhaps, at modest speed links (ADSL, DVB, or 25 Mbps domestic networks?), where the reduced latency for voice/video when multiplexed at finer grain may need the cut through cell size.

2.14 RECENT SIMPLIFIED APPROACHES TO SERVICE DIFFERENTIATION

Recently, a simpler model of service differentiation has emerged from LBL and MIT. The ideas are fairly simple and capitalise on recent advances on measurement-based admission and network pricing theory. Surprisingly, this ends up being a specification of service profiles, which are implemented at the ingress (or egress) to any area, where an area can be a backbone or an access net or whatever.

The service profile is 'accessed' simply by the 'user' (could be ingress/access router, or source host) setting the IP precedence bit (if they want low delay *too*, they set the ToS bit appropriately). The *rate* they send at determines the service profile (and therefore tariff, if appropriate). There was one *big* unsettled difference between the model Van Jacobson proposes and the more complex model that Wroclawski and Clark have devised.

Jacobson's scheme drops *all* packets above the service profile rate (so if you pay but the net is *not* congested, you do not get more than you paid for). For aggregated TCPs down such a pipe, this is not a problem, but a single TCP may not get good utilisation on this scheme (the goal is to create a disincentive for people to use the premium scheme during light load periods anyhow).

Clark and Wroclawski's scheme can do this, but can also specify a 'TCP rate', which then implements a complex filter/policy at the ingress, that 'understands' TCP dynamics and drops packets only for non-conforming TCPs (i.e. if TCP does slow start and congestion avoidance, their scheme for that particular profile will allow a sawtooth variation (not just a leaky bucket or burst tolerance, but a shaped burst tolerance)). The details are unclear on how to make this go fast, but there are some nice simulations.

The main problem with not dropping packets that exceed the service profile is what to do with them – in Clark's scheme, the precedence bit is cleared. This has the problem that they then *compete* on an equal footing with non-premium packets, and so can cause congestion downstream. Another problem is that they can arrive out of order with respect to the premium 'in-profile' packets. Some QoS routing researchers really like both schemes, since they can be implemted in two queues (or maybe four) and scale nicely (the nearer the backbone the router, the less that things have to be policed). RSVP might be used to 'install' profiles although it is more likely to be just a subscribe-time service. For alternative path QoS routing, it is also neat, since one only has to add a mechanism for distributing two (or four) sets of destination (or for multicast, source) based routes, which means it scales well.

2.15 SUMMARY

In this chapter we have looked at network service models and discovered that this is a complex area where there is a lot of debate on how to provide what is perceived as the need for guarantees for multimedia networked applications.

The very idea of guarantee is suspect to an engineer. In fact, what a network offers are services which provide probabilities of meeting some performance requirements. The performance bounds may involve more-or-less refined, individual offerings (i.e. to pairs or groups of users) or overall performance metrics to the set of typical users, or something between. The contract concerning performance statistics may be made some time in advance through subscription, or immediately before (or even remade during) each session. The costs of the various technical approaches to providing different performance bounds are not fully understood.

This area is extremely active in terms of research, standards development and technology deployment. However, an important aspect of it is the effect of pricing, which is outside the scope of this book. It is important to realise though, that the best technical solutions are often swept away by marketing.

CHAPTER THREE

Multicast

3.1 INTRODUCTION

When there is a requirement to send data to many receivers simultaneously, there are two traditional methods that can be used: repeated transmission and broadcast. Repeated transmission may be acceptable if the cost is low enough and delivery can be spread out over time, as with junk mail or electronic mailing lists. Otherwise a broadcast solution is required. With real time multimedia, repeated delivery is feasible, but only at great expense to the sender, who must invest in large amounts of bandwidth. Similarly, traditional broadcast channels have been very expensive if they cover significant numbers of recipients or large geographical areas. However, on the Internet, there is an alternative solution. IP multicast effectively turns the Internet into a broadcast channel, but one that anyone can send to without having to spend huge amounts of money on transmitters and government licences. It provides efficient, timely and global many-to-many distribution of data, and as such may become the broadcast medium of choice in the future.

The Internet is a datagram network. This means that anyone can send a packet to a destination without having to pre-establish a path. Of course, the boxes along the way must have either pre-computed a set of paths, or be pretty fast at calculating one as needed, and typically, the former approach is used. However, the sending host need not be aware of or participate in the complex route calculation; nor need it take part in a complex *signalling* or *call set-up* protocol. It simply addresses the packet to the right place, and sends it. As discussed briefly in Chapters 1 and 2, this may be a more complex procedure if the sending or receiving systems need more than the default performance that a path or network might offer, but it is the *default* model.

Adding multicast to the Internet does not alter the basic model. A sending host can still simply send, but now there is a new form of address, the multicast or host group address. Unlike unicast addresses, hosts can dynamically subscribe to multicast addresses and by so doing cause multicast traffic to be delivered to them. Thus the IP multicast *service model* can be summarised as:

1   Senders send to a multicast address.

2   Receivers express an interest in a multicast address.

3   Routers conspire to deliver traffic from the senders to the receivers.

Sending multicast traffic is no different from sending unicast traffic except that the destination address is slightly special. However, to receive multicast traffic, an interested host must tell its local router that it is interested in a particular multicast group address, which it does using the Internet group management protocol (IGMP).

Point-to-multipoint communication is nothing new. We are all used to the idea of broadcast TV and radio, where a shared medium (the RF spectrum) is partitioned amongst users (basically, transmitter or TV and radio station owners). It is a matter of regulation that there is typically only one particular sender of particular content on a particular frequency, although there are other parts of the RF spectrum given over to free use for multi-party communication (for example, police radio, citizen band radio, etc.).

The Internet multicast *model* (Deering, 1989) is very similar. The idea is to convert the mesh wide area network that is the Internet (whether the public Internet, or a private enterprise net, or intranet makes no difference to the model), into a shared resource for senders to send to multiple participants or groups.

To make this group communication work for large-scale systems (in the sense of a large number of recipients for a particular group, or in the sense of a large number of senders to a large number of recipients, or in the sense of a large number of different groups), it is necessary, both for senders and for the routing functions to support delivery to have a system that can be largely independent of the particular recipients at any one time. In other words, just as a TV or radio station do not know who is listening when, an Internet multicast sender does not know who might receive the packets it sends. If this sends alarm bells ringing about security, it should not. Unicast senders have no assurance about who receives their packets either. Assurances about disclosure (privacy) and authenticity of sender/recipient are largely separate matters from simple packet delivery models. We discuss these security matters in some detail in Chapter 10.

Basically, the model is an extension of the datagram model, and uses the fact that the datagram is a self-contained communications unit that not only conveys data from source to destination, but also conveys the source and destination, in other words, in some senses, datagrams *signal* their own path, both with a source and a destination address in every packet.

By adding a range of addresses for sending to a group, and providing independence between the address allocation and the rights to send to a group, the analogy between RF spectrum and the Internet multicast space is maintained. Some mechanism, as yet unspecified, is used to choose dynamically which address to send to. In Chapter 7, we will take a look at some protocols for carrying out this function, but suffice it to say for now that the idea is that somehow, elsewhere, the address used for a multicast session or group communication activity is chosen so that it does not clash with other uses or users, and is advertised. Imagine the equivalent in the RF spectrum. A new TV or radio station's manager (or multicast session creator) looks in a TV listings magazine, or in a government or regulatory body's publications (say a bulletin board) for a list of frequencies in use, and finds one that is free. We write to the TV listings magazine (the bulletin board) and have them advertise this new address. We can now safely send, and receivers find out where to 'receive on'.

It is *very important* to note that, unlike the RF spectrum, an IP packet to be multicast carries a unique source identifier, in that such packets are sent with the normal unicast IP address of the interface of the sending host they were sent from.

It is also worth noting that an address that is being used to signify a group of entities must surely be a logical address (or in some senses a name) rather than a topological or topographical identifier. We shall see that this means there must be some service that maps such a logical identifier to a specific set of locations in the same way that a local unicast address must be mapped (or bound) to a specific location. In the multicast case, this mapping is distributed. Note also that multicast Internet addresses are in some sense 'host group' addresses, in that they indicate a set of hosts to deliver to. In the Internet model there is a further level of multiplexing, that of transport-level ports, and there is room for some overlap of functionality, since a host may receive packets sent to multiple multicast addresses on the same port, or multiple ports on the same multicast address. We look at this further in Chapter 5.

This model raises a number of questions about address and group management, such as how these addresses are allocated. The area requiring most change, though, is in the domain of the routing. Somehow the routers must be able to build a distribution tree from the senders to all the receivers for each multicast group. The senders do not know who the receivers are (they just send their data), and the receivers do not know who the senders are (they just ask for traffic destined for the group address), so the routers have to do something without help from the hosts. We examine this in detail in section 3.4.

3.2 ROADMAP

The functions that provide the standard Internet multicast service can be separated into host and network components. The interface between these is provided by IP multicast addressing and IGMP group membership functions, as well as standard IP packet transmission and reception. The network functions are principally concerned with multicast routing, while host functions also include higher-layer functions such as the addition of reliability facilities in a transport-layer protocol. We cover each of these functions, in that order, in the rest of this chapter.

3.3 HOST FUNCTIONS

IGMP v1	IETF standard RFC 1112
IGMP v2	IETF proposed standard RFC 2236
IGMP v3	IETF work in progress

As we stated above, host functionality is extended through the use of the IGMP protocol. Hosts, and routers which we will look at later, must be able to deal with new forms of addresses. When IP version 4 addressing was first designed, it was divided into the classes shown in Table 3.1. Originally class A was intended for large

Table 3.1   Class D addresses are multicast.

Class	Addresses
A 0000	1.0.0.0 to 126.255.255.255
B 1000	128.0.0.0 to 191.255.255.255
C 1100	192.0.0.0 to 223.255.255.255
D 1110	224.0.0.0 to 239.255.255.255

networks, B for middle-sized networks and C for small networks. Class D was later allocated for multicast addresses. Since then, classless addressing has been introduced to solve Internet scaling problems, and the rules for classes A, B and C no longer hold, but class D is still reserved for multicast, and so all IPv4 multicast addresses start with the high-order 4 bit nibble 1110. In other words, from the 2^{32} possible addresses, 2^{28} are multicast. This means that there can be up to around 270 million different groups, each with as many senders as can get unicast addresses. This is many orders of magnitude more than the RF spectrum allows for typical analogue frequency allocations.[1]

For a host to support multicast, the host service interface to IP must be extended in three ways:

1   A host must be able to join a group. This means it must be able to reprogram its network level, and possibly, consequentially, the lower levels, in order to be able to receive packets addressed to multicast group addresses.

2   An application that has joined a multicast group and then sends to that group must be able to select whether it wants the host to loop back the packets that it sent so that it receives its own packets.

3   A host should be able to limit the scope with which multicast messages are sent. The Internet protocol contains a time to live field, used originally to limit the lifetime of packets on the network, both for safety of upper layers and for prevention of traffic overload during temporary routing loops. It is used in multicast to limit how 'far' a packet can go from the source. We will see below how scoping can interact with routing.

When an application tells the host networking software to join a group, the host software checks to see if the host is a member of the group. If not, it makes a note of the fact and sends out an IGMP join message. It also maps the IP address to a lower-level address and reprograms its network interface to accept packets sent to that address. There is a refinement here: a host can join 'on an interface'; that is, hosts that have more than one network card can decide which one (or more than one) they wish to receive multicast packets via. The implication of the multicast model is that it is 'pervasive' so that it is usually only necessary to join on one interface.[2]

Taking a particular example to illustrate the IP level to link level mapping process, if a host joins an IP multicast group using an ethernet interface, there is a mapping from the low 24 bits of the multicast address into the low 24 (out of 48) bits of the ethernet address. Since this is a many-to-one mapping, there may be multiple IP multicast groups occupying the same ethernet address on a given wire, though it may be made unlikely by the address allocation scheme (as discussed in Chapter 7). An ethernet LAN is a shared-medium network,[3] thus local addressing of packets to an ethernet group means that they are received by ethernet hardware and delivered to the host software, *only* of those hosts with members of the relevant IP group. This means that host software is generally saved the burden of filtering out irrelevant packets. Where there is an ethernet address clash, software can filter the packets efficiently.

How IGMP works can be summarised as follows:

1   When a host first joins a group, it programs its ethernet interface to accept the relevant traffic, and it sends an IGMP join message on its local network. This informs any local routers that there is a receiver for this group now on this subnet.

2   The local routers remember this information, and arrange for traffic destined for this address to be delivered to the subnet.

3   After a while, the routers wonder if there is still any member on the subnet, and send an IGMP query message to the multicast group. If the host is still a member, it replies with a new Join message unless it hears someone else do so first. Multicast traffic continues to be delivered.

4   Eventually the application finishes, and the host no longer wants the traffic. It reprograms its ethernet interface to reject the traffic, but the packets are still sent until the router times the group out and sends a query to which no one responds. The router then stops delivering the traffic.

Thus joining a multicast group is quick, but leaving can be slow with IGMP version 1. IGMP version 2 reduces the leave latency by introducing a 'leave' message, and an assorted set of rules to prevent one receiver leaving from disconnecting others. IGMP version 3 introduces the idea of *source-specific* joining and leaving whereby a host can subscribe (or reject) traffic from individual senders rather than the group as a whole, at the expense of more complexity and extra state in routers.

3.4 ROUTING AND ADDRESSING

Routers conspire to deliver packets in the Internet. Everything in any part of the Internet that wants to be reached must have an address. The address tells the computers in the Internet (hosts and routers) where something is topologically. Thus the address is also hierarchical. My computer's address is 128.16.8.88. We asked our Internet provider for a network number. We were given the number 128.16.x.y. We could fill in the x and y how we liked, to number the computers on our network. We divided our computers into groups on different LAN segments, and numbered the segments 1–256 (x), and then the hosts 1–256 (y) on each segment. When your organisation asks for a number for its net, it will be asked how many computers it has, and assigned a network number big enough to accommodate that number of computers. Nowadays, if you have a large network, you will be given a number of numbers.

Everything in the Internet must be reachable. The route to a host will traverse one or more networks. The easiest way to picture a route is by thinking of how a letter to a friend in a foreign country gets there.

You post the letter in a postbox. It is picked up by a postman (LAN), and taken to a sorting office (router). There, the sorter looks at the address, sees that the letter is for another country and sends it to the sorting office for international mail. This sorting office then carries out a similar procedure. And so on, until the letter gets to its destination. If the letter was for the same 'network' (i.e. local) then it would be delivered immediately. Notice the fact that all the routers (sorting offices) do not have to know all the details about everywhere, just about the next hop to go to. Notice the fact that the routers (sorting offices) have to consult tables of where to go next (for example, international sorting office). Routers chatter to each other all the time figuring out the best (or even just usable) routes to places.

The way to picture this is to imagine a road system with a person standing at every intersection who is working for the Road Observance Brigade. This person (Rob) reads the road names of the roads meeting at the intersection, and writes them down on a card, with the number 0 after each name. Every few minutes, Rob holds up the card to any neighbour standing down the road at the next intersection. If they are doing the same, Rob writes down their list of names, but adds 1 to the numbers read off the other card. After a while, Rob is now telling people about the neighbour's roads several roads away. Of course, Rob might get two ways to get somewhere – then, he crosses out the one with the larger number.

To support multicast, routers need to know where the recipients are (or possibly, where they are not). The first step in this is for routers to take part in the IGMP.

3.5 MULTICAST ROUTING

Given the multicast service model described above, and the restrictions that senders and receivers do not know each others' location or anything about the topology, how do routers conspire to deliver traffic from the senders to the receivers?

We shall assume that if a sender and a receiver did know about each other then they could each send unicast packets to the other. In other words, there is a network with bidirectional paths and an underlying unicast routing mechanism already running. Given this, there is a spectrum of possible solutions. At one extreme, we can flood data from the sender to all possible receivers and have the routers for networks where there are no receivers prune off their branches of the distribution tree. At the other extreme, we can communicate information in a multicast routing protocol conveying the location of all the receivers to the routers on the paths to all possible senders. Neither of these methods is terribly desirable on a global scale, and so the most interesting solutions tend to be hybrid solutions that lie between these extremes.

In the real world there are many different multicast routing protocols, each with its own advantages and disadvantages. We shall explain each of the common ones briefly, as a working knowledge of their pros and cons helps us to understand the practical limits to the uses of multicast.

3.5.1 Flood and prune protocols

DVMRP	IETF experimental standard RFC 1075
DM-PIM	IETF work in progress

These protocols are more correctly known as *reverse-path multicast* algorithms. When a sender first starts sending, traffic is flooded out through the network. A router may receive the traffic along multiple paths on different interfaces, in which case it rejects any packet that arrives on any interface other than the one it would use to send a unicast packet back to the source. It then sends a copy of each packet out of each interface except the one back to the source. In this way each link in the whole network is traversed at most once in each direction, and the data are received by all routers in the network. So far, this describes reverse-path *broadcast*. Many parts of the network will be receiving traffic although there are no receivers there. These routers know they have no receivers (otherwise IGMP would have told them) and they can then send prune messages back towards the source to stop unnecessary traffic flowing. Thus the delivery tree is pruned back to the minimal tree that reaches all the receivers. The final distribution tree is what would be formed by the union of shortest paths from each receiver to the sender, and so this type of distribution tree is known as a shortest-path tree.[4]

Two commonly used multicast routing protocols fall into the class: DVMRP (the distance vector multicast routing protocol) and DM-PIM (dense-mode protocol independent multicast). The primary difference between these is that DVMRP computes its own routing table to determine the best path back to the source, whereas DM-PIM uses that of the underlying unicast routing hence the term 'protocol independent'.

It should be fairly obvious that sending traffic everywhere and getting people to tell you what they do not want is not a terribly scalable mechanism. Sites get traffic they do not want (albeit very briefly), and routers not on the delivery tree need to store prune state. For example, if a group has one member in the UK and two in France, then routers in Australia still get some of the packets and need to hold prune state to prevent more packets arriving. However, for groups where most places actually do have receivers (receivers are 'densely' distributed), this sort of protocol works well, and so although these protocols are poor choices for a global scheme, they might be appropriate within some organisations.

3.5.2 MOSPF

MOSPF   IETF proposed standard RFC 1584

MOSPF is not really a category, but a specific instance of a protocol. MOSPF is the multicast extension to OSPF (open shortest path first) which is a unicast link-state routing protocol.

Link-state routing protocols work by having each router send a routing message periodically listing its neighbours and how far away they are. These routing messages are flooded throughout the entire network, and so every router can build up a map of the network which it can then use to build forwarding tables (using a Dijkstra algorithm) to decide quickly which is the correct next hop for sending a particular packet.

Extending this to multicast is achieved simply by having each router also list in a routing message the groups for which it has local receivers. Thus given the map and the locations of the receivers, a router can also build a multicast forwarding table for each group.

MOSPF also suffers from poor scaling. With flood-and-prune protocols, data traffic is an *implicit* message about where there are senders, and so routers need to store unwanted state where there are no receivers. With MOSPF there are *explicit* messages about where all the receivers are, and so routers need to store unwanted state where there are no senders. However, both types of protocol build very efficient distribution trees.

3.5.3 Centre-based trees

Rather than flooding the data everywhere, or flooding the membership information everywhere, algorithms in the centre-based trees category map the multicast group address to a particular unicast address of a router, and they build explicit distribution trees centred around this particular router. There are three main problems that need to be solved to get this approach to work:

1 How to perform the mapping from group address to centre address.

2 How to choose the location of the centre so that the distribution trees are efficient.

3 How to construct the tree given the centre address.

Different protocols have come up with different solutions to these problems. There are three centre-based tree protocols worth our exploring in a little detail because they illustrate different approaches. They are core-based trees (CBT), sparse-mode PIM (SM-PIM) and the border gateway multicast protocol (BGMP).

3.5.4 Core-based trees

Core-based trees   IETF experimental standard RFC 2201

CBT was the earliest centre-based tree protocol, and it is the simplest. When a receiver joins a multicast group, its local CBT router looks up the multicast address and obtains the address of the core router for the group. It then sends a Join message for the group towards the core. At each router on the way to the core, forwarding state is instantiated for the group, and an acknowledgement is sent back to the previous router. In this way, a multicast tree is built, as shown in Figure 3.1.

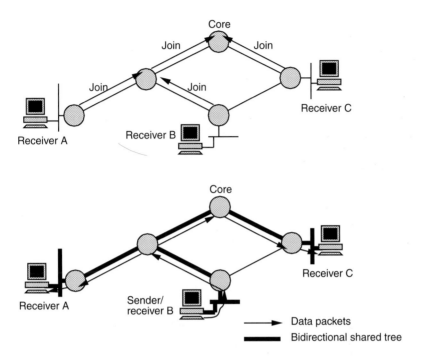

Figure 3.1 Formation of a CBT bidirectional shared tree.

If a sender (that is a group member) sends data to the group, the packets reach its local router, which forwards them to any of its neighbours that are on the multicast tree. Each router that receives a packet forwards it out of all it its interfaces that are on the tree except the one the packet came from. The style of tree that the CBT builds is called a bidirectional shared tree because the routing state is 'bidirectional' – packets can flow both up the tree towards the core and down the tree away from the core depending on the location of the source, and are 'shared' by all sources to the group. This is in contrast to unidirectional shared trees built by SM-PIM as we shall see later.

IP multicast does not require senders to a group to be members of the group, so it is possible that a sender's local router is not on the tree. In this case, the packet is forwarded to the next hop towards the core. Eventually the packet will either reach a router that is on the tree, or it will reach the core, and it is then distributed along the multicast tree.

CBT also allows multiple core routers to be specified which adds a little redundancy in case the core becomes unreachable. CBT never properly solved the problem of how to map a group address to the address of a core. In addition, good core placement is a hard problem. Without good core placement, CBT trees can be quite inefficient, and so CBT is unlikely to be used as a global multicast routing protocol.

However, within a limited domain, CBT is very efficient in terms of the amount of state that routers need to keep. Only routers on the distribution tree for a group keep forwarding state for that group, and no router needs to keep information about any source, and thus CBT scales much better than flood-and-prune protocols, especially for sparse groups where only a small proportion of subnetworks have members.

3.5.5 Sparse-mode PIM

SM-PIM   IETF experimental standard RFC 2117

The work on CBT encouraged others to try to improve on its limitations while keeping the good properties of shared trees, and sparse-mode PIM was one result. The equivalent of a CBT core is called a rendezvous point (RP) in PIM, but it serves largely the same purpose.

When a sender starts sending, irrespective of whether it is a member or not, its local router receives the packets and maps the group address to the address of the RP. It then encapsulates each packet in another IP packet (imagine putting one letter inside another, differently addressed envelope) and sends it unicast directly to the RP.

When a receiver joins the group, its local router initiates a Join message that travels hop-by-hop to the RP instantiating forwarding state for the group. However, this state is a unidirectional state – it can be used only by packets flowing from the RP towards the receiver, and not for packets to flow back up the tree towards the RP. Data from senders is de-encapsulated at the RP and flows down the shared tree to all the receivers.

The important advance that SM-PIM made over CBT was to realise that discovering who the senders are could be separated from building efficient trees from those senders to receivers.

Thus SM-PIM unidirectional trees are not terribly good distribution trees, but do start data flowing to the receivers. Once these data are flowing, a receiver's local router can then initiate a transfer from the shared tree to a shortest-path tree by sending a source-specific Join message towards the source, as shown in Figure 3.2. When data start to arrive along the shortest-path tree, a prune message can be sent back up the shared tree towards the source to avoid getting the traffic twice.

Unlike other shortest-path tree protocols such as DVMRP and DM-PIM where prune state exists everywhere there are no receivers, with SM-PIM, source-specific state exists only on the shortest-path tree. Also, low-bandwidth sources such as those sending RTCP receiver reports do not trigger the transfer to a shortest-path tree, which further helps scaling by eliminating unnecessary source-specific state.

Because SM-PIM can optimise its distribution trees after formation, it is less critically dependent on the RP location than CBT is on the core location. Hence the primary requirement for choosing an RP is load-balancing. To perform multicast-group to RP mapping, SM-PIM pre-distributes a list of candidates to be RPs to all routers. When a router needs to perform this mapping, it uses a special hash function to hash the group address into the list of candidate RPs to decide the actual RP to join. Except in rare failure circumstances, all the routers within the domain will perform the same hash and come up with the same choice of RP. The RP may or may not be in an optimal location, but this is offset by the ability to switch to a shortest-path tree.

The dependence on this hash function and the requirement to achieve convergence on a list of candidate RPs does, however, limit the scaling of SM-PIM. As a result, it is also best deployed within a domain, although the size of such a domain may be quite large.

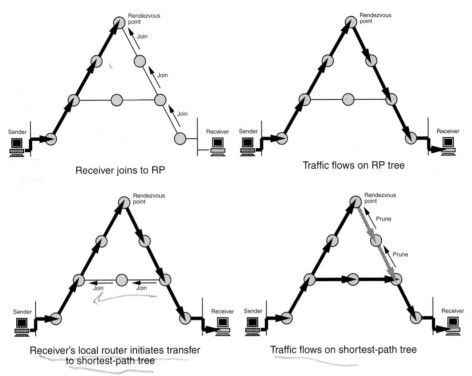

Receiver joins to RP

Traffic flows on RP tree

Receiver's local router initiates transfer to shortest-path tree

Traffic flows on shortest-path tree

Figure 3.2 Formation of a sparse-mode PIM tree.

3.5.6 Border gateway multicast protocol

BGMP   IETF work in progress

The border gateway multicast protocol (BGMP) is an attempt to design a true inter-domain multicast routing protocol; one that can scale to operate in the global Internet. DVMRP and DM-PIM will not do this because their flood-and-prune nature requires off-tree routers to keep per-source state. MOSPF will not do this because OSPF does not scale well enough, and MOSPF (which also distributes receivership information) scales worse. CBT and SM-PIM will not do this because the scalability of the mechanisms they use to perform group-to-RP mapping limits them.

BGMP was based on ideas from the intra-domain protocols above, but has a slightly different goal: it does not build trees of routers, but rather it builds bidirectional shared-trees of *domains*. Within a domain, any of the intra-domain multicast routing protocols can be used, and BGMP then provides multicast routing between the domains.

BGMP builds trees of domains that are similar to CBT trees of routers – they are bidirectional shared-trees built by sending explicit Join messages towards a root domain. However, BGMP can also build source-specific branches, which are similar in concept to source-specific trees in SM-PIM, but do not always reach as far as the

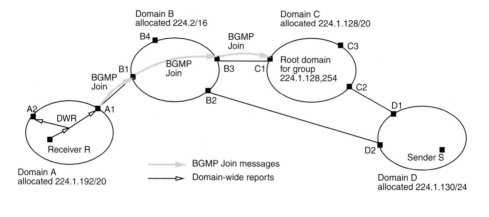

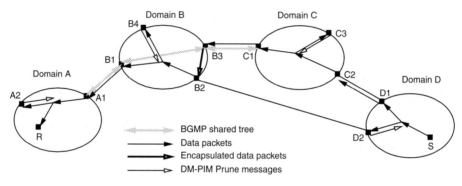

Figure 3.3   Formation of a BGMP shared tree.

source. The principal problem that prevents CBT and SM-PIM from scaling is that of mapping a multicast address to the unicast address of a rendezvous point or core. BGMP solves this problem through a close tie-in with a hierarchical multicast address allocation scheme called multicast address-set claim (MASC). MASC allocates ranges of multicast addresses to domains. These address ranges are distributed to border-routers worldwide as *group-routes* using BGP routing (which is used for unicast inter-domain routing). Such a group-route indicates the path to the root domain for that range of multicast addresses. To make this scale, MASC allocates the address ranges dynamically in a manner that can be aggregated, so the number of group-routes that need to be stored at each border router is relatively small.

Figure 3.3 illustrates how BGMP builds a distribution tree given that group-routes have already been distributed. In this case all the domains are running DM-PIM because this simplifies the example, but in reality they would likely be running a mixture of different protocols.

Receiver R joins the multicast group 224.1.128.254. Its local router sends a domain-wide report (DWR) to all the border routers in domain A. Router A1 discovers that the best route to the root for 224.1.128.254 is 224.1/16 received from its external peer router B1, so it sends a BGMP Join message to B1. Router B1 in turn looks up 224.1.128.254 and discovers its best route is 224.1.128/20 that it received from its internal peer router B3, so it sends a BGMP Join message to B3. B3 repeats the process and sends a BGMP Join to C1. Router C1 is a border

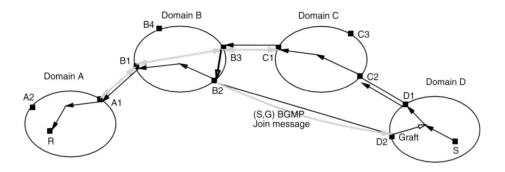

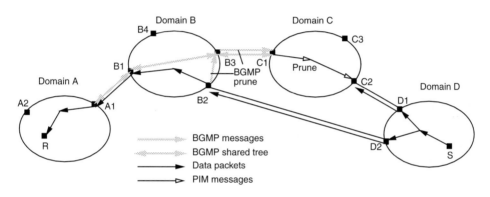

Figure 3.4 Forming a BGMP shortest-path branch.

router for the domain which has been allocated 224.1.128.254 (along with other groups), so the join message has now reached the root domain and need travel no further.

Now source S in domain D starts sending to 224.1.128.254. Its data flood through domain D and reach all the border routers. D2 is not on the best path to the root domain, so it sends a DM-PIM prune message back towards S, but router D1 is on the best path to the root domain. It has no state for group 224.1.128.254, but forwards the data anyway to C2. Router C2 forwards the data into the DM-PIM domain C, and they flood through the domain. Router C3 has no state for the group, and sends a prune in response, but router C1 is on the shared tree for the group, and so forwards the data to B3. B3 wishes to forward the data into B, but it is not on the best path back to S. If it merely multicast the data into B, routers within B would drop the data as DM-PIM requires the distribution tree to be source-based. Instead, it encapsulates the data and sends them to the correct entry router (as determined by its unicast routing table), in this case B2. B2 then decapsulates the data and multicasts them into domain B, where they flood through the domain. B1 in turn forwards the data along the shared tree to domain A and hence to R.

At this stage, as shown in the upper part of Figure 3.4, data are flowing from S to R along the shared tree. They have flooded through the domains along the path, but have been pruned back within the domains to just the minimal tree required to deliver the data. However, B3 is having to encapsulate the data to B2, which is undesirable as routers typically are not very good at encapsulation, and also as there is a better path that the data could have taken. As B2 is not on the shared tree, it is permitted to initiate a shortest-path branch by sending a source-specific Join message for source S to D2. When D2 receives this Join, it grafts itself onto the DM-PIM tree within domain D, and traffic starts to flow to B2. B2 then sends a BGMP prune to B3 and starts dropping the encapsulated packets to prevent it receiving two copies of the data. The prune will propagate up to the root domain if it encounters no other branch of the shared tree on the way.

The example above used dense-mode PIM within the domains, but any other inter-domain multicast routing protocol could be used instead. Each has its own set of rules for how to interoperate with BGMP, but at least each does not then need an additional set of rules for how to interoperate with every other intra-domain multicast routing protocol, which greatly simplifies things from an operational point of view.

Deciding where to put the root for any shared tree is a hard problem. BGMP places the root in the domain which has been allocated the multicast address. Hence if the session initiator obtains the address from its local multicast address allocation server, then the tree will be rooted in the session initiator's domain. For many uses of multicast, such as TV-style broadcasts, this is optimal. For other uses of multicast, with many senders, it may be less than optimal but it is still a reasonable default. Without knowing the receivership in advance, it is difficult to do better than this.

3.6 MULTICAST SCOPING

When applications operate in the global Mbone, it is clear that not all groups should have global scope. This is especially the case for performance reasons with flood-and-prune multicast routing protocols, but it also the case with other routing protocols for application security reasons and because multicast addresses are a scarce resource. Being able to constrain the scope of a session allows the same multicast address to be in use at more than one place so long as the scope of the sessions does not overlap.

Multicast scoping can currently be performed in two ways which are known as TTL scoping and administrative scoping. Currently, TTL scoping is most widely used, with only a few sites making use of administrative scoping.

3.6.1 TTL scoping

When an IP packet is sent, an IP header field called time to live (TTL) is set to a value between zero and 255. Every time a router forwards the packet, it decrements the TTL field in the packet header, and if the value reaches zero, the packet is dropped. The IP specification also states that TTL should be decremented if a packet is queued for more than a certain amount of time, but this is rarely implemented these days. With unicast, TTL is normally set to a fixed value by the sending host (64 and 255 are commonly used) and is intended to prevent packets looping for ever, and also forms a part of the formal proof that the TCP close semantics are safe.

With IP multicast, TTL can be used to constrain how far a multicast packet can travel across the Mbone by carefully choosing the value put into packets as they are sent. However, as the relationship between hop-count and suitable scope regions is poor at best, the basic TTL mechanism is supplemented by configured thresholds on multicast tunnels and multicast-capable links. Where such a threshold is configured, the router will decrement the TTL, as with unicast packets, but then will drop the packet if the TTL is less than the configured threshold. When these thresholds are chosen consistently at all of the borders to a region, they allow a host within that region to send traffic with a TTL less than the threshold, and to know that the traffic will not escape that region.

An example of this is the multicast tunnels and links to and from Europe, which are all configured with a TTL threshold of 64. Any site within Europe that wishes to send traffic that does not escape Europe can send with a TTL of less than 64 and be sure that its traffic does not escape.

However, there are also likely to be thresholds configured within a particular scope zone: for example, most European countries use a threshold of 48 on international links within Europe, and as TTL is still decremented each time the packet is forwarded, it is good practice to send European traffic with a TTL of 63, which allows the packet to travel 15 hops before it fails to cross a European international link.

3.6.2   Administrative scoping

There are circumstances where it is difficult to consistently choose TTL thresholds to perform the desired scoping. In particular it is impossible to configure overlapping scope regions as shown in Figure 3.5, and there are a number of other problems with TTL scoping. Hence administrative scoping has recently been added to the multicast forwarding code in both mrouted (Deering, 1988b) and most other router implementations. Administrative scoping allows the configuration of a boundary by specifying a range of multicast addresses that will not be forwarded across that boundary in either direction.

3.6.3   Scoping deployment

Administrative scoping is much more flexible than TTL scoping but suffers from a number of disadvantages. In particular, it is not possible to tell from the address of a packet where it will go unless all the scope zones that the sender is within

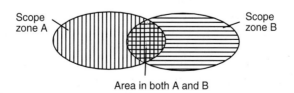

Scope zone A   Scope zone B

Area in both A and B

Figure 3.5   Overlapping scope zones possible with administrative scoping.

are known. Also, as administrative boundaries are bidirectional, one scope zone nested within or overlapping another must have totally separate address ranges. This makes their allocation difficult from an administrative point of view, as the ranges ought to be allocated on a top-down basis (largest zone first) in a network where there is no appropriate top-level allocation authority. Finally, it is easy to misconfigure a boundary by omitting or incorrectly configuring one of the routers – with TTL scoping it is likely that in many cases a more distant threshold will perform a similar task lessening the consequences, but with administrative scoping there is less likelihood that this is the case.

For these reasons, administrative scoping has been viewed by many network administrators as a speciality solution to difficult configuration problems rather than as a replacement for TTL scoping, and the Mbone still very much relies on TTL scoping.

3.7 RELIABLE MULTICAST TRANSPORT

Reliable multicast is sometimes regarded as something of an oxymoron. When people talk about 'reliable multicast' they usually mean a single protocol at a single 'layer' of a protocol stack, typically the transport layer, that can act as any layered protocol can: to provide common functionality for applications (higher layers) that need it. What is wrong with that? Possibly three things (or more): fate sharing, performance and semantics.

3.7.1 Fate sharing

Fate sharing in unicast applications means that so long as there is a path that IP can find between two applications, then TCP can hang on to the connection as long as they like. However, if either party fails, the connection certainly fails.

Fate sharing between multicast end points is a more subtle idea. Should 'reliability' extend to supporting the connection for k recipients failing? Clearly this will be application-specific (just as timing out on not getting liveliness out of a unicast connection is for TCP – we must permit per recipient timeouts/failures).

3.7.2 Performance

When A talks to B, the performance is limited by one path. Whatever can be done to improve the throughput (or delay bound) is done by IP (for example, load-sharing the traffic over multiple paths). When A talks to B,C,D,E,F, should the throughput or delay be that sustainable by the slowest or average?

3.7.3 Semantics

As well as performance and failure modes, n-way reliable protocols can have different service models. We could support reliable $1 - n$, reliable $n - 1$ and reliable $n - m$.

Table 3.2 Reliable multicast semantics.

	Recovery	Sequency	Dalliance
Network	Not in our Internet	Not in our Internet	intserv
Transport	One-to-many	y	Adaptive
Application	Many-to-many	Operation semantics	Adaptive

Applications such as software distribution are cited as classic $1 - n$ requirements. Telemetry is given as a $n - 1$ reliable protocol. Shared whiteboards are cited as examples of $n - m$.

Now the interesting thing is to look at the reliability functions needed in these. Both $1 - n$ and $n - 1$ are in effect *simplex* bulk transfer applications. In other words, the service is one where reliability can be dealt with by 'rounding up' the missing bits at the end of the transfer. Since this need not be especially timely, there is no need for this to be other than end-to-end, and application-based.[5]

On the other hand $n - m$ processes such as whiteboards need timely recovery from outages. The implication is that the 'service' is best done somewhat like the effect of having $\frac{1}{2}n(n - 1)$ TCP connections. If used in the WAN, the recovery may best be distributed, since requests for recovery will implode down the very links that are congested or error prone and caused the need for recovery.

There are different schemes for creating distributed recovery. If the application semantics are that operations (ALF packetsworths . . .) are sequenced in a way that the application can index them, then any member of a multicast session can efficiently help any other member to recover (examples of this include Handley's network text tool (Handley, 1995)). On the other hand, packet-based recovery can be done from data within the queues between network/transport and application, if they are kept at all members in much the same way as a sender in a unicast connection keeps a copy of all unacknowledged data. The problem with this is that *because* it is multicast, we do not have a positive acknowledgement system. Because of that, there is no way to inform *all* end points when they can safely discard the data in the 'retransmit' queue. Only the application really knows this.

This is not to say that there is not an obvious toolkit for reliable multicast support – it would certainly be good to have RTP-style media timestamps (determined by the application but filled in by the system). It would be good to have easy access to a timestamped-based receive queue so applications could use this to do all the above. It might be neat to have virtual token ring, expanding ring search, token tree and other toolkits to support retransmit 'helper' selection.

So, drawing a table of where we might put functions to provide reliability (retransmit), sequencing and performance (adaptive play-out, say, versus end-to-end, versus hop-by-hop delay constraint), we can see the picture set out in Table 3.2. We will revisit this in Chapter 5.

3.8 CALLING DOWN TRAFFIC ON A SITE

Multicast is a multiplier. It gives leverage to senders, but without their knowledge. Multicast (and its application-level cousin, the CU–SeeMe reflector)[6] can 'attract' more traffic to a site than it can cope with on its Internet access link. A user can do this by inadvertently joining a group for which there is a high-bandwidth sender, and then 'going for a cup of tea'. This problem will be averted through access control, or through mechanisms such as charging which may result from the deployment of real time traffic support as described in Chapter 2.

3.9 SUMMARY

In this chapter we have looked at multi-destination packet delivery services, for circuit, and packet, and packet over circuit-based networks. We have looked at the various routing systems that are used to devise delivery trees over which multimedia data can be sent for the purposes of group communication.

The main lessons are that:

1   If you have group communication, network support through multicast will in general reduce traffic significantly.

2   The IP multicast model is very powerful, and is much more convenient than the point–multipoint VC services in other networks. It is, however, hard to implement the former over the latter efficiently.

3   Large-scale use of multicast may require some form of aggregation of IP-level multicast tree indices (state in Mbone routers). We do not know how to do this at all.

4   Policy and QoS support in multicast routing are not yet available technologies.

In the next chapter, we look at how to reduce the amount of data that is sent so that they do not swamp our network.

Notes

1 In the next version of IP, IP version 6, the address space is 16 bytes (or octets) in size, and the address space for multicast has been allocated as starting with eight '1' bits. Interworking between IPv4 and IPv6 multicast address sessions is relatively straightforward compared with unicast addresses, since they are already dynamic entities, so that there are already ways for hosts and routers to interact to establish receiver membership locations.

2 There may be some interaction with firewalls here, and this is discussed in Chapter 10.

3 Even when this is not really the case, such as with a hub-switched ethernet, it maintains the illusion of such.

4 Strictly speaking it is a *reverse* shortest path tree – typically the routers do not have enough information to build a true *forward* shortest path tree.

5 Yes, telemetry could be real timeish, but we are trying to illustrate major differences clearly for now.

6 CU–SeeMe is a popular Mac and PC-based Internet video conferencing package that currently does not directly use IP multicast.

CHAPTER FOUR

Coding and Compression

4.1 INTRODUCTION

In this chapter we look at multimedia content from the informational point of view. A key problem with multimedia is the sheer quantities of data that result from naive digitisation of audio, image or video sources. Other problems involve quality, representation of metadata such as timing and relationships between different media and so on.

There are a variety of compression techniques commonly used in the Internet and other systems to alleviate the storage, processing and transmission (and reception) costs for such data.

We start by building a framework for understanding the systems requirements and components in dealing with multimedia flows – to start with, we look at the nature of the information and its use, leading to discussion of general principles of loss-free and lossy compression. We look at simple lossless schemes such as run length encoding and systems based on the statistics of frequency of occurrences of codewords such as Huffman codes. We look at substitutional or dictionary-based schemes such as the Lempel–Ziv family of algorithms. Then we look at transform-based schemes and the way in which controlled loss of quality can be achieved using these.

We contrast data, audio, still image and moving image, covering the ideas of redundancy in images, sound and motion, We look at the cycles within the data that lead to the signal processing models used by engineers, including those in computer-generated and naturally occurring data, leading to model-based coding and compression, including future schemes such as wavelet, vector quantisation, fractal and hierarchical use of lossy schemes.

We look at audio compression. Audiophiles often use the term 'compression' in another way – to refer to the reduction in dynamic range of an audio signal: for example, some noise reduction systems use compression and expansion devices so that the noise with respect to signal at low power levels (quiet bits) of a piece of music are less noticeable. This is quite different from compression of the amount of data needed to represent a signal at all. We look at the effect of the network on the design of coding and compression schemes – loss of synchronisation, data, reordering and duplication all lead to the need for recovery ponts in the datastream and place limits on the timeframes that compression (and decompression) can operate over at sender and receiver ends for interactive applications.

We then discuss the main approaches and standards for multiplexing of audio and video between sender and recipient. Finally we cover the performance of some example systems.

4.2 ROADMAP

Figure 4.1 illustrates the components of a system to capture, code, compress, transmit, decompress, decode and display multimedia data. The rest of this chapter describes each of the components in this diagram, moving approximately from left to right across the picture. We cover some example cases of coding and compression schemes along the way.

4.3 SYSTEM COMPONENTS

We mentioned in Chapter 1 that multimedia data originate in some analogue form. However, all data are eventually turned into some (typically repetitive) digital code, and the statistics of the digital code are of great interest when we want to think about compressing a set of such data. The statistics are important at several levels of granularity.

Even text input from a given language has several levels of interest, such as characters, words and grammatical structure. In a similar way, speech or music signals have repetitive structure which shows correlation at several levels of detail. Images may have some structure, although in natural images this tends to be very subtle (fractal). Moving images clearly have at least two timescales of interest, owing partly to the nature of the input and display devices (and the human eye), the scanline and the frame.

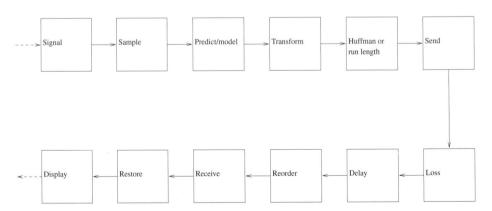

Figure 4.1 Roadmap of Chapter 4.

Thus coding and compression go hand in hand. We choose some levels of granularities at which to code an input signal or message – this determines the initial input buffer size over which we run our code. It is this which, for real time applications, determines the codec delays. This also determines the number of quanta or different values for each 'letter of the alphabet' in the input buffer.

The selection of these two (or more) timescales may be determined long in advance for some data types. For example, for text in a given language and alphabet there are large sets of samples that are amenable to analysis, so we can find nearly optimal digital representations of the data in terms of storage. However, there may be other factors that affect our design of a code. For example, a variable length code for the English alphabet could be devised that used fewer bits for the average block of text than a fixed-length codeword such as 7 bit ASCII. On the other hand, it may be more efficient in computing terms to trade off a small overhead (even as much as 50%) in storage for speed of processing and to choose a fixed-length code – which is what has been done in practice for text.

For audio, while a speech input signal is composed of a stream of phonemes, words and sentences, it is relatively hard to build an intermediate representation of this, so typically we start with a set of fixed-length samples of short timespans of the signal and work from there.

Similarly with a still (or single image from a moving) image, we choose to sample the input scene at typically fixed horizontal and vertical intervals giving a 2D image of a given resolution. We make a design decision when we choose the number of levels (quantisation) of the samples (the familiar 8 bit versus 24 bit colour display is such a decision – 1 or 3 bytes of storage per pixel of the image).

4.4 NATURE OF THE SIGNAL

We must distinguish between raw data and information, but such a distinction is quite a subtle business. 'Information' refers to that part of a signal that constitutes *useful* items of knowledge for some user.

Thus, depending on the user, some part of a signal may be regarded as less useful. This means that there may be *redundancy* in the data. In some cases, the redundancy is unambiguous (for example in the easy case of simple repetition) where data are coded in some grossly inefficient manner.

Depending on the source, and on the form of the signal, we may know something about the statistics of the contents in advance, or we may have to do some online analysis if we are to remove redundancy. The performance of online analysis will depend on the range and accuracy over which the signal repeats itself – in other words, the block size.

How much data we can store in a compression algorithm that does online analysis will be affected by how much delay we are allowed to incur (over and above the delay 'budget' for transmission and reception), and the CPU load incurred processing larger chunks of the signal.

Finally, redundancy is in the eye of the beholder: we are rarely obliged to keep the original signal with 100% integrity since human frailty would mean that even without an Internet path between light or sound source and a person, it is likely that the receiver would miss some parts of a signal in any case. This latter point is extremely *task dependent*.

4.4.1 Analogue-to-digital conversion: sampling

An input signal is converted from some continuously varying physical value (for example, pressure in air, or frequency or wavelength of light), by some electromechanical device into a continuously varying electrical signal. This signal has a range of amplitude, and a range of frequencies that can present. This continuously varying electrical signal can then be converted to a *sequence* of digital values, called samples, by some analogue-to-digital conversion circuit. Figure 4.2 illustrates this process.

There are two factors which determine the accuracy with which the digital sequence of values captures the original continuous signal: the maximum rate at which we sample and the number of bits used in each sample. This latter value is known as the quantisation level and is illustrated in Figure 4.3.

The raw (uncompressed) digital data rate associated with a signal, then, is simply the sample rate times the number of bits per sample. To capture all possible frequencies in the original signal, Nyquist's theorem shows that the digital rate must be twice the highest frequency component in the continuous signal. However, it is often not necessary to capture all frequencies in the original signal – for example, the voice is comprehensible with a much smaller range of frequencies than we can actually hear. When the sample rate is much lower than the highest frequency in the continuous signal, a band-pass filter which allows only frequencies in the range actually needed, is usally put before the sampling circuit. This avoids possible ambiguous samples ('aliases').

4.4.2 Constructing a signal out of components

One view of the input signal illustrated in Figure 4.2 is that it is made up of a number of contributing signals – mathematically, we can consider any reasonable set of orthogonal signals as components, but the easiest ones to use are sine functions.

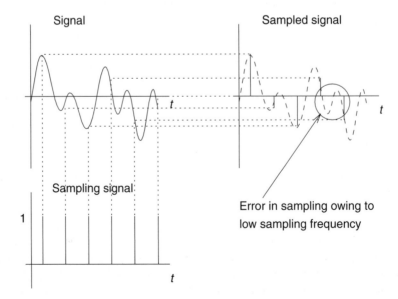

Figure 4.2   Sampling a continuous signal.

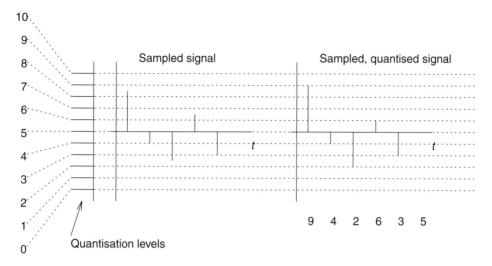

Figure 4.3 Quantisation of samples.

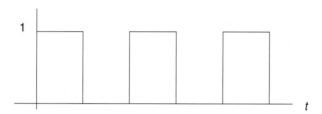

Figure 4.4 Square wave.

One extreme case often used to illustrate this is the square wave signal. In Figure 4.4, we show a square wave. If this were made out of a number of sine waves with different frequencies, the contribution of each frequency would be as illustrated in Figure 4.5.

The way then that we build up the square wave *constructively* out of a set of sine waves of different frequencies can be seen in the progression of Figures 4.6–4.9.

It may seem odd that a simple 'on–off' signal takes a lot of contributions, but then the point is that this method of representing the continuous signal is general, and can represent *any* input signal.

Input data can be transformed in a number of ways to make it easier to apply certain compression techniques. The most common transform in current techniques is the discrete cosine transform (DCT). This is a variant of the discrete Fourier transform, which is, in turn, the digital (discrete) version of the continuous Fourier transform.

As described earlier, any signal (whether a video or audio signal) can be considered a periodic wave. If we think of a sequence of sounds, these sounds are a modulation of an audio wave; similarly, the scan over an image or scene carried out by a camera conveys a wave which has periodic features in time (in the timeframe of the scene, as well as over multiple video frames in the moving picture). It is possible to convert from the original signal as a function of time, to the *Fourier series*,

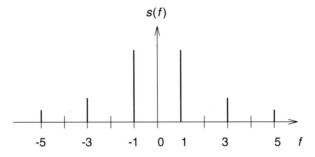

Figure 4.5 Spectrum of a square wave.

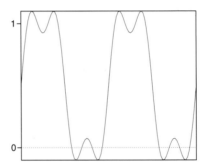

Figure 4.6 Square from one sine wave.

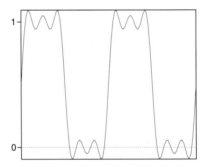

Figure 4.7 Square from two sine waves.

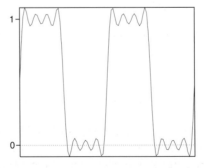

Figure 4.8 Square from three sine waves.

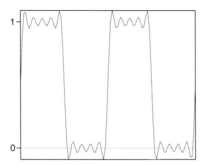

Figure 4.9   Square from four sine waves.

which is the sum of a set of terms, each being a particular *frequency* (or wavelength). You can think of these terms or coefficients as being the *contribution* of a set of base pure 'sine wave' frequencies (also known as the spectral density), that together make up the actual signal:

$$g(\omega) = K_1 \int_{-\infty}^{+\infty} f(t) \exp(-j\omega t)\, d\omega \quad \text{where } K_1 = 1$$

and

$$f(t) = K_2 \int_{-\infty}^{+\infty} g(\omega) \exp(-j\omega t)\, dt \quad \text{where } K_1 = \pi/2$$

You can imagine these sweeping through a typical audio signal as shown in Figure 4.10 below, and 'pulling out' a spectrum (see Figure 4.11) or set of coefficients that represents the contribution of each frequency to that part of the signal strength.

4.5 LOSSLESS DATA COMPRESSION

There is a huge range of data compression techniques – these are of some interest to the multimedia systems designer, but there are many good books on them already. Suffice it to say that three common techniques used are run length encoding (removing repetitions of values and replacing them with a counter and single value), Huffman coding, and dictionary techniques such as the Lempel–Ziv family of substitutional compression algorithms.

4.5.1 Run length compression

Run length coding is fairly simple to implement and, as with all lossless schemes, its performance depends heavily on the input data statistics. Computer-generated binary files are often very amenable to this type of compression, for example with a codeword size of 1 bit, or a byte or a word often leading to elimination of many or all 1s or all 0s in successive fields. The nice feature of this scheme is that it incurs very little delay at sender or receiver. Note that this and other schemes do incur a variable output bit/symbol rate.

4.5.2 Huffman compression

Huffman coding is the most widespread way of replacing a set of values of fixed-size code words with an optimal set of different sized code words based on the statistics of the input data. The way a Huffman code is constructed involves constructing a frequency distribution of the symbols. This is then used to decide the new compressed representation for each symbol. The easiest way to do this is to consider the case for compressing alphabetic text, with symbols drawn from characters in an alphabet with 256 letters. If these are all equally likely to occur, then it is hard to compress the data. However, if there is a severe skew in the frequency distribution in typical data (texts in this alphabet) then we can use more bits to represent the most frequently occurring characters or code word values, and more bits for the less commonly occurring ones, with some compression gain.

So, how to build this new coding scheme for the alphabet? The classic scheme is to construct a tree from the frequency distribution, taking pairs of characters/code word values at a time from the least frequently occurring values in the frequency chart, and adding a bit position to the string representation for them, with value 1 for one, 0 for the other, then moving to the next least commonly occurring; eventually, the most commonly occurring two values take two bits, one to say which is which, and one to say that it is one of these two values, or that it is one of the 254 other values. And so on.

This scheme is optimal in only one case, which is when the probability of occurrences of code word values is distributed as a set of inverse powers of $\frac{1}{2}$, i.e. $\frac{1}{2}$, $\frac{1}{4}$, $\frac{1}{8}$, $\frac{1}{16}$ etc. Otherwise the scheme is less and less good.

A generalisation of Huffman coding that avoids this latter problem is arithmetic coding, which uses binary fraction representations in building the coding tree. In practice, this can be computationally expensive.

If one is transmitting Huffman (or arithmetic) compressed data, one must also share the same codebook as sender and receiver: the list of codes and their compressed representation must be the same at both ends. This can be done on a case by case basis, but is usually based in long-term statistics of the data (for example, the frequency of occurrence of the letter 'ee' in the written English language is a well known example of this sort of statistic).

4.5.3 Dictionary approaches to compression

A completely different approach is to look at the data *as they arrive* and form a dictionary on the fly. As the dictionary is formed, it can be used to look up new input, dynamically; and if the new input existed earlier in the stream, the dictionary position can be transmitted instead of the new input codes. These schemes are known as 'substitutional' compression algorithms, and there are two patented families of schemes invented by Ziv and Lempel in the 1970s that cover a broad class of the ideas here.

In essence, the dictionary is constructed as a data structure that holds strings of symbols that are found in the input data, together with short bitstring entry numbers. Whenever an entry is not found, it is added to the dictionary in a new position, and the new position and string sent. This means that the dictionary is constructed dynamically at the receiver, hence there is no need to carry out statistics or share a table separately.

A second family of Lempel–Ziv dictionary-based compression schemes is based on the idea of a sliding window over the input text. The compression algorithm consists of searching for substrings ahead in the text, in the current window. This approach constrains the size of the dictionary, which could otherwise grow in an unbounded way.

4.5.4   Continuous data: sample rates and quantisation

In the next two sections we look at audio and then video coding and compression. Here, one is concerned with the initial fidelity of the signal which is tied up with the sampling mechanism – the number of samples per second, and the number of bits per sample (quantisation levels) – in other words, one has to choose an accuracy right at the beginning, and this represents an opportunity for compression even before we have got to the digital domain. After this, there are a number of other techniques, including the lossless ones just described, which are applicable.

4.6   AUDIO

Devices that encode and decode audio and video as well as compress and decompress are called codecs, or CODer/DECoders. Sometimes, these terms are used for audio, but mainly they are for video devices.

Voice coding techniques take advantage of features of the voice signal. In the time domain, we can see from Figures 4.10 and 4.11 that there is much similarity between adjacent speech samples – this means that a system that sends only differences between sample values will achieve some compression. We can see that there are a lot more values in samples with low intensity, than with high. This means that we could use more bits to represent the low values than the high ones. This could be done in a fixed way and A-law and μ-law encodings do just this by choosing a logarithmic encoding. Or we could adapt to the signal; APCM does this. These

Figure 4.10   The author saying 'smith'.

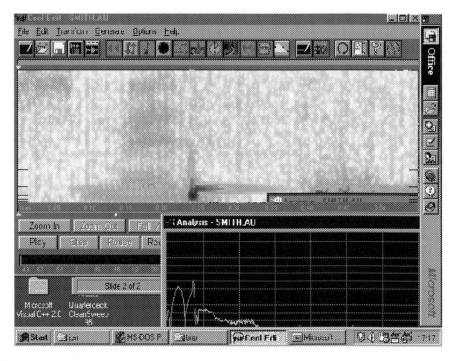

Figure 4.11 Typical voice spectrum.

techniques can be combined, and the ADPCM (adaptive differential pulse code modulation) achieves 50% savings over basic PCM with no apparent loss of quality, and relatively cheap implementation.

More ingenious compression relies on two things: an appreciation of the actual *model* of speech and a model of the listener. Such techniques usually involve recognising the actual speech production and synthesising a set of filters which are transmitted to the receiver and used to reconstruct sound by applying them to raw 'sound' from a single frequency source and a white noise generator – examples of codecs that are based on this idea are linear predictive coding (LPC) and CELP (code excited linear predictor). Including a model of how humans perceive sound ('psycho acoustics') leads to more expensive, but highly effective, compression such as is used in MPEG audio codecs.

4.6.1   Audio input and output

Audio signals to and from the real (analogue) world have a less immediately obvious mapping to the digital world. Audio signals vary depending on the application. Human speech has a well understood spectrum and set of characteristics, whereas musical input is much more varied, and the human ear and perception and cognition systems behave rather differently in each case. For example, when a speech signal degrades badly, humans make use of comprehension to interpolate. This may be harder or easier to do with music depending on levels of expertise and familiarity with the style or idiom.

Basically, for speech, the analogue signal from a microphone is passed through several stages. Firstly, a band-pass filter is applied, eliminating frequencies in the signal that we are not interested in (for example, for telephone quality speech, above 3.6 kHz).[1] Then the signal is sampled, converting the analogue signal into a sequence of values, each of which represents the amplitude of the analogue signal over a small, discrete time interval. This is then quantised, or mapped into one of a set of fixed values – for example, for telephone quality speech, one of 2^8, or 256 possible values. These values are then coded (represented in some standard form) for transmission or storage. The process at the receiver is simply the reverse.

There are a number of features of the speech signal that enable it to be compressed, and we look at some of these in the next section.

4.6.2 Audio output

Audio output is generally made by some physical process interacting with the air (in space, of course, there is no sound). The air conveys the sound to your ear (or to a microphone or other input device).

To produce output from a computer, we need to take a digital signal, convert it to analogue, and use that to drive a loudspeaker. Many microcomputers now feature fairly standard hi-fi amplifiers and stereo speaker systems.

Sounds can be created purely digitally (from synthesisers) or partly digitally (from samples) or naturally from the surrounding world (wind in the trees, rain on the roof), or from analogue musical instruments or from human speech.

Audio output by people

People generate sounds by breathing air through the vocal chords, which resonate, and then controlling the production of sound by varying the shape of their vocal tract, mouth, tongue and so on. For the purposes of communication, speech is generally more useful than music, and happens to use a constrained part of the frequency and power range that humans are capable of generating – and a much more constrained part of the range than they are capable of hearing. Typically, we can generate sounds over a dynamic range of 40 decibels. For recognisable speech, the vast majority of important sounds are in the frequency range 60–8000 Hz (compared with music which is typically audible up to nearly 20 kHz).

Speech is made up of sound units called *phonemes* (the smallest unit of distinguishable sound). These are specific to a language, so for example, we find that English and Japanese each have phonemes that the other language does not (for example, 'l' and 'r' – hence the difficulty in learning to pronounce a distant language). We illustrate some of the international phonetic alphabet for British English with example words in Table 4.1.

Phonemes are vowels or consonants, where vowels are either pure or diphthongs (made of two sounds), and consonants may be semi-vowel, fricative (use teeth to make), plosive (use lips) or nasal (use nose). Other factors influencing the sound we make are stress (change of strength), rhythm and pace, and intonation (pitch).

Table 4.1 International phonetic alphabet for British English.

Vowels	Diphthongs	Semi-vowels	Nasals	Fricatives	Affricatives	Plosives
/i/ heed	/gi/ buy	/w/ was	/m/ am	/s/ sail	/dg/ jaw	/b/ bat
/I/ hid	/ai/ by	/r/ ran	/n/ an	/S/ ship	/tj/ chore	/d/ disc
/e/ head	/au/ bow	/l/ lot	/n/ sang			
/ae/ had	/ao/ bough	/j/ yacht				

4.6.3 Audio input by people

We hear mainly through our ears which respond over a frequency range of around 20 khz. Stereo is important to many human actions and even the phase difference between signals arriving from the same source at each ear (as well as simple timing, since sound moves so slowly compared with light) gives us good directional hearing, although mainly at high frequencies. As people get older, their high frequency accuracy decreases quite markedly, although this does not usually affect speech recognition until old age.

4.6.4 Summary of audio and video input and output

Data (files etc.) are typically compressed using simple schemes such as run length encoding, or statistically based Huffman codes or dictionary-based substitutional schemes such as the Lempel–Ziv algorithms. Audio and video are loss tolerant, so can use cleverer compression that discards some information. Compression of 400 times is possible on video – useful given the base uncompressed data rate of a 25 frames per second CCIR 601 image is 140 Mbps.[2] There are many standards for this now, including schemes based on PCM, such as ADPCM, or on models such as LPC, and MPEG audio. Note that lossy compression of audio and video is not acceptable to some classes of user (for example, radiologist, or air traffic controller).

It is sometimes said that 'the eye integrates while the ear differentiates'. What is meant by this is that the eye responds to stronger signals or higher frequencies with cumulative reaction, while the ear responds less and less (i.e. to double the pitch, you have to double the frequency, so we hear a logarithmic scale as linear, and to double the loudness, you have to increase the power exponentially too).

A video codec can be anything from the simplest A2D device, through to something that does picture preprocessing, and even has network adapters built into it (i.e. a videophone). A codec usually does most of its work in hardware, but there is no reason not to implement everything (except the A2D capture) in software on a reasonably fast processor.

The most expensive and complex component of a codec is the compression/decompression part. There are a number of international standards, as well as any number of proprietary compression techniques for video.

4.6.5   The ITU (was CCITT) audio family

The fundamental standard upon which all videoconferencing applications are based is G.711, which defines pulse code modulation (PCM). In PCM, a sample representing the instantaneous amplitude of the input waveform is taken regularly, the recommended rate being 8000 samples per second (50 ppm). At this sampling rate, frequencies up to 3400–4000 Hz are encodable. Empirically, this has been demonstrated to be adequate for voice communication, and, indeed, seems to provide marginally acceptable music quality. The samples taken are assigned one of 212 values, the range being necessary in order to minimise signal-to-noise ratio (SNR) at low volumes. These samples are then stored in 8 bits using a logarithmic encoding according to either of two laws (A-law and μ-law). In telecommunications, A-law encoding tends to be more widely used in Europe, whilst μ-law predominates in the United States. However, since most workstations originate outside Europe, the sound chips within them tend to obey μ-law. In either case, the reason that a logarithmic compression technique is preferred to a linear one is that it more readily represents the way humans perceive audio. We are more sensitive to small changes at low volume than the same changes at high volume; consequently, lower volumes are represented with greater accuracy than high volumes.

ADPCM

Adaptive differential pulse code modulation, ADPCM (G.721) allows for the compression of PCM-encoded input whose power varies with time. Feedback of a reconstructed version of the input signal is subtracted from the actual input signal, which is then quantised to give a 4 bit output value. This compression gives a 32 kbps output rate. This standard was recently extended in G.726 , which replaces both G.721 and G.723 , to allow conversion between 64 kbps PCM and 40, 32, 24, or 16 kbps channels. G.727 is an extension of G.726 and issued for embedded ADPCM on 40, 32, 24, or 16 kbps channels, with the specific intention of being used in packetised speech systems utilising the packetised voice protocol (PVP) defined in G.764.

The encoding of higher quality speech (50 Hz–7 kHz) is covered in G.722 and G.725, and is achieved by utilising sub-band ADPCM coding on two frequency sub-bands; the output rate is 64 kbps.

LPC

Linear predictive coding (LPC) is used to compress audio at 16 kbps and below. In this method the encoder fits speech to a simple, analytic model of the vocal tract. Only the parameters describing the best-fit model are transmitted to the decoder. An LPC decoder uses those parameters to generate synthetic speech that is usually very similar to the original. The result is intelligible but robotic-sounding speech.

CELP

Code excited linear predictor (CELP) is quite similar to LPC. The CELP encoder does the same LPC modelling but then computes the errors between the original speech and the synthetic model and transmits both model parameters and a very compressed representation of the errors. The compressed representation is an index into an excitation vector (which can be thought of as a 'code book' shared between encoders and decoders). The result of CELP is a much higher quality speech at low data rate.

MPEG audio

High-quality audio compression is supported by MPEG. MPEG I defines sample rates of 48 kHz, 44.1 kHz and 32 kHz. MPEG II adds three other frequencies: 16 kHz, 22.05 kHz and 24 kHz. MPEG I allows for two audio channels where as MPEG II allows five audio channels plus an additional low-frequency enhancement channel.

MPEG defines three compression levels: audio layers I, II and III. Layer I is the simplest, a sub-band coder with a psycho-acoustic model. Layer II adds more advanced bit allocation techniques and greater accuracy. Layer III adds a hybrid filterbank and non-uniform quantisation. Layers I, II and III give increasing quality/compression ratios with increasing complexity and demands on processing power.

4.7 STILL IMAGE

A picture is worth a thousand words. But an image, uncompressed, is worth many megabytes.

4.7.1 How big is a single frame of video?

First we consider the spatial size of analogue video when compared with the common formats for digital video standards. A PAL television displays video as 625 lines and an NTSC television displays 525 lines. Current televisions have an aspect ratio of 4:3, giving PAL a spatial resolution of 833×625, and NTSC a resolution of 700×525, not all of which is visible. Most common formats for digital video are related to the visible area for each of the television standards. The size of video when using the international standard H.261, found in CCITT (1990), is 352×288 for the common interchange format (CIF), 176×144 for the QCIF (quarter CIF) and 704×576 for the SCIF (super CIF), where a CIF image is one-quarter the size of the visible area of a PAL image. For NTSC-derived formats 640×480, 320×240, and 160×120 are common. Figure 4.12 shows the spatial size of these common resolutions with respect to a PAL TV image.

It can be seen from Figure 4.12 that digital images are all smaller than current television sizes. Moreover, television images are significantly smaller than current workstation screen sizes which are commonly of the order 1200×1000 pixels. Digital video utilises even less of a workstation screen. Owing to this significant size difference, some observers have commented that digital video often looks like 'moving postage stamps' on modern workstations.

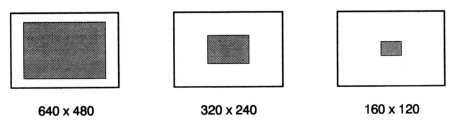

| 640 x 480 | 320 x 240 | 160 x 120 |

Figure 4.12   The spatial size of digital video compared with a PAL TV image.

For digital video, as with analogue video, a new frame is required every $\frac{1}{25}$ second for PAL and every $\frac{1}{30}$ second for NTSC. If we assume that there are 24 bits per pixel in the digital video and 30 frames per second, the amount of disk space required for such a stream of full-motion video is shown in Table 4.2. The table is presented for the amount of time the digital video is shown and for a given spatial size in pixels.

We can see that 1 hour of video with a resolution of 640 × 480 would consume 97 GB of disk space, which is significantly larger than most storage devices. An equivalent amount of analogue video (i.e. a 1 hour video), which has a higher resolution and also contains audio, would only take between one-half and one-quarter of a 120 minute or a 240 minute video cassette, respectively. However, although there are devices that can store this amount of data, there are currently no digital storage devices which could store 97 GB on half a device which is the size of a video cassette.

In order to reduce the amount of data used for digital video, it is common to use compression techniques, such as the international standards H.261, MPEG (Hoffman *et al.*, 1994), or to use proprietary techniques such as nv encoding (Frederick, 1994) or CellB (Sun Microsystems Computer Corp., 1993). Rowe has also estimated the amount of space used when compression techniques are used (Rowe and Smith, 1992). Table 4.3 shows the space needed when compressing video of size 640 × 480 pixels, and Table 4.4 shows the space used when compressing video of size 320 × 240 pixels. Both tables present data for a given scale factor of

Table 4.2   The amount of data for full-motion digital video.

Time:Size	640 × 480	320 × 240	160 × 120
1 second	27 Mb	6.75 Mb	1.68 Mb
1 minute	1.6 Gb	400 Mb	100 Mb
1 hour	97 Gb	24 Gb	6 Gb
1000 hours	97 Tb	24 Tb	6 Tb

Source: Rowe and Smith, 1992

Table 4.3   The amount of data for compressed video of size 640 × 480.

Time v. scale	None	3:1	25:1 (JPEG)	100:1 (MPEG)
1 second	27 MB	9 MB	1.1 MB	270 kB
1 minute	1.6 GB	540 MB	65 MB	16 MB
1 hour	97 GB	32 GB	3.9 GB	970 MB

Table 4.4 The amount of data for compressed video of size 320 × 240.

Time v. scale	None	3:1	25:1 (JPEG)	100:1 (MPEG)
1 second	6.75 MB	2.25 MB	270 kB	68 kB
1 minute	400 MB	133 MB	16 MB	4 MB
1 hour	24 GB	8 GB	1 GB	240 MB

compression and for the time the video is shown. The 97 GB used for the 1 hour of 640 × 480 video can be reduced to approximately 1 GB when compression is done at a scale factor of 100:1.

Although the tables show compression factors for MPEG, the H.261 standard uses a discrete cosine transform encoding function which is similar to that used in MPEG, therefore we can expect the compression ratios to be of a similar order of magnitude. In reality, when encoding real video the compression factor is not constant but variable because the amount of data produced by the encoder is a function of motion. However, these figures do give a reasonable estimation of what can be achieved.

It is significant that with digital video it is possible to dramatically reduce the amount of data generated even further by reducing the perceived frame rate of the video from 30 frames per second (fps) down to 15 or even 2 fps. This can be achieved by explicitly limiting the number of frames or through a bandwidth limitation mechanism. In many multicast conferences the bandwidth used is between 15 and 64 kbps. Although the reduced frame rate video loses the quality of full-motion video, it is perfectly adequate for many situations, particularly in multimedia conferencing.

There are a large number of still image formats and compression schemes in use in the network today. Common schemes include:

- *TIFF and GIF*: These both use compression schemes based on the Lempel–Ziv type of algorithm described earlier.

- *JPEG*: This is from the Joint Photographic Experts Group in the International Organisation for Standardisation (ISO).

The first two of these still image schemes are discussed elsewhere in great detail. JPEG is interesting as it is the same baseline technology as used partly in several popular moving image compression schemes. The JPEG standard's goal has been to develop a method for continuous-tone image compression for both colour and greyscale images. The standard defines four modes:

- *Sequential*: In this mode each image is encoded in a single left-to-right, top-to-bottom scan. This mode is the simplest, and is the one most implemented in both hardware and software implementation.

- *Progressive*: In this mode the image is encoded in multiple scans. This is helpful for applications in which transmission time is too long and the viewer prefers to watch the image building in multiple coarse-to-clear passes.

- *Lossless*: The image here is encoded to guarantee exact recovery of every source image sample value. This is important to applications where any small loss of image data is significant. Some medical applications do need that mode.

- *Hierarchical*: Here the image is encoded at multiple resolutions, so that low-resolution versions may be decoded without having to decode the higher-resolution versions. This mode is beneficial when transmission is over packet switched networks. Only the data significant for a certain resolution determined by the application can be transmitted, so more applications can share the same network resources. In real time transmission cases (for example, an image pulled out of an information server and synchronised with a real time video clip), a congested network can start dropping packets containing the highest resolution data, resulting in a degraded quality of the image instead of delay.

JPEG uses the discrete cosine transform to compress spatial redundancy within an image in all of its modes apart from the lossless one where a predictive method is used instead.

As JPEG was designed for the compression of still images, it makes no use of temporal redundancy which is an important element in most video compression schemes. Thus, despite the availability of real time JPEG video compression hardware, its use will be quite limited owing to its poor video quality.

4.8 MOVING IMAGE

4.8.1 Video input and output

Before you can digitise a moving image, you need to know what the analogue form is, in terms of resolution and frame rate. Unfortunately, there are three main standards in use. PAL is used in the UK, while NTSC is used in the United States and in Japan, and SECAM is used mainly in France and Russia. The differences are in number of lines, frame rate, scan order and so forth. PAL is used most widely: it uses 625 lines, and has a line rate of 50 Hz. NTSC and SECAM use 525 lines and a line rate of 59.94 Hz. These all differ in number of lines, frame rate, interlace order and so on. There are also a number of variants of PAL and NTSC (for example, I/PAL is used in the UK and Ireland, while M/NTSC is the ITU designation for the scheme used in the United States and Japan).

Colour

Colour is very complex. Basically, light is from a spectrum (continuum), but we typically manipulate colours by manipulating discrete things like pens, or the coloured dots of phosphor on a CRT which emit light of a given intensity but at a single colour, when hit by an electron of a given energy. There are several ways of mixing discrete colours to get a new colour that has the right appearance to the human eye. The human eye does not perceive a spectrum, but rather all colours as combinations of three so-called primary colours: red (435 nm), green (546 nm) and blue (700 nm).

These primaries can be added to produce secondaries: magenta, cyan and yellow. (The roles of primary and secondary are reversed in pigments, as opposed to in light, since the concern of a dyemaker is with which colour is absorbed rather than which is transmitted). Most multimedia users use colour far too much, however, in natural situations, it is very rich – this is a strange paradox.

Colour input by humans

The human eye can perceive a very wide range of colours compared with the range of greyscales. It actually has different sensors for colour and for monochrome. Colour is detected by cones, cells in the retina that distinguish a range of different signals, while monochrome is dealt with by rods. Rods are actually sensitive to much lower light levels (intensity/power), and are particularly good at handling motion. Cones are specialised to higher light levels (hence colour vision does not work in dim light such as during dawn, dusk and twilight).

Colour input by computers

A colour input device such as a video camera has a similar set of sensors to cones. These respond to different wavelengths with different strengths. In essence, a video camera is a digital device, based around an array of such sensors, and a clock that sweeps across them in the same way that the electron gun in the back of a TV or computer display is scanned back and forth, and up and down, to refresh the light emission from the dots on the screen. So, for a single, still frame, a scan produces an array of reports of intensity, one element for each point in the back of the camera. For a system with three colour sensor types, you get an array of triples, values of intensity of light of each of the sensors. This is then converted into an analogue signal for normal analogue recording. Some devices are emerging where the values can be input directly to a computer rather than converted to analogue, and then have to be converted to digital again by an expensive frame grabber or video card. Given that the range of intensities the human eye can perceive is not huge, they are usually stored digitally in a small number of bits – most usually 8 per colour – hence a 'true' colour display has 24 bits, 8 bits each for R, G and B. RGB is the most commonly used computing colour model. CMY is just [1] − [RGB], and vice versa. [0,0,0] is black, and [255,255,255] is white.

Colour output by computers and other devices

Image or video output is just the reverse of input. Thus an area of memory is set aside for the 'frame buffer'. Data written here will be read by the video controller, and used to control the signal to the display's electron gun for intensity of each of the colours for the corresponding pixel. By changing what is in the frame buffer once per scan time, you get motion/animation. So in order to play back digital video from disk, typically you read it from disk to the frame buffer at the appropriate rate, and you have a digital VCR (presumably with digital video tapes).

'Video RAM' (VRAM) is not usually quite the same as other memory since it is aimed at good row then column scans rather than true RAM access.

VRAM stores n bits of each of RGB. If $n = 8$, it is known as 'true colour'. An n less than 8 can have colour maps, values then are typically indexes to tables. These colour maps lead to flicker or false colour. An $n = 1$ is just plain monochrome.

Towards compressed video

Video compression can take away the requirement for very high data rates and move video transmission and storage into a regime similar to that for audio. In fact, in terms of tolerance for poor quality, it seems that humans are better at adapting to poor visual information than poor audio information. A simple-minded calculation shows the amount of data you might expect, and is shown in Table 4.5.

The liberal estimate yields 75 MBps, or 600 Mbps – this is right on the limit of modern transmission capacity. Even in this age of deregulation and cheaper telecoms, and larger, faster disks, this is profligate. On the other hand, for a scene with a human face in it, as few as 64 pixels square, 10 frames per second might suffice for a meaningful image. The cautious estimate yields 122 kBps, or just under 1 Mbps – this is achievable on modern LANs and high-speed WANs but still is not friendly.

Notice that in the latter example, we did two things to the picture.

1   We used less 'space' for each frame by sending less 'detail'.
2   We sent frames less frequently since little is moving.

This is a clue as to how to go about improving things. Basically, if there is not much information to send, we avoid sending it. Both spatial and temporal domain compression are used in many of the standards.

If a frame contains a lot of image that is the same, maybe we can encode this with fewer bits without losing any information (run length encode, use logically larger pixels etc.). On the other hand, we can take advantage of other features of natural scenes to reduce the amount of bits – for example, nature is very fractal, or self-similar: there are lots of features, sky, grass, lines on face etc. that are repetitive at any level of detail. If we leave out some levels of detail, the eye (and human visual cortex processing) ends up being fooled a lot of the time. The way that the eye and the ear work (integration versus differentiation) means that video and audio compression are very different things.

Hierarchical coding

Hierarchical coding is based on the idea that coding will be in the form of a quality hierarchy where the lowest layer of hierarchy contains the minimum information for intelligibility. Succeeding layers of the hierarchy add increasing quality to the scheme.

This compression mechanism is ideal for transmission over packet switched networks where the network resources are shared among many traffic streams and delays, losses and errors are expected.

Table 4.5 Estimates for uncompressed video data rate.

Liberal estimate	Cautious estimate
1024 × 1024 pixels	64 × 64 pixels
3 bytes per pixel (24 bit RGB)	3 bytes per pixel (24 bit RGB)
25 frames per second	10 frames per second

Packets will carry data from only one layer. Consequently, packets can be marked according to their importance for intelligibility for the end-user. The network would use this information as a measure of what sorts of packet may be dropped or delayed and what should take priority. It should be noted that priority bits already exist in some protocols such as the IP protocol.

Hierarchical coding will also be ideal to deal with multicasting transmission over links with different bandwidths. To deal with such a problem in a non-hierarchical encoding scheme, either the whole multicasting traffic adapts to the lowest bandwidth link capabilities thus degrading the video/audio quality where it could have been better or causing the low link to suffer congestion. Sites thus affected will lose some of the intelligibility in their received video/audio. With hierarchical coding, low-level packets can be filtered out whenever a low bandwidth link is encountered thus preserving the intelligibility of the video/audio for the sites affected by these links and still delivering a better quality to sites with higher bandwidth.

Schemes that are now in relatively commonplace use include H.261 for videotelephony, MPEG for digital TV and VCRs and JPEG for still images. Most current standards are based on one simple technique, so let us look at that first:

- That last idea was that levels of detail can be sent at different rates or priorities.

- This can be useful if there are different users (e.g. in a TV broadcast, or Internet multicast).

- It can also be useful for deciding what to lose in the face of overload, lack of disk storage etc.

- Many of the video encodings (and still picture standards) are well suited to this.

Sub-band coding

Sub-band coding is given as an example of an encoding algorithm that can neatly map onto hierarchical coding. There are other examples of hierarchical encoding but none of them is a standard or as widely used as the international standards such as H.261 and MPEG.

Sub-band coding is based on the fact that the low spatial frequencies components of a picture carry most of the information within the picture. The picture can thus be divided into its spatial frequencies components and then the coefficients quantized thereby describing the image band according to their importance (lower frequencies being more important). The most obvious mapping is to allocate each sub-band (frequency) to one of the hierarchy layers. If interframe coding is used, it has to be adjusted so as not to create any upward dependencies.

In the discrete cosine world, we can replace $\sin(\omega t) + j \cos(\omega t)$ with just the $\cos(t)$, and the integrals become sums. Parameter t just references a token or symbol in the original digital spatial sample (for an image). Of course, an image is two-dimensional, which means we have to do the transform for two spatial co-ordinates, rather than one temporal co-ordinate.

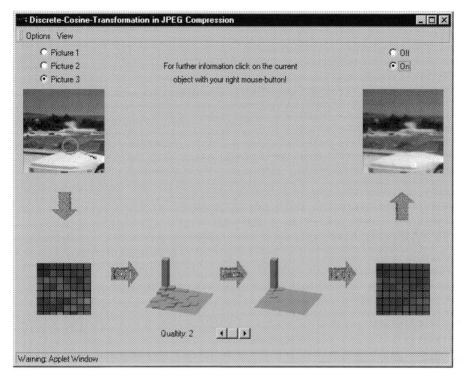

Figure 4.13 Some examples of DCT'd data.

So to transform a block of image data, 8×8 pixels square, into the *frequency domain*, we apply:

$$\text{DCT}[i,j] = \sum_{x=0}^{7} \sum_{y=0}^{7} \cos(2\pi(xi + yj)) f(x, y)$$

Let us have a look at how this works in practice. In Figure 4.13 we can see some artificial images and their transforms. In the transform, we can see how a given artifact in the input appears. For example, the lower left corner of the DCT represents the DC component (average), whilst the corners represent horizontal, vertical and other frequency information.

Finally, we should observe that there is a set of well known optimisations of the discrete Fourier and cosine transforms, based on *decimation in time*. In essence, these all stem from the facts that there is a lot of symmetry in the transform and that the relationship $x = 2, i = 1$ gives the same cosine value as $x = 1, i = 2$.

4.8.2 H.261

H.261 is the most widely used international video compression standard for video conferencing. This ITU (was CCITT) standard describes the video coding and decoding methods for the moving picture component of a audiovisual service at the rate of $p \times 64$ kbps where p is in the range 1 to 30. The standard targets and is really suitable for applications using circuit switched networks as their transmission channels. This is understandable as ISDN with both basic and primary rate access was the communication channel considered within the framework of the standard.

H.261 is usually used in conjunction with other control and framing standards such as H.221, H.230 H.242 and H.320, of which more later.

H.261 source images format

The source coder operates on only non-interlaced pictures. Pictures are coded as luminance and two colour difference components (Y, Cb, Cr). The Cb and Cr matrices are half the size of the Y matrix.

H.261 supports two image resolutions, QCIF which is 144×176 pixels and, optionally, CIF which is 288×352.

The three main elements in an H.261 encoder as illustrated in Figure 4.14 are prediction, block transformation quantisation and entropy coding.

Prediction   H.261 defines two types of coding: *intra* coding where blocks of 8×8 pixels each are encoded only with reference to themselves and are sent directly to the block transformation process, and *inter* coding where frames are encoded with respect to another reference frame.

A prediction error is calculated between a 16×16 pixel region (macroblock) and the (recovered) correspondent macroblock in the previous frame. Prediction errors of transmitted blocks (criteria of transmission are not standardised) are then sent to the block transformation process:

- Blocks are inter or intra coded.
- Intra-coded blocks stand alone.
- Inter-coded blocks are based on predicted error between the previous frame and this one.
- Intra-coded frames must be sent with a minimum frequency to avoid loss of synchronisation of sender and receiver.

H.261 supports motion compensation in the encoder as an option. In motion compensation a search area is constructed in the previous (recovered) frame to determine the best reference macroblock. Both the prediction error and the motion vectors specifying the value and direction of displacement between the encoded macroblock and the chosen reference are sent. Neither the search area nor the method of computing the motion vectors is subject to standardisation; both horizontal and vertical components of the vectors must have integer values in the range -15 to $+15$ though.

In block transformation, intra-coded frames as well as prediction errors will be composed into 8×8 blocks. Each block will be processed by a two-dimensional FDCT function. If this sounds expensive, there are fast table driven algorithms and it can be done in software quite easily, as well as very easily in hardware.

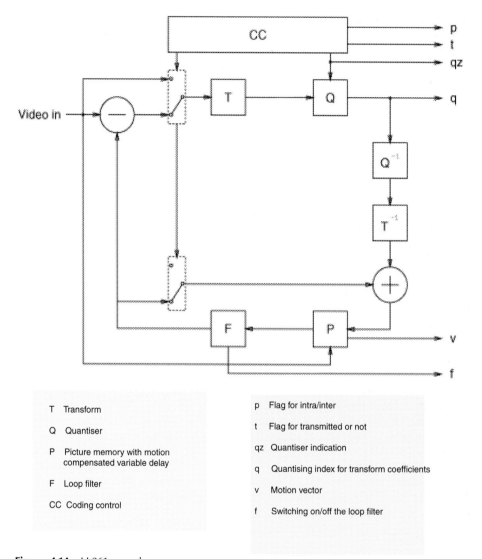

Figure 4.14 H.261 encoder.

T Transform	p Flag for intra/inter
Q Quantiser	t Flag for transmitted or not
P Picture memory with motion compensated variable delay	qz Quantiser indication
	q Quantising index for transform coefficients
F Loop filter	v Motion vector
CC Coding control	f Switching on/off the loop filter

Block transformation quantisation and entropy coding The purpose of this step is to achieve further compression by representing the DCT coefficients with no greater precision than is necessary to achieve the required quality. The number of quantisers are one for the intra DC coefficients and 31 for all others.

Entropy coding involves extra compression (non-lossy) and is done by assigning shorter code words to frequent events and longer code words to less frequent events. Huffman coding is usually used to implement this step.

In other words, for a given quality, we can lose coefficients of the transform by using fewer bits than would be needed for all the values. This leads to a coarser picture. We can then entropy code the final set of values by using shorter words for the most common values and longer ones for rarer ones (like using 8 bits for three-letter words in English).

H.261 multiplexing

The video multiplexer structures the compressed data into a hierarchical bitstream that can be universally interpreted. The hierarchy has four layers:

- Picture: corresponds to one video picture (frame).
- Group of blocks: corresponds to one-twelfth of CIF pictures or one-third of QCIF.
- Macroblock: corresponds to 16 × 16 pixels of luminance and the two spatially corresponding 8 × 8 chrominance components.
- Block: corresponds to 8 × 8 pixels.

H.261 error correction framing

An error correction framing structure is described in the H.261 standard. The frame structure is shown in Figure 4.14. The BCH (511,493) parity is used to protect the bitstream transmitted over ISDN and is optional to the decoder. The fill bit indicator allows data padding thus ensuring the transmission on every valid clock cycle.

4.8.3　H.263

H.263+ is a new addition to the ITU H series and is aimed at extending the repertoire to video coding for low bit rate communication. This makes it eminently suitable to a wide variety of Internet access line speeds, and therefore also probably reasonably friendly to many Internet service providers' backbone speeds.

Existing audiovisual standards and video and the basic technology of CCD camera and of television and general CRT dictate frame grabbing at some particular resolution and rate. The choice of resolution is complex. One could have fixed number of pixels, and aspect ratio, or allow a range of choice of line rate and sample rates. H.261 and MPEG chose the latter.

The line rate (also known as picture clock frequency, PCF) is 30 000/1001 or about 29.97 Hz, but one can also use multiples of this. The chosen resolution for H.263 is $dxdy$ luminance and chrominance is just one-half of this in both dimensions. H.263+ then allows for sub-QCIF which is 128 × 96 pixels, QCIF 176 × 144 pixels, CIF 352 × 288 pixels, 4CIF (SCIF in the INRIA ivs tool) 704 × 576 pixels and 16CIF 1408 × 1152 pixels. The designer can also choose a pixel aspect ratio; the default is 288/3:352/4 which is 12:11 (as per H.261). The picture area covered by standard formats has an aspect ratio of 4:3.

Luminance and chrominance sample positions are as per H.261, discussed earlier in this chapter. The structure of the coder is just the same too, although there are now two additional modes called the slice and picture block modes.

A block is 16 × 16 Y and 8 × 8 Cb and Cr each. The group of block, or GOB, refers to k × 16 lines. GOBs are numbered using a vertical scan starting with 0 to k, depending on the number of lines in picture. For example, normally, when *lines* is less than 400, then k is 1. The number of GOBs per picture then is 6 for sub-QCIF, 9 for QCIF, 18 for CIF (and for 4CIF and 16CIF because of special rules).

Prediction works on intra, inter, B, PB, EI or EP (the reference picture is smaller).

The macroblock is 16 lines of Y, and the corresponding 8 each of Cb and Cr motion vectors of which we can receive one per macroblock.

There is some provision for other technology – we could envisage an 'intelligent' device in camera, and detect only 'objects' and motion. This is some way off in the future and anyhow can be done after the event with general software intelligence after dumb capture and compression (using compression for hints).

H.263, then, extends H.261 over a lower bit rate (not just the $p \times 64$ kbps design goal) and adds features for better quality and services, but the basic ideas are the same:

1   Intra- and inter-frame compression.

2   DCT block transform plus quantisation.

There are, then, a number of basic enhancements in H.263 including:

1   Continuous presence multipoint and video multiplex mode – basically 4 in 1 sub-bitstream transmission. This may be useful for conferences, telepresence, surveillance and so on.

2   Motion vectors can point outside picture.

3   Arithmetic as well as variable length coding (VLC).

4   Advanced prediction mode, which is also known as overlapped block motion compensation, uses four 8×8 blocks instead of one 16×16: this gives better detail.

5   PB frames known as combined predictive and bidirectional frames (like MPEG II).

6   Forward error correction (FEC) to help with transmission loss; advanced intra coding to help with interpolation; deblocking filter mode to remove blocking artifacts.

7   Slice structured mode (reorder blocks so slice layer instead of GOB layer is more delay and loss tolerant for packet transport).

8   Supplemental enhancement information, freeze/freeze release and enhancement and chroma key (use external picture as merge/background etc. for mixing).

9   Improved PB mode, including two-way motion vectors in PB mode.

10   Reference picture selection

11   Temporal, SNR and spatial scalability mode; this allows receivers to drop B frames for example; gives potential heterogeneity amongst receivers of multicast.

12   Reduced resolution update; independent segment decoding; alternate inter VLC mode.

13   Modified quantisation mode (can adjust up or down the amount of quantisation to give fine quality/bit rate control.

Chroma keying is a commonly used technology in TV, for example, for picture in picture/superimpose etc., for weather people and so on. The idea is to define some pixels in an image as transparent or semi-transparent and instead of showing these, a reference, background image is used (compare transparent GIFs in the Web). We need an octet per pixel to define the keying colour for each of Y, Cb and Cr. The actual choice when there is no exact match is implementor defined.

4.8.4   MPEG

The aim of the MPEG II video compression standard is to cater for the growing need for generic coding methods for moving images for various applications such as digital storage and communication. So, unlike the H.261 standard which was designed specifically for the compression of moving images for video conferencing systems at $p \times 64$ kbps, MPEG is considering a wider scope of applications:

- Aimed at storage as well as transmission
- Higher cost and quality than H.261
- Higher minimum bandwidth
- Decoder is just about implementable in software
- Target 2 Mbps to 8 Mbps really
- The 'CD' of video(?)

MPEG source images format

The source pictures consist of three rectangular matrices of integers: a luminance matrix (Y) and two chrominance matrices (Cb and Cr).

The MPEG supports three formats:

- *4:2:0 format*: In this format the Cb and Cr matrices shall be one-half the size of the Y matrix in both horizontal and vertical dimensions.
- *4:2:2 format*: In this format the Cb and Cr matrices shall be one-half the size of the Y matrix in horizontal dimension and the same size in the vertical dimension.
- *4:4:4 format*: In this format the Cb and Cr matrices will be of the same size as the Y matrix in both vertical and horizontal dimensions.

Looking at some video capture cards (for example, Intel's PC one) it may be hard to convert to this, but then this is aimed at digital video tape and video-on-demand.

MPEG frames

The output of the decoding process, for interlaced sequences, consists of a series of fields that are separated in time by a field period. The two fields of a frame may be coded independently (field pictures) or can be coded together as a frame (frame pictures).

Figure 4.15 shows the intra, predictive and bidirectional frames that MPEG supports.

An MPEG source encoder will consist of the following elements:

- Prediction (three frame times)
- Block transformation
- Quantisation and variable length encoding

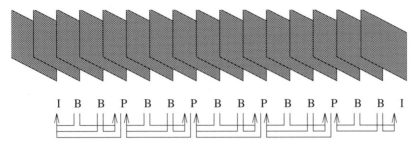

Figure 4.15 MPEG frames.

MPEG prediction

MPEG defines three types of picture:

- *Intrapictures (I-pictures)*: These pictures are encoded only with respect to themselves. Here each picture is composed onto blocks of 8 × 8 pixels each that are encoded only with respect to themselves and are sent directly to the block transformation process.

- *Predictive pictures (P-pictures)*: These are pictures encoded using motion-compensated prediction from a past I-picture or P-picture. A prediction error is calculated between a 16 × 16 pixels region (macroblock) in the current picture and the past reference I- or P-picture. A motion vector is also calculated to determine the value and direction of the prediction. For progressive sequences and interlaced sequences with frame coding, only one motion vector will be calculated for the P-pictures. For interlace sequences with field coding two motion vectors will be calculated. The prediction error is then composed to 8 × 8 pixels blocks and sent to the block transformation.

- *Bidirectional pictures (B-pictures)*: These are pictures encoded using motion-compensated predictions from a past and/or future I-picture or P-picture. A prediction error is calculated between a 16 × 16 pixels region in the current picture and the past as well as future reference I-picture or P-picture. Two motion vectors are calculated: one to determine the value and direction of the forward prediction, the other to determine the value and direction of the backward prediction. For field-coding pictures in interlaced sequences, four motion vectors will thus be calculated.

It should be noted that a B-picture can never be used as a prediction picture.

The method of calculating the motion vectors as well as the search area for the best predictor is left to be determined by the encoder.

MPEG block transformation

In block transformation, intra-coded blocks as well as prediction errors are processed by a two-dimensional DCT function.

- *Quantisation*: The purpose of this step is to achieve further compression by representing the DCT coefficients with no greater precision than is necessary to achieve the required quality.

- *Variable length encoding*: Here extra compression (non-lossy) is done by assigning shorter code words to frequent events and longer code words to less frequent events. Huffman coding is usually used to implement this step.

MPEG multiplexing

The video multiplexer structures the compressed data into a hierarchical bitstream that can be universally interpreted.

The hierarchy has four layers:

- *Videosequence*: This is the highest syntactic structure of the coded bitstream. It can be looked at as a random access unit.
- *Group of pictures*: This is optional in **MPEG II** and corresponds to a series of pictures. The first picture in the coded bitstream has to be an I-picture. Group of pictures does assist random access. It can also be used at scene cuts or in other cases where motion compensation is ineffective. Applications requiring random access, fast-forward or fast-reverse playback may use a relatively short group of pictures.
- *Picture*: This corresponds to one picture in the video sequence. For field pictures in interlaced sequences, the interlaced picture will be represented by two separate pictures in the coded stream. The two pictures will be encoded in the same order as will occur at the output of the decoder.
- *Slice*: This corresponds to a group of macroblocks. The actual number of macroblocks within a slice is not subject to standardisation. Slices do not have to cover the whole picture. It is a requirement that if the picture was used subsequently for predictions, then predictions shall only be made from those regions of the picture that were enclosed in slices.

  Macroblock: (1) A macroblock contains a section of the luminance component and the spatially corresponding chrominance components. A 4:2:0 macroblock consists of six blocks (4Y, 1 Cb, 1Cr). A 4:2:2 macroblock consists of eight blocks (4Y, 2 Cb, 2 Cr). A 4:4:4 macroblock consists of twelve blocks (4Y, 4Cb, 4Cr). (2) Block which, as with H.261, corresponds to 8×8 pixels.

MPEG picture order

It must be noted that in MPEG the order of the pictures in the coded stream is the order in which the decoder processes them. The reconstructed frames are not necessarily in the correct form of display. The example in Table 4.6 shows such a case at the encoder output, in the coded bitstream and at the decoder input, and at the decoder output.

Since the order of pictures at the decoder is not always in the display order, this leads to potential for delays in the encoder/decoder loop. This is also true of H.261 – at its highest compression ratio, it may incur as much as 0.5 seconds delay – not very pleasant for interactive use.

Table 4.6 MPEG source, encoder and decoder frame sequence.

At the encoder input										
12	3	4	5	6	78	9	10	11	12	13
IB	B	P	B	B	PB	B	I	B	B	P

At the encoder output										
14	2	3	7	5	610	8	9	13	11	12
IP	B	B	P	B	BI	B	B	P	B	B

At the decoder output										
12	3	4	5	6	78	9	10	11	12	13

Scalable extensions

The scalability tools specified by **MPEG II** are designed to support applications beyond those supported by single-layer video. In a scalable video coding, it is assumed that given an encoded bitstream, decoders of various complexities can decode and display appropriate reproductions of coded video. The basic scalability tools offered are: data partitioning, SNR scalability, spatial scalability and temporal scalability. Combinations of these basic scalability tools are also supported and are referred to as hybrid scalability. In the case of basic scalability, two layers of video, referred to as the lower layer and the enhancement layer, are allowed; in hybrid scalability up to three layers are supported.

MPEG extensions include:

- *Spatial scalable extension*: This involves generating two spatial-resolution video layers from a single video source such that the lower layer is coded by itself to provide the basic spatial resolution and the enhancement layer employs the spatially interpolated lower layer and carries the full spatial resolution of the input video source.

- *SNR scalable extension*: This involves generating two video layers of the same spatial resolution but different video qualities from a single video source. The lower layer is coded by itself to provide the basic video quality and the enhancement layer is coded to enhance the lower layer. The enhancement layer, when added back to the lower layer, regenerates a higher-quality reproduction of the input video.

- *Temporal scalable extension*: This involves generating two video layers where the lower one is encoded by itself to provide the basic temporal rate and the enhancement layer is coded with temporal prediction with respect to the lower layer. These layers, when decoded and temporally multiplexed, yield full temporal resolution of the video source.

- *Data partitioning extension*: This involves the partitioning of the video-coded bitstream into two parts. One part will carry the more critical parts of the bitstream such as headers, motion vectors and DC coefficients; the other part will carry less critical data such as the higher DCT coefficients.

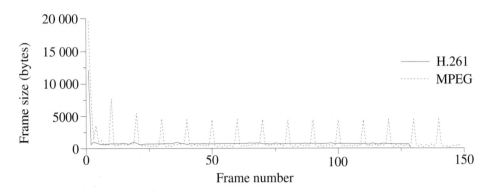

Figure 4.16   H.261 versus MPEG data rates.

- *Profiles and levels*: Profiles and levels provide a means of defining subsets of the syntax and semantics and thereby the decoder capabilities to decode a certain stream. A profile is a defined subset of the entire bitstream syntax that is defined by MPEG II. A level is a defined set of constraints imposed on parameters in the bitstream.

To constrain the choice pragmatically, five MPEG II profiles and four levels of quality are defined. However, it is important to realise that specification is of an encoded stream rather than of an actual compression and decompression mechanism. This leaves lots of options open to the implementor. Profiles allow us to scope these choices (as in other standards, e.g. in telecommunications). This is important, as the hard work (expensive end) is the encoder, while the stream as specified is generally easy to decode however it is implemented. Figure 4.16 shows a comparison of the data rate of an H.261 and an MPEG coder.

MPEG II is now an ISO standard. Owing to the forward and backward temporal compression used by MPEG, a better compression and better quality can be produced. As MPEG does not limit the picture resolution, high resolution data can still be compressed using MPEG. The scalable extensions defined by MPEG can map neatly on the hierarchical scheme explained in Chapter 2. The out-of-order processing which occurs in both encoding and decoding can introduce considerable latencies. This is undesirable in video telephony and video conferencing.

Prices for hardware MPEG encoders are high at the moment although this should change in the near future. The new SunVideo board (see below) supports MPEG I encoding. Software implementation of MPEG I decoders are already available.

MPEG III and IV

MPEG III was going to be a higher-quality encoding for HDTV. It transpired after some studies that MPEG II at higher rates is pretty good, and so MPEG III has been dropped.

MPEG IV is aimed at the opposite extreme – that of low bandwidth or low storage capacity environments (for example, PDAs). It is based around model-based image coding schemes (i.e. knowing what is in the picture). It is aimed at up to 64 kbps.

4.8.5 Region coding

Intel's digital video interactive (DVI) compression scheme is based on the region encoding technique. Each picture is divided into regions which in turn are split into subregions and so on, until the regions can be mapped onto basic shapes to fit the required bandwidth and quality. The chosen shapes can be reproduced well at the decoder. The data sent are a description of the region tree and of the shapes at the leaves. This is an asymmetric coding which requires a large amount of processing for the encoding and less for the decoding.

DVI, although not a standard, started to play an important role in the market. Sun prototype DIME board used DVI compression and it was planned to be incorporated in the new generation of Sun VideoPix cards. This did not happen, however. Intel cancelled the development of the V3 DVI chips. Sun's next generation of VideoPix, the SunVideo card, does not support DVI. The future of DVI is in doubt.

4.8.6 Wavelet, vector quantisation and fractal compression

Wavelet, vector quantisation and fractal compression are three techniques which are emerging from the research community for improved quality or compression or even both.

Briefly, wavelets are a generalisation of the Fourier transforms, vector quantisation is a generalisation of the quantisation mechanism, and fractal is a generalisation of an information-free object-based compression scheme. All three are compute intensive, although there are many people working on codecs (hardware and software) and we will probably see some low-cost high-quality results soon.

4.9 MULTIPLEXING AND SYNCHRONISING

In networked multimedia standards, the *multiplexing function* defines the way that multiple streams of different or the same media of data are carried from source to sink over a channel. There are at least three completely different points in this path where we can perform this function: (1) we can design a multimedia codec which mixes together the digitally coded (and possibly compressed) streams as it generates them, possibly interleaving media at a bit-by-bit level of granularity; (2) we can design a multiplexing layer that mixes together the different media as it packetises them, possibly interleaving samples of different media in the same packets; or (3) we can let the network do the multiplexing, packetising different media streams completely separately.

The approaches have different performance benefits and costs, and all three approaches are in use for Internet multimedia. Some of the costs are what engineers call 'non-functional' ones, which derive from business cases of the organisations defining the schemes.

There are a lot of players ('stakeholders') in the multimedia marketplace. Many of them have devised their own system architectures – not the least of these are the ITU, ISO, DAVIC and the IETF. The ITU has largely been concerned with videotelephony, whilst DAVIC has concerned itself with digital broadcast technology, and the IETF has slowly added multimedia (store and forward and real time) to its repertoire.

Each group has its own mechanism or family of mechanisms for identifying media in a stream or on a store, and for multiplexing over a stream. The design criteria were different in each case, as were the target networks and underlying infrastructures. This has led to some confusion which will probably persist for a few years.

Here we look at the four major players and their three major architectures for a multimedia stream. Making sense out of this jungle was the brave goal of Apple and Microsoft, and we briefly discuss their earlier attempts to unravel this puzzle. Microsoft has made recent changes to its architecture at many levels; this is discussed in its product specifications and is not covered here.

To cut to the chase, the ITU defines a bit-level interleave or multiplex appropriate to low-cost, low-latency terminals and a bit pipe model of the network, while ISO MPEG group defines a codec-level interleave appropriate to digital multimedia devices with high-quality, but possibly higher-cost, terminals (it is hard to leave out a function); finally, the DAVIC and Internet communities define the multiplexor to be the network, although DAVIC assumes an ATM network whereas the Internet community assumes an IP network as the fundamental layer.

The Internet community tends to try to make use of anything that it is possible to use, so that if an ITU or DAVIC or ISO codec is available on an Internet-capable host, someone, somewhere, will at some time devise a way to packetise its output into IP datagrams. The problem with this is that it means that for the non-purist approaches of separate media in separate packets, there are potentially then several layers of multiplexing. In a classic paper, David Tennenhouse describes the technical reasons why this is a very bad architecture for communicating software systems (Tennenhouse, 1989). Note that this is not a critique of the ISO MPEG, DAVIC or ITU H.320 architectures: they are beautiful pieces of design fit for a particular purpose; it is merely an observation that it is better to unpick their multiplex in an Internet-based system. It certainly leads to more choice regarding where to carry out other functions (for example, mixing, resynchonisation, trans-coding, etc.). In the next subsections we describe these schemes in some detail.

4.9.1   IETF multiplex

The IETF addresses a broad range of scenarios but, in laboratories and high-tech companies at least, access is via local area networks, and backbone speeds are appreciable. Thus a more loose approach has evolved, although mechanisms for mapping this and optimising it for lower-speed networks are not ignored.

There are at least two separate mechanisms for naming multimedia content:

- *MIME content-type*: MIME (multi-purpose Internet mail extension) is used to wrap content that is retrieved from the World Wide Web, and typically transferred using SMTP (the simple mail transfer protocol, used for Internet email) or HTTP (hypertext transfer protocol) used for Web server to browser communication. In either case, this is for non-real time communication.

- *RTP payload types*: RTP payload types indicate what media type and encoding are in use in a real time Internet session.

Neither case has an explicit multiplexing and synchronisation protocol. Instead, in the MIME case, we retrieve all the media and then play them using a single local clock. In the RTP case, each stream has a source timestamp, and external clock synchronisation can be used to play out separately sourced streams with lip synchronisation. This is discussed more in Chapter 5.

4.9.2 ITU multiplex

The ITU sees its remit as providing quality video telephony over the typical telephone companies' infrastructure. Owing to the low speed of typical access lines, this has led to a tightly specified multiplex for audio and video, and data being added in an external manner.

Typically, ITU protocols (at least on lower-speed access networks up to around T1 or megastream) run over synchronous networks, so that the clock for the media can be reasonably assumed to be that of the transmission system.

The framing structure for H.261 is H.221, which includes a FEC scheme, as shown in Figures 4.17 and 4.18.

H.221 is the most important control standard when considered in the context of equipment designed for ISDN, especially current hardware video codecs. It defines the frame structure for audiovisual services in one or multiple B or H0 channels

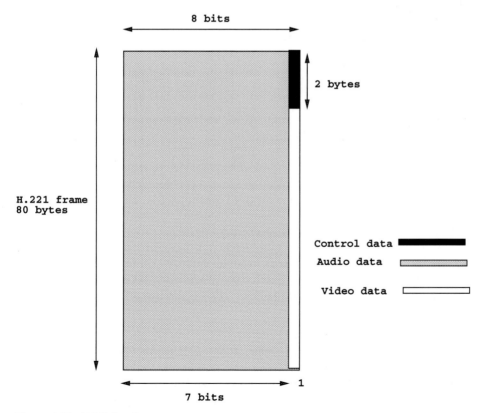

Figure 4.17 H.221 framing.

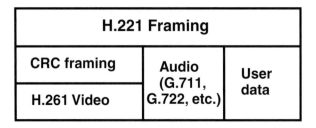

Figure 4.18 H.320 structure.

or a single H11 or H12 channel at rates of between 64 and 1920 kbps. It allows the synchronisation of multiple 64 or 384 kbps connections and dynamic control over the subdivision of a transmission channel of 64 to 1920 kbps into smaller subchannels suitable for voice, video, data and control signals. It is designed mainly for use within synchronised multiway multimedia connections, such as video conferencing.

H.221 was designed specifically for usage over ISDN. A lot of problems arise when trying to transmit H.221 frames over PSDN.

Owing to the increasing number of applications utilising narrow- (3 kHz) and wideband (7 kHz) speech together with video and data at different rates, a scheme is recommended by this standard to allow a channel that accommodates speech and optionally video and/or data at several rates and in a number of different modes. Signalling procedures for establishing a compatible mode upon call set-up, to switch between modes during a call and to allow for a call transfer, are explained in this standard.

Each terminal would transfer its capabilities to the other remote terminal(s) at call set-up. The terminals will then proceed to establish a common mode of operation. Terminal capabilities consist of: audio capabilities, video capabilities, transfer rate capabilities, data capabilities, terminals on restricted networks capabilities, and encryption and extension-BAS capabilities.

The H.230 standard is concerned mainly with the control and indication signals needed for the transmission of frame-synchronous video or requiring rapid response. Four categories of control and indication signal have been defined: first, one related to video; second, one related to audio; third, one related to maintenance purposes; and last, one related to simple multipoint conferences control (signals transmitted between terminals and MCUs, as specified in H.231).

H.320 covers the technical requirements for narrowband telephone services defined in the H.200/AV.120 series recommendations, where channel rates do not exceed 1920 kbps. There is now convergence work between this group and the AVT and MMusic groups in the IETF. This is discussed further in Chapter 6.

4.9.3   ISO MPEG multiplex – DMIF

The MPEG committee has defined the Delivery Multimedia Integration Framework (DMIF), to provide the multiplexing and synchronisation services necessary for the various MPEG coding schemes.

The DMIF specification compares the overall design to FTP. There is a DMIF application interface (DAI) and the DMIF network interface (DNI). The application uses the DAI to establish a session, and the DMIF layer maps this through to the DNI to signal the appropriate network resources. How this happens is very application-pattern dependent. For example, an application for local storage is quite different from one for remote interaction. Network channels are called *transmuxes*, and a general model of mapping elementary MPEG streams onto these channels is defined, together with a specific mapping for low-latency, low-overhead (i.e. multiple streams per network channel), in the TransMux channel model in the standard.

Other models are possible, but not specified – for example, a stream per channel in keeping with the IETF model would be feasible. This could then be mapped to an RTP flow, perhaps multicast and perhaps reserved using RSVP. This is currently being explored for remote retrieval using RTSP and for interactive use in the relevant IETF working groups.

4.9.4 The DAVIC multiplex

The Digital Audio Video Interactive Council (DAVIC) has chosen standards from the ISO MPEG work for its transmission of digital broadcast television and radio. The MPEG systems stream conveys a system clock that allows play-out of the multiplex.

4.9.5 Proprietary multiplexes

Apple and Microsoft have both defined standards for their respective systems to accommodate video, namely Quicktime, and the Multimedia PC architecture. However, in both cases, they are more concerned with defining a usable API so that program developers can generate applications that interwork quickly and effectively. Thus, Quicktime and Video for Windows both specify the ways that video can be displayed and processed within the framework of the GUI systems on the Apple and MS-Windows systems. However, neither specifies a unique video encoding. Rather, they assume that all kinds of encodings will be available through hardware codecs or through software, and thus they provide metasystems that allow the programmer to name the encoding, and provide translations.

4.10 STANDARDS AND FUTURES

Although we have mentioned that H.261 can be considered the most widely used video compression standard in the field of multimedia conferencing, it has its limitations as far as its suitability for transmission over PSDN is concerned. H.261 does not map naturally onto hierarchical coding. A few suggestions have been made as to how this can happen, but as a standard there is no support of that. H.261 resolution is fine for conferencing applications. Once more quality-critical video data need to be compressed, the upper limit optional CIF resolution can start to show its inadequacy.

4.11 PERFORMANCE

Here we take a look at some performance aspects of coding and compression of multimedia in packet networks. First we look at the sorts of compression ratio that can be achieved. Then we take a look at the effect of network behaviour on received media streams. Finally we carry out a back-of-the-envelope analysis of a particular compression algorithm to see what levels of CPU costs are involved.

4.11.1 Typical compression achieved

The amount of compression that can (and should) be achieved for a given medium depends very much on the actual requirements of the user and the user's given task.

MPEG I and II aim for compression down to storage and transmission over digital broadcast networks, so several megabits per second are worth considering. H.261 is aimed at interactive Internet telpehony, so the target operating environment is the digital telephone net, at one to several multiples of 64 kbps. H.263 and MNPEG IV are aimed at lower capacity for each case, so we can envisage a range of a few tens of kilobits per second up to several megabits (some users report that motion JPEG for a broadcast-quality result typically takes near to 20 Mbps maximum).

4.11.2 Effects of network loss and delay on video

The effects of variable network behaviour on audio or video are quite hard to estimate. Typically, a play-out buffer will be set given the delays in the encoder, compressor, decoder, decompressor and transmission, and the overall delay budget, to put a drop-dead deadline on arrival of packets over the Internet.

Packets are either lost in transit or reordered or delayed so that some simply do not make it. The loss distributions in the Internet are complex, and change as the network evolves. However, the degradation of the received and perceived signal will increase with compression and loss – since the compression exploits redundancy, it removes the signal's very tolerance for loss. Lossy compression is worse since it reduces the signal to its bare essential components.

The designer of a compression scheme for packet transmission has two possible approaches to this problem: firstly, careful choice of compression scheme and ratio, to minimise the impact of loss for the average delivered rate; secondly, the use of smart protection by re-adding redundancy to the packets in a way that is designed to protect against packet loss.

Suffice it to say that under heavy load there are significant losses and that the losses are quite often spatially and temporally correlated (that is to say, if a packet is lost, it is more likely that the next one to the same place will be lost, and that packets destined for similar areas of the network are also more likely to be lost).

The size of a packet in the Internet for audio or video might typically be in the range 320–1500 bytes. This means that the loss of media data is quite significant even for only a single lost packet.

There are various enhancement approaches to protecting the media stream by clever mapping of the data into packets. One can go further and add general packet-level FEC codes, or even media-specific FECs (Hardman *et al.*, 1995), or, when the delays are sufficiently low, or in a playback situation, recover from loss using retransmission strategies. Some users propose a hybrid of media-specific FEC and retransmission.

Finally, it remains to be seen if new, scalable codecs might be devised which, combined with intelligent distribution of the compressed media data over a sequence of packets, lead to better quality results in the face of the Internet's current curious, and somewhat pathological, loss behaviour.

4.12 PROCESSING REQUIREMENTS FOR VIDEO COMPRESSION

In this section we present a brief analysis of the complexity of implementing a lossy video compression algorithm in software. We use an example loosely based on the H.621 scheme.

There has been some disagreement about just how many MIPs[3] it takes to compress to a particular bandwidth.

Rather than look in detail at the exact standard, let us take a hypothetical coding standard, called VRUM (video reduction for usable multimedia). This takes a nominal 1024 pel square true colour (24 bit per pel) video frame sequence, at 25 frames per second (75 MBps), and compresses as follows:

- *Intra-frame coding*: Divide the 1024 × 1024 area into 8 × 8 blocks and run a discrete cosine transform (16 384 times).
- *Inter-frame coding*: Meanwhile, for interframe coding consider:
  - difference each 8 × 8 area with same area in previous frame;
  - For i=1 to 8 frames in sequence,
    For each neighbour block in successive frames
    if neighbour == current block offset by i pels
        send motion vector for this block for all 8 frames
        (and 1st DCT coded block, of course)

Obviously, a naive implementation of this could be very expensive, but there are a number of very obvious optimisations (not the least is not to bother calculating DCT on blocks that either have not changed or have simply moved and have motion vectors being sent).

Now, DCT looks like this:

```
for (x=0..7, y=0..7)
f(x,y) = 1/4 Sum(i=0..7, j=0..7) C(i) C(j)
Cos(pi (2x+1) i/16)
Cos(pi (2y+1) j/16)


C(k) = 1/root2 for i=0, else 1


The range of f is -256..255.
```

We can precalculate all discrete cosine values for the 256 possible input values (i.e. only have a table lookup of 256 × 2 entries for the transform itself). We could go further and have a table of sums of cosines, but let us just leave it here for now.

This then gives each block taking

```
8*8 * (add + (8*8 (2 table lookups) + multiply))
= 64 * 130 = 8320
```

So for full inter-frame coded stream of 25 frames each taking

```
16384 blocks, this takes
25*16384*8320 =
3407872000 = 3000 MIPs
without any differencing...
```

However, if a significant number of blocks are similar, then we need to look at the relative cost of differencing with 'DCT-ing'. Differencing 16 384 blocks can be done with a simple-minded compare (cmp):

```
blkcmp()
for(i=0..7, j=0..7)
    pel = i*8+j
    if (frame[seq][block[pel]]) != frame[seq-1][block[pel]]
return false
return true
```

Since a pel is 3 bytes, this is 3 'compares' times 64 to find true, or on average (whatever that is) a lot less to find false. This gives a result of roughly 196 instructions, to avoid 8320 DCT instructions.

In other words, if we run a simple blk cmp, and get some proportion n of blocks the same, we reduce the MIP count to:

$$n \times 196 + \{(1 - n)(8320 + (p \times 196))\} \times 25 \times 16\,384$$

where p is the proportion that a changed block has changed, which (for largish n) is approximately:

$$(1 - n) \times 3000\,\text{MIPs}$$

For $n = \frac{2}{3}$ (for example, head and shoulders view) we are now down to 1000 MIPs.

To reduce further, we should consider precalculating some subset of the DCT cosine products, but would need to then check that we do not have too high a memory requirement. Now, the searches are a bit more complex. Each search is just like the differencing code, only it costs more as we have to do it across eight frames, and across ± 8 in x and y directions, i.e. $16 \times 16 \times 8$ times as much. However, this is incrementing only once per new frame, so in effect it is calculated only across the 16×16 moves.

In fact, if we roll this into the difference code (since a motion vector of $0, 0$ is the same as an unchanged block), we have $16 \times 16 \times 196$ instructions to see if a block is unchanged, and moved or unmoved. This results in around 50 176 instructions. So now we get:

$$\{n \times 50\,176 + (1 - n)(8320 + (q \times 50\,176))\} \times 25 \times 16\,384 \tag{4.1}$$

where q is the proportion that a changed block has changed (whether moved or not); q is probably very small. Unfortunately, this is rather worse than the mere intra-coded frame. However, when doing the differencing, we can cache all previous points reached in previous blocks, so we need only run another 196 instructions per frame per block and we get back to the previous result: $(1 - n) \times 3000\,\text{MIPs}$. For $n = 0.9$, this then gets us to around 300 MIPs.

■ Note that, for H.261, input is defined to be CCIR 601, which is 720×486, not 1024 square, i.e. a further factor of three smaller in area.

■ In addition, your comparisons are on a byte-by-byte basis. You could take into consideration a 32 bit word size.

■ It is hard to see how you can use the results of previous comparisons in doing the differencing. The origin of the new block with respect to the old is changed for each iteration: the two have nothing in common.

■ If you reduce the frame rate to 5 Hz, then there will be less correspondence between frames, and the motion compensation will give you less in terms of compression. Since it is optional for the encoder in the H.261 standard, why not just difference? This may mean slightly less compression but there is a big benefit in terms of computation. (On the other hand, maybe not – differences will be detected quicker.)

Now the implementation results on modest performance PC processors achieve five frames per second (i.e. one-fifth our frame rate) and one-quarter CIF on a 30 MIPs machine, which confirms our approximate analysis.

Arguments like these have been behind the design of the Intel MMX (multi-media extensions) to the PC processor, and Sun Microsystems Visual Instruction Set – along the lines of RISC arguments for running conventional programs, there are a few possible additional instructions that are frequently used and which can make a big difference to performance.

4.13 SUMMARY

In this chapter we have looked at video and audio coding and compression techniques. We have also introduced some preliminary ideas in conferencing and conference control protocols, by virtue of their being part of one of the dominant standards for compression, namely the H.320 family: more of this in Chapter 6. Important lessons for people using multimedia include:

1   Multimedia is large. The same amount of information can often be represented for human consumption in text taking far less storage or transmission than in graphical form.

2   Multimedia is highly redundant, and compresses very successfully.

3   Human perception is frail, and cognition smart. We can take advantage of it. Note that the auditory and visual systems, however, are quite different, with persistence, averaging and so on happening at different stages in each.

4   Users of some critical applications cannot tolerate any artifacts, and therefore prefer lossless compression – examples are typically in the area of medical imaging (radiology, ultrasound, functional imaging from magnetic resonance imaging, and so on).

5   There are a number of ways to multiplex a set of media together, and a set of engineering trade-offs associated with these. Different industries have made different choices for good reasons. However, this means that in the Internet we have to unpick some of the multiplexes chosen in the broadcast and telephony industries before gaining the advantages of the Internet's full generality.

6   Last but not least, it is very important that the more sophisticated the compression technique (at least for video) the harder it is in processing terms; but decompression is massively less expensive than compression. This means that one-to-many applications are cost effective.

Notes

1   This also has the effect of eliminating *aliases*, which are harmonic, or higher frequencies, which appear at the same intervals as the actual frequencies that we want to have in our digital signal, but more frequently.
2   To be more precise, the CCIR 601 standard defines a raw 4:3 rate of the fully digitised TV signal as 270 Mbps, including the non-visible lines, the time for interframe synchronisation and so on. Without all this redundant information, the pure PAL and NTSC visible components can be coded uncompressed at 143 and 177 Mbps, respectively.
3   MIPs: million instructions per second – a common measure of CPU performance, too simple for subtle work but good enough for back-of-the-envelope estimates.

PART TWO

Middleware

The advent of the Internet, with novel facilities such as multicast, has led to the separation of the protocols used for conference media streams from the protocols used to set up and control various aspects of a conference, such as membership, session information, media activity, floor control and so on, as we shall see in the next few chapters.

The usefulness of the IP multicast service has made itself felt in the control protocols too. A number of sites have used multicast as the way to disseminate control information within a conference. Again, as with the media streams, the advantages in terms of scalability are manifold.

Alongside the multicast group used to carry the media themselves, another associated multicast group can be used to disseminate this control information. The model is that of a computer bus on which messages can be placed and received by any device attached to the backplane. This bus model is used in two related ways:

1   The LBL tools (Jacobson, 1994a) use this as a local bus to distribute information among applications at a given site to co-ordinate the control activities that are common. For example, if a user runs a video, audio and a whiteboard application, there is little point in each of these applications sending activity messages separately. They can be combined. Also, when a user is participating in multiple conferences, the co-ordination of ownership of devices such as exclusive use audio input and output can be carried out through messages on the local conference control bus.

2   UCL researchers have carried this, and the basic wide area session message use of multicast, to a general extreme, where the entire Mbone is used to co-ordinate all conference control messages using a conference control channel. This is illustrated below as the multicast control bus.

The local bus can also be used to carry out receiver synchronisation. If a machine is receiving different media streams with different delay variations that belong in the same session, then the adaptive play-out buffer sizes can be exchanged by multicasting their status on the local Mbone (local to the receiver machine only), and used to add in a constant so that all streams are played out in synchronisation, with no need for any complex end-to-end protocol to carry out complex delay bound calculations, as is used in many other systems.

The growth in the Mbone has led to some navigation difficulties (just as there are in the World Wide Web, and in Usenet News Groups). This has led to the creation of a session directory service. This has several functions:

1   A user creating a conference needs to choose a multicast address that is not in use. The session directory system has two ways of doing this: firstly, it allocates addresses using a pseudorandom strategy based on how widespread the conference is going to be according to the user, and where the creator is; secondly, it multicasts the session information out, and if it detects a clash from an existing session announcement, it changes its allocation. This is currently the main mechanism for the management of allocation and listing of dynamic multicast addresses.

2   Users need to know what conferences there are on the Mbone, what multicast addresses they are using, and what media are in use on them. They can use the session directory messages to discover all of this. The latest versions of multicast include a facility for administrative scoping, which allows session creators to designate a logical region of interest outside of which traffic will not (necessarily) flow. This is used mainly to limit the network capacity used rather than as a privacy enhancement, since there is little guarantee that someone does not subvert the Internet multicast routing anyhow, so it cannot give a guarantee of protection against accidental or deliberate disclosure. It can, however, protect co-operating users and sites from being overrun by irrelevant video and audio traffic.

3   Furthermore, the session directory tools currently implemented will launch applications for the user.

Conference control (Schooler, 1992) refers to the set of tasks concerned with managing the tools that mediate between users. This includes controlling access and membership, controlling starting and stopping media including co-ordinating this with any floor control mechanism, reporting activity by a user of a given media type, and so on.

Early conference control systems in the Internet were modelled around telephony and the T.120/T.GCC style of management, where each and every control action is specified for a unique participant, and each and every action is specified to each and every participant. Such systems were aimed at closed, secure, managed, and generally floor-controlled (chaired) conferences. Often, the conference control architecture was dictated by the low-level network call control model, or even by the media distribution technology (as with MCU-based T.120-based video conference systems).

The Mbone style of conferencing separates out this functionality, but in no way precludes using tight coupling of control actions, participants and media. Indeed, the use of the local and wide area bus model to propagate control actions leads naturally to efficient scaling of all styles of conference. Yet again, we note the user expectation is of potential dynamics in membership and quality of conferences. This is an advantage over hardwired groups and quality, since it is less constraining to designers of conferencing tools. They can always add constraints later.

The use of a single approach that seamlessly scales from small to large systems, from homogeneous, to heterogeneous, and from one style of use to another is clearly a desirable engineering goal.

The following chapters look at these various technologies.

CHAPTER FIVE

Transport Protocols

5.1 INTRODUCTION

In the Internet, the user datagram protocol, UDP, is used to carry interactive or real time multimedia data around. UDP is chosen not only because it is lightweight, but also because it interposes no unpredictable or unnecessary functions between the application and the network.

Multimedia transport protocols do not have to be complex or 'heavyweight', in the sense that an all-purpose transport protocol such as the transmission control protocol, TCP, is heavyweight. In fact, TCP is not really heavyweight, but it does have, albeit parsimoniously, mechanisms for flow control, reliability and ordering, that are counterproductive for multimedia traffic. It is also impossible to use in a scalable way for many-to-many communication (Paliwoda and Crowcroft, 1988).

The goal of transport protocols is to provide both end-to-end services that are specific to some modest range of applications and specific services that are not common to all applications and are therefore not required in the network service.

However, UDP, being designed originally for lightweight management tasks such as local time and name lookup services, does not always provide enough functionality for multimedia data transport. Multimedia transport protocols need to provide hooks for a common set of multimedia services that can be distinguished quite clearly from conventional data services, for example:

- A basic framing service is needed, defining the unit of transfer, typically common with the unit of synchronisation (in keeping with the application-layer framing principle (Clark and Tennenhouse, 1990)).

- Multiplexing may be needed, since we may wish not only to identify separate media in separate streams, but also to stack media together in the same IP packets.

- Timely delivery is needed where possible, and can be traded off against reliability. This means that it is unlikely in most scenarios that an error detection and timeout/retransmission-based error recovery scheme is appropriate. Instead, we would usually employ media-specific forward error recovery.[1]

- Synchronisation is a common service to almost all networked multimedia applications, so providing a common timestamping framework seems like a good component of a transport protocol, especially since it is between the sender (who knows media sample times) and the receiver (who has to play out media in the right order, and without gaps, gasps or unnecessary jitters) that the synchronisation is needed. Synchronisation is also needed between different media; this is discussed later in this chapter.

The basic unit of transfer in the Internet is the IP packet, which carries application data, and a transport protocol header preceded by the IP header. Packets are demultiplexed at the host based on the transport protocol port numbers and routed in the network-based IP addresses.

RTP, the preferred carrier/framing protocol for multimedia traffic, is carried on top of UDP. It has the potential for further multiplexing information, since it carries source identifiers. The main other item in the RTP header is the media timestamp (for the sample carried) which is formatted specifically for each media type. This is used for the play-out and synchronisation algorithms. RTCP, the real time control protocol, is used to convey additional information such as participant details and statistics of packet arrivals and loss. It is typically sent on one UDP port number higher than the UDP port used for the associated RTP packets.

One might envisage using the Internet to provide a rich medium for a distributed orchestra or even a cattle auction. However, there are limits imposed by the speed of light, to the end-to-end and round-trip delays, however fast the lines and switching, and however ingenious the implementation of RTP. Musicians require extremely short delays between hearing each other, and reacting, and reacting to the reaction. Consider, for example, a *rallentando* when an entire orchestra slows down the beat evenly: this may require delays of a few tens of milliseconds *at most*. This precludes such activities over distances of more than a few hundred miles at absolute best.

5.2 ROADMAP

The transport protocol for multimedia provides some functions that are rather different from those for elastic reliable data transfer, although some of the functions could be seen as analogous.

RTP provides payload identification, multiplexing and feedback from receivers to senders of reception conditions. It also provides hooks for synchronisation, both within and between streams. There are requirements from some applications for some levels of reliability – we have touched on these in Chapter 3, and revisit them at the end of this chapter.

5.3 TCP ADAPTION ALGORITHMS

TCP adaption	IETF proposed standard RFC 2001
RTP	IETF proposed standard RFC 1889

Before we look at the mechanisms to multimedia adaption, it is worth explaining how the current system survives at all for data flows. It is in essence achieved by degrading everyone's performance smoothly as load increases (rather than blocking access) that the current Internet continues to function. This is done through a variety of adaption algorithms, both for data and for multimedia applications. Adaption in protocols was first introduced in TCP in around 1988 (Jacobson, 1988).

Adaption in TCP is both to the round-trip time, in order to dynamically tune retransmit timers for reliable delivery, and of the send rate in order to adapt to the achievable transfer rate between the sender and receiver (possible owing to network bottlenecks or receiver interface performance problems). The same techniques can often be applied in other protocols, in particular for multimedia services to operate over time-varying network services.

Adaption to delay at the receiver can be used for two purposes:

1   Adaptive play-out buffer to smooth play-out so that a fixed-rate media device (for example, within a single video frame scan or a dumb CBR audio device) is not starved of data, or overrun.

2   Syncronisation of streams from different sources (timestamps) can be achieved at a receiver.

The first of these is done by looking at the inter-arrival time (IAT) variation and calculating a rolling average. This is needed to deal with the fact that there are variations in network delay for two reasons:

1   Other traffic causes the long-term average to vary.

2   Bursts of one's own traffic cause ones own delay to vary quickly.

The usual algorithm for this is an exponential weighted moving average. Assume we measure the arrival time for each (ith) packet as IAT_i then the simple average would be: $\sum_{i=1}^{n} IAT_i$, divided by the number of packets. But since the average is not fixed, we give the most recent measurements a lot more weight than the older ones by using:

$$\overline{IAT_i} = IAT_i \times \alpha + (1 - \alpha) \times \overline{IAT_{i-1}}$$

In other words, we give alpha's worth of credence to the latest measurement, and only $1 - \alpha$ to *all* the previous ones. It is only a coincidence that the equation for a rolling (moving) average for IAT estimation is the same as the one for TCP's RTT estimation. It is worth noting, however, that in both cases the requirement is only for local clocks not to drift too fast so that the measurement of successive arrival times of packets is accurate with respect to the previous ones; no clock synchronisation is needed.

This is sometimes not used, as it includes all the past, and if there is a fundamental change in the network (for example, a reroute) then a system that eliminates outlying points quickly may be better. Henning Sculzrinne's paper suggests a 'band-pass filter' approach to the estimation of average IAT, based on taking only the sum of the smallest of a set of measurements recently, over the number of them.

Once you have an average IAT, then you can calculate the current required play-out buffer since it is roughly twice the variation in inter-arrival times.

Given two streams, to synchronise their play-out at a receiver we need to know the delay from each source to each destination, and the clock offsets in case the clocks in the two (or more) senders are out of step with the receiver. This requires the exchange of packets including each sender's statement of the current clock from its view. Assume that the delay in each direction on the net is the same (and if you do not then it is impossible to solve this):

1   Send a packet from s to d with source time in it (t_1) and it arrives at d when d's clock reads t_2.

2   Send the packet back to s with t_1, t_2 and t_3, the time on d's clock when it sends it.

3   s gets the response at t_4 by its clock.

4   If s and d have clocks that differ by offset, and the network delay is d, then

$$t_4 = t_3 + \text{Offset} + \text{Delay}$$

but

$$t_2 = t_1 - \text{Offset} + \text{Delay}$$

so

$$\text{Delay} = \frac{t_4 + t_2 - t_3 + t_1}{2}$$

Offset can be calculated similarly. We then do this for several goes, and keep a mean and variance.

5.4 PLAY-OUT ALGORITHMS

For a variety of reasons, samples may arrive at different times from when they were sent – this variation can be coped with so long as the mean rate of delivery of samples is maintained, and the variation is a second-order (less important) effect compared with the delivery delay. A play-out buffer can accommodate a fixed variation in arrival. If the arrival rate itself varies, it is possible to use an adaptive play-out buffer, which is continually recalculated.

As explained above, the Internet currently provides no guarantees. The throughput and delay along a path can vary quite drastically as other traffic comes and goes. When the network is overloaded, packets get lost, leaving gaps in the information flow at a receiver. This is illustrated below. Two basic techniques have emerged to deal with these two problems:

1   Audio, video and other interactive application receivers generally use an adaptive play-out scheme.

2   Senders are generally adaptive to reported network conditions, falling back to lesser quality as the network becomes more highly loaded, and increasing the quality and subsequent load only as the network is perceived to have more spare capacity.

The way these two techniques work is quite ingenious, but once seen, relatively simple (Jacobson, 1994a). All sources that are generating information with time structure use a protocol called RTP, the real time protocol, which places a media timestamp in each packet that is sent. All receivers use this time stamp for two purposes, as follows.

The inter-arrival time distribution is monitored. If the delay on the path varies, it will probably vary fairly smoothly, with some sort of reasonable probability distribution. By monitoring the mean difference between inter-arrival times, and adding

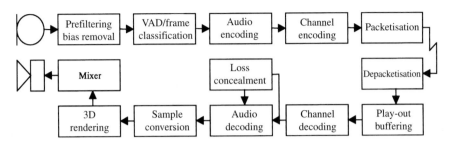

Figure 5.1 Typical media tool data flows.

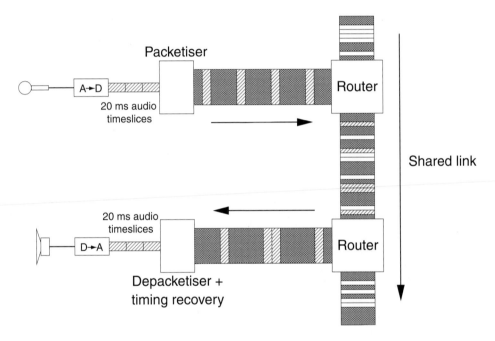

Figure 5.2 End-to-end requirement for play-out adaption.

this to a play-out buffer that is used to delay sending data between the receiving application and the output device (video window, audio, whiteboard, etc.), the receiver can be assured to a high degree of chance that it will not be starved of data.

Figure 5.1 shows the components of a play-out buffer. These include the mixing of streams from multiple sources, which can also be used to synchronise media. In Figure 5.2, we can see the reason for this requirement graphically displayed: interference from other traffic causes jitter within the network.

Receivers monitor gaps in the inter-arrival times (that correspond to missing data, as opposed to just, say, silence in an audio stream). Periodically, Mbone applications report the statistics about particular sources by multicasting a report to the same group. A sender/source can use this report to calculate whether the network appears congested or not. The scheme used to adjust the sending rate is basically that used in TCP but must be implemented by degrading the quality of the input media for audio and video – many video compression schemes are easily altered to permit this. The total amount of traffic generated by these quality reports is constrained to be a constant percentage of any conference session (typically around five conditions) so that as a conference grows, the number of samples of different parts of the net gets better and better, hence the quality of information in fact improves, even though the quantity from any given receiver decreases. The receivers use the reception of other receivers' reports to give an estimate of the number of receivers, and hence to reduce the frequency with which they send reports in a fully distributed way.

5.5 MPEG SYSTEMS

We have discussed the MPEG multiplex earlier in Chapter 4. MPEG systems' part is the control part of the MPEG standard. It addresses the combining of one or more streams of video and audio as well as other data into a single or multiple stream which is suitable for storage or transmission. Figure 5.3 shows a simplified view of the MPEG control system.

5.5.1 Packetised elementary stream (PES)

PES consists of a continuous sequence of PES packets of one elementary stream. The PES packets would include information regarding the elementary clock reference and the elementary stream rate. The PES is not defined for interchange and interoperability though. Both fixed-length and variable-length PES packets are allowed.

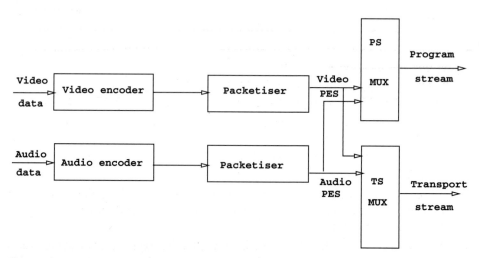

Figure 5.3 MPEG systems stream.

5.6 TRANSPORT AND PROGRAM STREAMS

There are two datastream formats defined: the transport stream, which can carry multiple programs simultaneously and which is optimised for use in applications where data loss may be likely (for example, transmission on a lossy network), and the program stream, which is optimised for multimedia applications, for performing systems processing in software, and for MPEG I compatibility.

5.6.1 Synchronisation

The basic principle of MPEG system coding is the use of timestamps which specify the decoding and display time of audio and video and the time of reception of the multiplexed coded data at the decoder, all in terms of a single 90 kHz system clock. This method allows a great deal of flexibility in such areas as decoder design, the number of streams, multiplex packet lengths, video picture rates, audio sample rates, coded data rates, digital storage medium or network performance. It also provides flexibility in selecting which entity is the master time base, while guaranteeing that synchronisation and buffer management are maintained. Variable data rate operation is supported. A reference model of a decoder system is specified which provides limits for the ranges of parameters available to encoders and provides requirements for decoders.

5.7 RTP

The real time protocol is the Internet standard for conveying media streams between interactive participants.

5.7.1 RTP packet format

The first twelve octets are present in every RTP packet, while the list of CSRC identifiers is present only when inserted by a mixer. With reference to Figure 5.4:

- *Version (V)*: 2 bits. This field identifies the version of RTP. The version defined by this specification is two (2).
- *Padding (P)*: 1 bit. If the padding bit is set, the packet contains one or more additional padding octets at the end which are not part of the payload.
- *Extension (X)*: 1 bit. If the extension bit is set, the fixed header is followed by exactly one header extension.
- *CSRC count (CC)*: 4 bits. The CSRC count contains the number of CSRC identifiers that follow the fixed header.
- *Marker (M)*: 1 bit. The interpretation of the marker is defined by a profile. It is intended to allow significant events such as frame boundaries to be marked in the packet stream.
- *Payload type (PT)*: 7 bits. This field identifies the format of the RTP payload and determines its interpretation by the application.

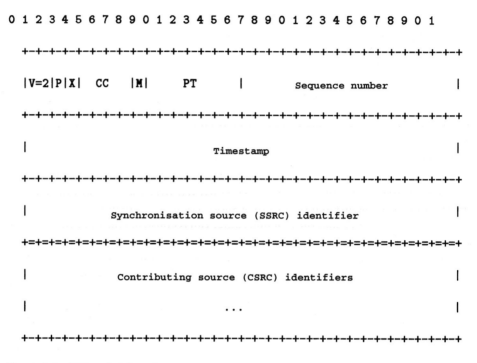

Figure 5.4 RTP packet format.

- *Sequence number*: 16 bits. The sequence number increments by one for each RTP data packet sent, and may be used by the receiver to detect packet loss and to restore packet sequence.
- *Timestamp*: 32 bits. The timestamp reflects the sampling instant of the first octet in the RTP data packet. The sampling instant must be derived from a clock that increments monotonically and linearly in time to allow synchronisation and jitter calculations.
- *SSRC*: 32 bits. The SSRC field identifies the synchronisation source.
- *CSRC list*: 0 to 15 items, 32 bits each. The CSRC list identifies the contributing sources for the payload contained in this packet. The number of identifiers is given by the CC field. If there are more than 15 contributing sources, only 15 may be identified. CSRC identifiers are inserted by mixers, using the SSRC identifiers of contributing sources.

5.7.2 RTP header compression

The combination of the IP, UDP and RTP control information adds up to a significant overhead for small media samples, particularly over low-speed links, which are in common use by the domestic and small office user dialling up their Internet service provider at a few tens of kilobits per second. An Internet protocol datagram has a 20 byte header, while the UDP header is 8 bytes (source and destination ports, plus length and checksum field). The RTP header adds 12 bytes to this, making a total of 40 bytes of control for a single sample, in some cases (especially where sampling/serialising delay is a problem) as little as 20 ms worth of 8 kHz speech.

Luckily, by far the common case of such usage is as stated when dialling up an ISP, where the access router is connected to a high-speed backbone. There is already a technique for reducing the overhead of packets in such circumstances, designed for compressing *TCP/IP headers* specified in RFC 1144 by Jacobson (1990). Casner and Jacobson (1998) adapted this technique to RTP headers, noting certain particular differences.

The technique consists of two parts: noting fields in the packet headers that do not change over the life of a flow, and noting that there are few flows at the 'edge of the network' so that such information can be conveyed over the first hop by a single packet and subsequently referred to by a short 'connection identifier' which serves to index the full state so that the first hop router can reconstruct the full Internetwork packet. In RTP, it turns out that there are also fields that change only by the same amount from each packet to the next, except in exceptional circumstances, so that this second-order information can also be stored in the compression state vector at the first-hop routers. Note also that this compression state is 'soft state' in that it can be recovered simply by loss since the packet conveys enough implicit information that end-to-end checksums are still computed, and hopwise recomputed from the state vector and from the remaining data in the compressed header. In other words, if the router resets, or the route changes, or the end system radically alters state, the invalid checksum causes a reset of the compressed state and an exchange of a full packet recreates the necessary state anew. The work is still in progress, although there are several implementations in common use, and shows a typical reduction to a header size of 3–4 bytes (better than tenfold reduction in control overhead).

5.7.3   RTP multiplexing

There are a number of circumstances in which one might wish to carry multiple media flows within a single RTP data payload between two points. The two most important cases are IP paths between Internet telephony gateways and special hardware devices such as codecs with non-negotiable multiplexed media.

There are at least two ways to multiplex data in RTP packets. One could (for example, in the telephony case) assume that all the samples have the same payload type and are simply offset in different end-to-end flows. Here we need a mapping table in the gateways that indicates the offset for each payload type and a list of the flows in each packet. The second approach might be a more generic one (suggested by Mark Handley recently in work in progress), which is to adapt the ideas from the previous section concerning RTP header compression and to allow for multiple compressed headers within a single RTP packet, one for each of the samples. This latter approach would not use precisely the same compression algorithm, since the fields differ for different reasons, but would permit multiple different media to be efficiently encapsulated in a single packet. This might address both types of application of RTP multiplexing more effectively.

5.7.4 RTCP packet format

RTCP is the real time transport control protocol, which may be used as a lightweight companion to RTP to convey a number of statistics and other information about an RTP flow between recipients and senders.

The header is illustrated in Figure 5.5.

- *SR or RR*: The first RTCP packet in the compound packet must always be a report packet to facilitate header validation. This is true even if no data have been sent or received, in which case an empty RR is sent, and even if the only other RTCP packet in the compound packet is a BYE.

- *Additional RRs*: If the number of sources for which reception statistics are being reported exceeds 31, the number that will fit into one SR or RR packet, then additional RR packets should follow the initial report packet.

- *SDES*: An SDES packet containing a CNAME item must be included in each compound RTCP packet. Other source description items may optionally be included if required by a particular application, subject to bandwidth constraints.

- *BYE or APP*: Other RTCP packet types, including those yet to be defined, may follow in any order, except that BYE should be the last packet sent with a given SSRC/CSRC. Packet types may appear more than once.

5.7.5 Payloads

There are quite a few payloads defined for RTP, ranging from ones designed to carry video and audio formerly available on hardware codecs only, such as MPEG, H.261 and the various CCITT/ITU voice coding schemes, through to some more generic payloads designed to carry redundantly coded audio such as that used by INRIA's freephone, and UCL's rat tools.

There has been some discussion in the IETF of a payload for multiplexed media within a single stream (such as the way the MPEG systems stream of H.221 framed stream emerge in a single bitstream from a hardware codec). To date, the disadvantages of this have outweighed any perceived advantage.

5.7.6 RTCP scaling properties and timer considerations

The intention and original design goal of RTCP messages was for them to act as a distributed source of lightweight session data that would allow a range of highly fault-tolerant and reasonable scale mechanisms to be built including:

1 *Membership*: RTCP reports carry the identifier of participants. There are also 'bye' messages which indicate the departure of a participant.

2 *Loss statistics*: RTCP reports convey information about packet losses. These could be used not only as health reports but also to select a codec or compression level for sources capable of adaption.

```
 0 1 2 3 4 5 6 7 8 9 0 1 2 3 4 5 6 7 8 9 0 1 2 3 4 5 6 7 8 9 0 1

+-+-+-+-+-+-+-+-+-+-+-+-+-+-+-+-+-+-+-+-+-+-+-+-+-+-+-+-+-+-+-+-+

|V=2|P|   RC   |   PT=SR=200   |   Header     Length             |



+-+-+-+-+-+-+-+-+-+-+-+-+-+-+-+-+-+-+-+-+-+-+-+-+-+-+-+-+-+-+-+

|                         SSRC of sender                        |

+=+=+=+=+=+=+=+=+=+=+=+=+=+=+=+=+=+=+=+=+=+=+=+=+=+=+=+=+=+=+=+=+

|             NTP timestamp, most significant word              |  Sender

+-+-+-+-+-+-+-+-+-+-+-+-+-+-+-+-+-+-+-+-+-+-+-+-+-+-+-+-+-+-+-+-+  Info

|             NTP timestamp, least significant word             |

+-+-+-+-+-+-+-+-+-+-+-+-+-+-+-+-+-+-+-+-+-+-+-+-+-+-+-+-+-+-+-+-+

|                         RTP timestamp                         |

+-+-+-+-+-+-+-+-+-+-+-+-+-+-+-+-+-+-+-+-+-+-+-+-+-+-+-+-+-+-+-+-+

|                     Sender's packet count                     |

+-+-+-+-+-+-+-+-+-+-+-+-+-+-+-+-+-+-+-+-+-+-+-+-+-+-+-+-+-+-+-+-+

|                     Sender's octet count                      |

+=+=+=+=+=+=+=+=+=+=+=+=+=+=+=+=+=+=+=+=+=+=+=+=+=+=+=+=+=+=+=+=+

|                 SSRC_1 (SSRC of first source)                 |  Report

+-+-+-+-+-+-+-+-+-+-+-+-+-+-+-+-+-+-+-+-+-+-+-+-+-+-+-+-+-+-+-+-+  Block 1

| Fraction lost |       Cumulative number of packets lost       |

-+-+-+-+-+-+-+-+-+-+-+-+-+-+-+-+-+-+-+-+-+-+-+-+-+-+-+-+-+-+-+-+

|             Extended highest sequence number received         |

+-+-+-+-+-+-+-+-+-+-+-+-+-+-+-+-+-+-+-+-+-+-+-+-+-+-+-+-+-+-+-+-+

|                     Inter-arrival jitter                      |

+-+-+-+-+-+-+-+-+-+-+-+-+-+-+-+-+-+-+-+-+-+-+-+-+-+-+-+-+-+-+-+-+

|                        Last SR (LSR)                          |

+-+-+-+-+-+-+-+-+-+-+-+-+-+-+-+-+-+-+-+-+-+-+-+-+-+-+-+-+-+-+-+-+

|                  Delay since last SR (DLSR)                   |

+=+=+=+=+=+=+=+=+=+=+=+=+=+=+=+=+=+=+=+=+=+=+=+=+=+=+=+=+=+=+=+=+

|                 SSRC_2 (SSRC of second source)                |  Report
```

Figure 5.5   Real time control protocol.

RTCP reports are designed to be sent periodically, with a frequency inversely proportional to the number of members. This can be set to constrain the bandwidth consumed by RTCP to be a known fixed fraction of the total capacity required for a many-to-many session. For multimedia conferencing this is an excellent solution for many applications requirements for such data. However, there are three circumstances where this approach creates a problem: firstly, when a session starts, the members do not know the number of other members – initial membership for a scheduled session could rise sharply, leading to a flood of initial packets; secondly, this effect can also happen for 'bye' messages; finally, for sessions where there is some form of floor control, or few senders compared with recipients, the fact that the RTCP reports are multicast means that they arrive at all participants – this may still represent a non-trivial fraction of the capacity to a given participant – in some cases, the state for large membership may impact on memory for small multicast devices (Internet telephones).

5.8 SYNCHRONISATION

First, some definitions:

1 *Intra-stream synchronisation*: Inside a stream, need to know where in the 'time structure' a bit goes.

2 *Inter-stream synchronisation*: For example, we are watching two people and want to see their reactions to what they see of a third.

3 *Inter-media synchronisation*: This is just lip synchronisation.

5.8.1 Intra-stream synchronisation

Intra-stream synchronisation is a base part of the H.261 and MPEG coding systems. H.221 and MPEG systems specify not only an encapsulation of multiple streams, but also how to carry timing information in the stream. In the Internet, the RTP media-specific timestamp provides a general-purpose way of carrying out the same function.

5.8.2 Inter-stream synchronisation

The easiest way of synchronising between streams at different sites is based on providing a globally synchronised clock. There are two ways this might be done:

1 Have the network provide a clock. This is used in H.261/ISDN-based systems. A single clock is propagated around a set of codecs and MCUs.

2 Have a clock synchronisation protocol, such as NTP (the network time protocol) or DTS (digital time service). This operates between all the computers in a data network and continually exchanges messages between the computers to monitor clock offsets network delays.

Alternatively, the media streams between sites could carry clock offset information, and the media timestamps with arrival times could be used to measure network delays, the clocks adjusted accordingly and then used to insert a baseline delay into the adaptive play-out algorithms so that the different streams are all synchronised.

5.8.3 Inter-media synchronisation

Options include having a global clock provided from the network or using clock synchronisation between computers. Or we could simply carry a clock in all packets and use it for the clock synchronisation calculation in the manner of NTP/DTS.

More generally, we could encapsulate the media in the same transmission stream. This is very effective but may entail computationally expensive labour at the recipient unravelling the streams. H.221 works like this but, since it is designed to introduce only minimal delay in doing so, is a bit-level framing protocol and is very hard to decode rapidly. Some recipients may not want or be capable of displaying all media (or have the capacity to receive all without disruption to some or other stream).

Alternatively, we could use much the same scheme as is used to synchronise different sources from different places. However, since media from the same source are timestamped by the same clock, the offset calculation is a lot simpler and can be done in the receiver only – basically, messages between an audio decoder and a video decoder can be exchanged inside the receiver and used to synchronise the play-out points.

This latter approach assumes that the media are timestamped at the 'real' source (i.e. at the point of sampling, not at the point of transmission) in order to be accurate.

5.9 RELIABLE MULTICAST TRANSPORT

Reliable multicast transport was dealt with at some length in section 3.7 of Chapter 3. We revisit and expand upon the subject here.

5.9.1 Congestion avoidance for reliable multicast applications

One of the big research areas not quite complete in this topic is how to achieve flow and congestion control (or avoidance) for reliable multicast applications.

There are a number of options when confronted with a congested link or receiver, and sending to a group; it depends on the nature of the application which is the best option. The options can be seen as spanning a spectrum, from sending at the slowest rate, sending at the average or median, and sending at the fastest.

Where we choose in this spectrum to run our algorithm depends on the nature of error recovery, the timeframe of the session, and the congestion. For example, a reliable multicast protocol being used to pre-fetch data for Web caches is a performance enhancement only to normal Web access, so it can run at the average rate and simply leave behind receivers that are too slow (and can choose to leave the receiver group if they cannot keep up). In fact, such an application could be pretty tolerant of the group changing throughout a session. On the other hand, distributing a set of slides to a distributed class might require one to run at the minimum rate to be fair to the students.

The global congestion picture is not at all clear, either, for reliable multicast (or unreliable for that matter). For example, TCP's classic congestion control algorithm (Jacobson, 1988) achieves a level of fairness for relatively long-lived unicast congestion, and even manages to allow the network to run at high utilisation. For a set of multicast 'connections', it is not at all clear that the same scheme will be stable enough, since there are multiple senders and recipients, some sharing links – there may be multiplier effects that mean that an even more cautions back-off is needed than TCP's.

5.9.2   Reliable multicast framework

One of the authors [MJH] has proposed a framework within which we can consider reliable multicast protocol work. In this, he describes the categories of parameters of the system:

1   Number of sources: 1-to-n, n-to-m, or other.
2   Transmitter start time: Is there one? Is there one for each receiver marked at join time?
3   Real timeness: What are the latency constraints on delivery of data from source to one, any or all receivers?
4   Consistency.

He lists as non-factors both congestion control and ordering, since both can be done orthogonally to the above categorisation. He then groups applications into five main areas:

1   Bulk transfer (VR database, Usenet News, etc.):
    (a) one-to-many
    (b) relaxed real time
    (c) synchronised start time
    (d) file (object) level consistency
2   Live data feeds (stock exchange, etc.):
    (a) one source
    (b) no start time
    (c) quasi real time
    (d) may need synchronised consistency
3   Resilient (streamed server data, like RTSP from video/audio from Web site):
    (a) one data source
    (b) no start time
    (c) stream consumed in near real time
    (d) non-consistency

4   Shared applications (wb, nte, etc.):

(a) distributed data set

(b) all sites fold most

(c) relaxed consistency

(d) many sources of changed

5   Hybrid – some applications (in general, the distributed interactive simulation systems) may be a hybrid of all of the above.

This is discussed further in Chapter 8 where we look at some applications that require specific reliable multicast semantics.

5.10   SUMMARY

In this chapter we have looked at transport (end-to-end) protocols. To some extent, the term is meaningless for multimedia, and especially for multiple participant multimedia systems, in the normal protocol layering sense. The 'ends' of a flow in a multimedia service are the sampling devices, and so the protocol system must reach right into the depths of the application at source and sink. Ideally, it must be possible to fill in (and extract) fields from the transport protocol header, from control status registers in media devices, if we wish to minimise delays and provide the best possible stream synchronisation.

For some supporting applications, such as whiteboards, some slightly more conventional protocol is required for reliability, yet we can see that the notion of reliability is a slippery one when it comes to group and human communication.

Note

1 There are exceptional circumstances where automatic repeat request protocols may be useful for multimedia, for instance on LANs where the delay incurred may be tolerable. However, these are usually networks that have relatively low error rates, and FEC may be more acceptable here too. The main specialist area where ARQ might really be needed is wireless LANs.

CHAPTER SIX

Session Directories, Advertisement and Invitation Protocols

6.1 INTRODUCTION

In this chapter we look at how multimedia sessions are set up. In principle, no formal session set-up mechanisms are needed for multicast communication – senders send to a group address, receivers subscribe to the same address, and communication ensues. In practice, we normally need a means for users that wish to communicate to discover which multicast address to use, to discover which protocols and codecs to transmit and receive with, and simply to discover that a session is going to take place at all. Sometimes email has served these purposes, but typically we require more integrated mechanisms that are designed specifically with session initiation in mind and which hide most of the details from the users.

There are several complementary mechanisms for initiating sessions, depending on the purpose of the session, but they can be broadly divided into invitation and announcement mechanisms. A traditional example of an invitation mechanism would be making a telephone call, which is in essence an *invitation* to participate in a private session. A traditional example of an announcement mechanism is the television guide in a newspaper, which *announces* the time and channel that each programme is broadcast. In the Internet, in addition to these two extremes, there are also sessions that fall in the middle, such as an invitation to listen to a public session, and announcements of private sessions to restricted groups.

6.2 ROADMAP OF THE PROTOCOLS

There are two families of protocol for setting up multimedia sessions: the IETF family of protocols, and the ITU family of protocols. There is some overlap between these two families, and some reuse of IETF protocols in the ITU family. The reason for the overlap is that the different standards groups started work from different points, and slowly expanded their area of applicability so that now there are two ways to do some things. In the long run, the market will no doubt decide which protocol is chosen for a particular task, but for now the picture is a little confusing.

In the IETF arena, work started in the area of loosely coupled large-scale multicast multimedia conferences. In the ITU arena, work started with ISDN-based circuit switched video conferencing, and was expanded to extend ISDN conferencing over packet switched LANs within companies.

At the time, wide-area Internet telephony seemed a long way off because, while multicast offered great advantages for large conferences, the Internet was a poor environment to provide high-quality calls that compete with the traditional telephone system.

In practice, it seems that the latent demand for convergence of data and telephony networks was larger than either group foresaw, and rapidly both sets of protocols started to be applied to Internet telephony and small wide-area video conferences. Hence, although the protocols were not designed as competitors, that is the situation we find ourselves in today.

In this chapter we shall discuss the IETF family of protocols, including the session description protocol (SDP), the session announcement protocol (SAP) and the session initiation protocol (SIP). In Chapter 7 we will discuss the ITU's H.323 family of protocols. In some environments we envisage that hybrids will be widely used, for example using SIP to initiate an H.323 conference. However, at the time of writing it is not yet clear exactly what form such hybrids will take.

6.3 IETF PROTOCOLS FOR SETTING UP SESSIONS

Generally speaking there are two ways to set up a session, although hybrids of the two are possible: announce the session to all possible participants, or invite just those participants you wish to be in the session.

To announce a session to all possible participants, the session announcement protocol is used. This sends out announcement information to anyone who is listening to the right multicast group, giving them information about the session.

To invite someone into a session, the session initiation protocol is used. This sends an invitation to participate in a session to a specific user.

Both of these protocols carry the description of the session in a precise format called the session description protocol. This is not really a protocol, but a well defined format for describing which media are in a session, information about the protocols and formats that the session will use, and enough information to decide whether or not to participate in the session.

6.4 SESSION DESCRIPTION PROTOCOL (SDP)

SDP   IETF proposed standard (RFC 2327)

A session description expressed in SDP is a short, structured, textual description of the name and purpose of the session, and the media, protocols, codec formats, timing and transport information that are required to decide whether a session is likely to be of interest and to know how to start media tools to participate in the session.

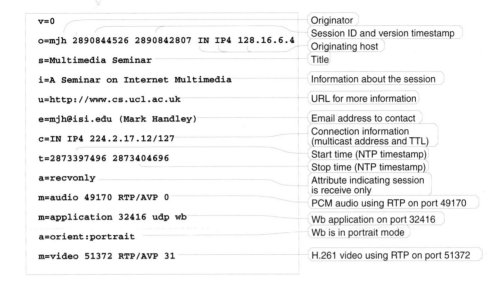

Figure 6.1   Annotated SDP session description.

SDP is purely a format for session description – it does not incorporate a transport protocol, and is intended to use different transport protocols as appropriate, including the session announcement protocol (see section 6.5), session initiation protocol (section 6.6), real time streaming protocol (see Chapter 9), electronic mail using the MIME extensions, and the hypertext transfer protocol (HTTP).

Although SDP is not intended to be read by humans, it is relatively easily understood. An example session description is shown in Figure 6.1.

Even without the annotation, it would be easy to guess that this session is entitled Multimedia Seminar, that it will use audio, video and an application called wb, and that someone called Mark Handley is responsible for the session.

However, this SDP also indicates the precise timing of the session (the 't=' line gives start and stop times), that the session is multicast to group 224.2.17.12 with a TTL of 127, the audio is 8 kHz μ-law carried by RTP to UDP port 49170, the video is H.261 encoded, also over RTP but to port 51372, and the whiteboard program should be started up in portrait mode using port 32416.

Thus SDP includes the *session name* and a description of its *purpose*, the *times* the session is active, the *media* constituting the session, and information to receive those media (addresses, ports, formats and so on).

As resources necessary to participate in a session may be limited, some additional information may also be desirable, including information about the bandwidth to be used by the conference and contact information for the person responsible for the session.

In general, SDP must convey sufficient information to be able to join a session (with the possible exception of encryption keys) and to announce the resources to be used to non-participants that may need to know.

Timing information

Sessions may be either bounded or unbounded in time. Whether or not they are bounded, they may be active only at specific times.

SDP can convey an arbitrary list of start and stop times bounding the session. For each bound, repeat times such as 'every Wednesday at 10am for one hour' can be specified.

This timing information is globally consistent, irrespective of local time zone or daylight saving time because it is given in UTC. Modifiers can be specified to uniquely apply offsets if the session crosses a change to or from daylight saving time.

Media descriptions

A session description is composed of general information that applies to the whole session (such as the timing) followed by sections that are specific to each medium. Thus in the description in Figure 6.1, the 'a=orient:portrait' line applies to the 'application/wb' medium, whereas the 'a=recvonly' applies to the whole session.

For each medium, SDP includes the type of media (video, audio, etc.), the transport protocol (RTP/UDP/IP, H.320, etc.), the format of the media (H.261 video, MPEG video, etc.), and media- or codec-specific attributes.

For an IP multicast session, the multicast address for that medium and the transport port are also conveyed. This address and port are the destination address and destination port of the multicast stream, whether being sent, received, or both.

For an IP unicast session, the remote address for the media stream and the transport port for the contact address are given. This makes sense in the context of an invitation such as SIP, where the person making the call gives information about where the person being called should send his audio and video streams. The response to the invitation would then give similar information about where the caller should send her audio and video streams.

6.4.1 SDP syntax

An SDP session description consists of a number of lines of text of the form:

< type >=< value >

<type> is always exactly one character and is case-significant; *<value>* is a structured text string whose format depends on *<type>*. In general, *<value>* is either a number of fields delimited by a single-space character or a free-format string.

A session description consists of a session-level description (details that apply to the whole session and all media streams) and optionally several media-level descriptions (details that apply only to a single media stream). The session-level part starts with a *v=* line and continues to the first media-level section. The media description starts with an *m=* line and continues to the next media description or to the end of the whole session description. In general, session-level values are the default for all media unless overridden by an equivalent media-level value.

The individual fields have the following meanings, and must be in this order, with '*' indicating an optional field:

v=   Protocol version
o=   The owner/creator and session identifier
s=   Session name
i=*   Session information
u=*   URI of description
e=*   Email address
p=*   Phone number
c=*   Connection information
b=*   Bandwidth information

One or more time descriptions

z=*   Time zone adjustments
k=*   Encryption key
a=*   *Zero or more* session attributes

Zero or more media descriptions

Each time description consists of a t= field, optionally followed by one or more r= fields.

t=   Time the session is active
r=*   *Zero or more* repeat times

Each media description consists of a m field, with other optional fields providing additional information:

m=   Media name and transport address
i=*   Media title
c=*   Connection information
b=*   Bandwidth information
k=*   Encryption key
a=*   *Zero or more* media attributes

   The connection (c=) and attribute (a=) information in the session-level section applies to all the media of that session unless overridden by connection information or an attribute of the same name in the media description. For instance, in Figure 6.1, all the media inherited the multicast address 224.2.17.12.
   The main way to extend SDP, other than by registering new codecs through the MIME registry, is by using attributes. Adding new SDP fields to the list above is not possible without revising the SDP protocol specification.

6.4.2   SDP: summary

SDP originated for announcing multicast sessions, and it serves that task well. It was not originally intended to deal with unicast sessions, but it works well enough in the context of SIP and RTSP. It was certainly never intended to be a content *negotiation* mechanism, because it lacks any clean way to group different options together into capability sets. Although it can serve this role, when it does so the limitations of its original design purpose start to show.

SDP is in widespread use in SAP, SIP, H.332, and RTSP, and has even been proposed for use in the context of advanced television.

6.5 SESSION ANNOUNCEMENT PROTOCOL (SAP)

SAP   IETF experimental standard

The session announcement protocol (SAP) must be one of the simplest protocols around. To announce a multicast session, the session creator merely multicasts packets periodically to a well known multicast group carrying an SDP description of the session that is going to take place. People that wish to know which sessions are going to be active simply listen to the same well known multicast group, and receive those announcement packets. The protocol gets a little more complex when we take security and caching into account, but basically that is it.

The SAP packet format (for IPv4) is shown in Figure 6.2. The *message type* (MT) field indicates whether this packet announces a session or deletes an announcement. One bit (E) indicates whether or not the payload is encrypted, and one bit (C) indicates whether or not the payload is compressed. The combination of 'Message ID hash' and 'Original source' is supposed to provide a unique announcement ID that can be used to identify this particular version of this particular session. This is useful for caching or for ignoring packets that we previously failed to decrypt, but this announcement ID is not guaranteed to be unique. Care must also be taken to check the packet length and, periodically, to check the packet contents themselves.

SAP announcements can be authenticated by including a digital signature of the payload in the optional *authentication header*. Both PGP and PKCS#7-based digital signatures are supported in the SAP protocol, although currently not many announcements are authenticated. As multicast-based sessions become more popular and people attempt to subvert them, this will, no doubt, change.

SAP announcements can also be encrypted. However, this does not mean that the standard way to have small, private wide-area conferences will be to announce them with encrypted SAP – the session initiation protocol is a more appropriate mechanism for such conferences. The main uses for encrypted SAP announcements would

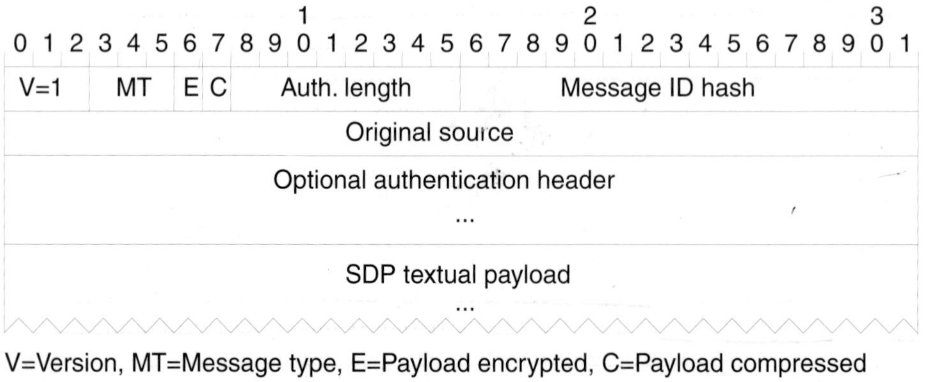

```
            1                   2                   3
 0 1 2 3 4 5 6 7 8 9 0 1 2 3 4 5 6 7 8 9 0 1 2 3 4 5 6 7 8 9 0 1
+-------+-------+---+-------------------+---------------------------+
| V=1   | MT    |E C| Auth. length      | Message ID hash           |
+-------+-------+---+-------------------+---------------------------+
|                       Original source                            |
+------------------------------------------------------------------+
|                  Optional authentication header                  |
|                              ...                                 |
+------------------------------------------------------------------+
|                      SDP textual payload                         |
|                              ...                                 |
~~~~~~~~~~~~~~~~~~~~~~~~~~~~~~~~~~~~~~~~~~~~~~~~~~~~~~~~~~~~~~~~~~~~~~
```

V=Version, MT=Message type, E=Payload encrypted, C=Payload compressed

Figure 6.2   Session announcement packets.

appear to be in intranet environments where the SAP announcements would bother few additional people, or for very large sessions where members are charged to participate. In the latter case, it would probably be a good idea to provide an additional level of access control beyond SAP encryption because it is easy for one misbehaving participant to leak an SAP key to other potential participant unless the keys are embedded in hardware, as they are with satellite television smart cards.

The announcement rate for SAP is quite low, with typically several minutes between repeated announcements of the same session. Thus a user starting an SAP receiver will have to wait a few minutes before seeing all the sessions. This is normally solved by caching: either by running an SAP receiver in the background all the time to keep the cache up to date, or by going to a local SAP proxy on start-up and requesting a cache download.

It should be clear that although SAP will scale to any number of receivers, it will not scale to huge numbers of sessions. It is currently an IETF experimental standard, which reflects this belief that we will eventually need to replace it with something different. In the meantime though, it is a great way to bootstrap the use of IP multicast, and with appropriate caching, SAP will be acceptable with up to a few thousand sessions advertised.

SAP should be used for sessions of some public interest where the participants are not known in advance. If you know whom you want in your session, a better mechanism is to invite them explicitly using SIP.

6.6 SECTION INITIATION PROTOCOL (SIP)

SIP   IETF proposed standard

In the near future, if you make a telephone call, it is quite likely that the session initiation protocol will be what finds the person you are trying to reach and causes their telephone to ring. SIP is all about calling people and services.

The most important way that SIP differs from making an existing telephone call (apart from being an IP-based protocol) is that you may not be dialing a number at all. Although SIP can call traditional telephone numbers, SIP's native concept of an address is an SIP URL, which looks very like an email address.

When you email joe@gadgets.com, as a user you have no real idea which computer at gadgets.com your email will eventually reach, or indeed, if Joe is currently contracting at another company, your message may even be forwarded there. All you wanted to do was to send a message to Joe.

The SIP authors believe that making a telephone or multimedia call should be similar: you want to call Joe, but you do not care exactly which 'phone' Joe uses to answer your call. SIP solves this problem by combining user location with the request to set up the call. It might seem that these should be separate, but this is not the case – the routing the call takes may depend on who is trying to make the call. If Joe's sister calls him while he is out at lunch, he might want the call to be routed to his cellphone, but if his boss makes the same call, the call gets routed to his voice-mail. For privacy reasons, performing user location without actually making the complete call is simply unacceptable to many people.

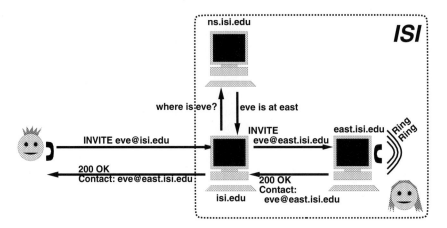

Figure 6.3   SIP request being relayed.

So how does SIP do this? SIP makes extensive use of proxy servers, each of which looks at the call request, looks up whatever local information it has about the person being called (i.e. the *callee*), performs any security checks that it has been asked by the callee or her organisation to make, and then routes the call onward.

When I call jane@euphoric-state.edu, my computer (or telephone exchange) looks up euphoric-state.edu in the domain name system (DNS) and looks for an SIP service record giving the address of the SIP server (in this case sip.euphoric-state.edu) for Euphoric State University. It then sends the SIP request to that machine. At sip.euphoric-state.edu, the server consults a database and discovers that Jane is a staff member in the computer science department, and that the SIP server for CS is sipgw.cs.esu.edu. It then sends the SIP request on to sipgw.cs.esu.edu, which again consults a database. This new database happens to be built dynamically by SIP clients registering when people log on. It turns out that Jane is a professor, and computer science professors never adopt new technology early so her workstation is not capable of multimedia conferencing. Instead, sipgw.cs.esu.edu routes the call to her regular telephone and it acts as a gateway into the department PBX.

The example above uses proxies that *relay* the SIP call. This is illustrated in Figure 6.3. Relaying is often performed when the gateway or firewall to a site wishes to hide any search that goes on internally from the caller's machine.

An alternative to relaying is *redirection*, which is illustrated in Figure 6.4. Redirection makes the caller's machine do any additional work, so it makes life easier for the proxy server. This might be appropriate when the callee has moved outside of the local network of the proxy.

If you do know the machine the callee is using, you can also send the request there directly without going through any proxies, but some sites may insert a proxy in the path anyway because the proxy is on their firewall machine.

Figure 6.5 shows a complete SIP call, with the arrows indicating SIP requests and responses passing backward and forward. In this case the SIP Invite request for eve@isi.edu is sent to isi.edu, but is then redirected to eve@east.isi.edu. A new Invite request is then made, which succeeds in finding Eve and causes her telephone to ring, which is reported back to the caller. When Eve picks up the

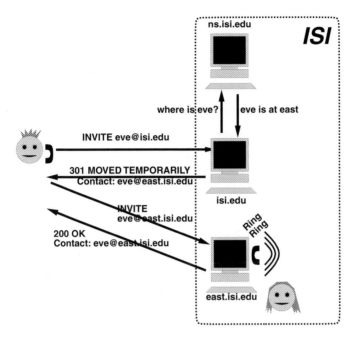

Figure 6.4 SIP request being redirected.

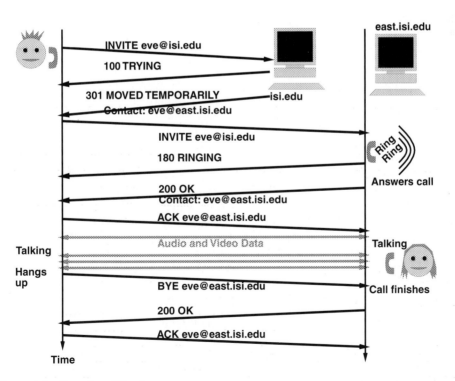

Figure 6.5 Complete SIP call.

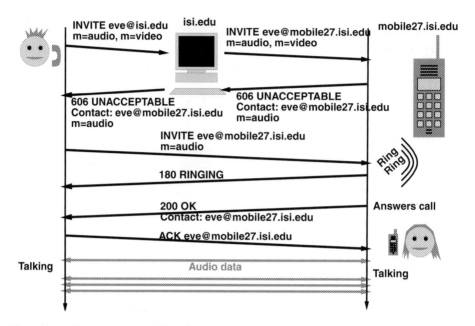

Figure 6.6 SIP 'negotiation' of media parameters.

telephone, the request is completed with a 200 OK response, which is in turn acknowledged, and a voice call is set up. Multimedia information is now exchanged using RTP for as long as they continue to chat. After they have finished their conversation, the caller hangs up, and this causes a SIP Bye request to be sent, which proceeds to close down the call.

SIP can set up many types of call, not just telephone calls, because it was designed originally for setting up multimedia conferences. However, the world can be a very heterogeneous place, and the person making a call may not be able to predict what equipment is available at the other end to receive the call. For example, I may make a videophone call to you, and although you may have an equivalent videophone on your desk, it happens that you are out of the office when I call. Instead my call is redirected to your cellphone, which unfortunately does not yet support video conferencing, but it could perfectly well support an audio call.

This is illustrated in Figure 6.6. The original call attempt requests an audio/video call, and is relayed to mobile27.isi.edu. Mobile27 is a cellphone, and so it rejects the call with a 606 Unacceptable response code indicating that an audio-only call is possible. A new call attempt is made suggesting an audio call, and then everyone is happy.

6.6.1 SIP protocol details

SIP is a text-based protocol with syntax much like the hypertext transfer protocol (HTTP) and real time streaming protocol (RTSP). An SIP Invite request looks something like Figure 6.7.

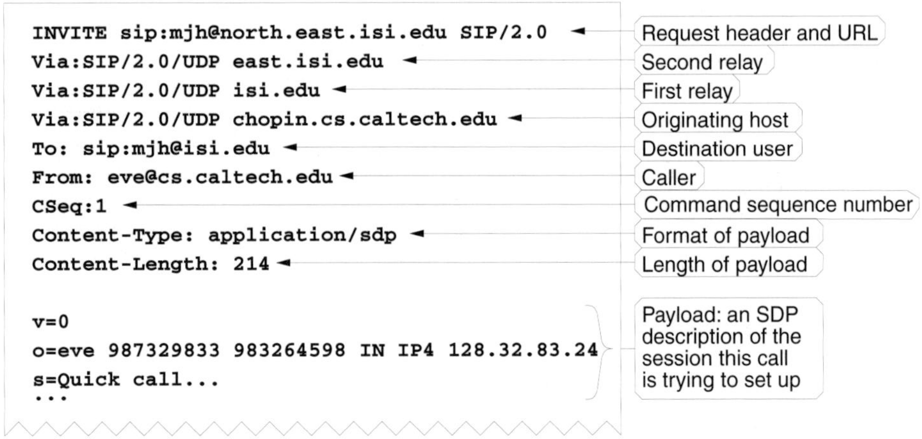

```
INVITE sip:mjh@north.east.isi.edu SIP/2.0  ◄        Request header and URL
Via:SIP/2.0/UDP east.isi.edu  ◄                     Second relay
Via:SIP/2.0/UDP isi.edu ◄                           First relay
Via:SIP/2.0/UDP chopin.cs.caltech.edu ◄            Originating host
To: sip:mjh@isi.edu ◄                               Destination user
From: eve@cs.caltech.edu ◄                          Caller
CSeq:1 ◄                                            Command sequence number
Content-Type: application/sdp ◄                     Format of payload
Content-Length: 214 ◄                               Length of payload


v=0                                                 Payload: an SDP
o=eve 987329833 983264598 IN IP4 128.32.83.24       description of the
s=Quick call...                                     session this call
...                                                 is trying to set up
```

Figure 6.7   SIP 'invite' request.

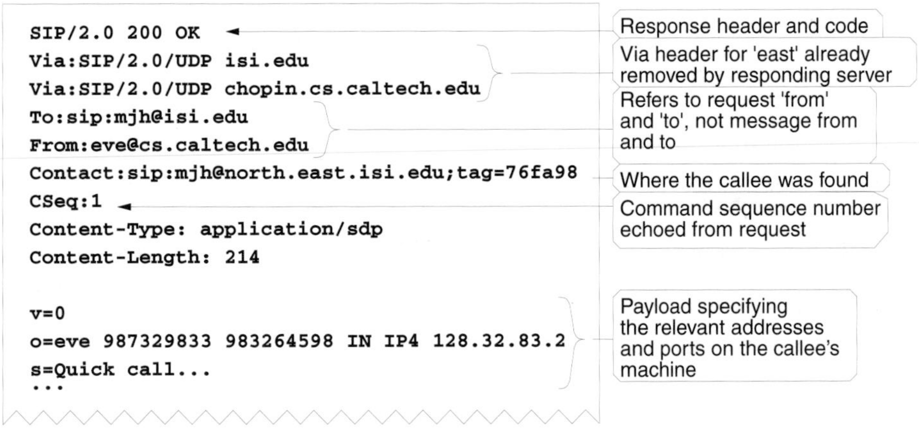

```
SIP/2.0 200 OK  ◄                                   Response header and code
Via:SIP/2.0/UDP isi.edu                             Via header for 'east' already
Via:SIP/2.0/UDP chopin.cs.caltech.edu               removed by responding server
To:sip:mjh@isi.edu                                  Refers to request 'from'
From:eve@cs.caltech.edu                             and 'to', not message from
                                                    and to
Contact:sip:mjh@north.east.isi.edu;tag=76fa98       Where the callee was found
CSeq:1 ◄                                            Command sequence number
Content-Type: application/sdp                       echoed from request
Content-Length: 214


v=0                                                 Payload specifying
o=eve 987329833 983264598 IN IP4 128.32.83.2        the relevant addresses
s=Quick call...                                     and ports on the callee's
...                                                 machine
```

Figure 6.8   SIP message response.

Typically, the payload is an SDP description of the session that the caller wishes to set up. The via fields indicate the path taken by the request through proxies so far, with the first via field indicating the most recent proxy traversed and the last one indicating the caller's host. In this case Eve sent the message from chopin.cs.caltech.edu, it has traversed isi.edu and east.isi.edu, and is currently being sent to north.east.isi.edu as indicated in the request URL.

A response to this message indicating that 'mjh' does want to talk might look like Figure 6.8.

The response code 200 indicates success (many other response codes are possible). When north.east.isi.edu sent this response, it removed the first via field (east.isi.edu) and then sent the response to east. In this way the response retraces the path through a chain of proxies that the request took.

SIP supports several request *methods* as shown in Table 6.1. The use of 'invite', 'bye', 'ack' and 'register' methods is shown in Figures 6.3 to 6.6.

Table 6.1   Request methods supported by SIP.

Request method	Purpose
Invite	Invite the callee into a session
Options	Discover the capabilities of the receiver
Bye	Terminate a call or call request
Cancel	Terminate incomplete call requests
Ack	Acknowledge a successful response
Register	Register the current location of a user

Table 6.2   SIP response code categories.

Response class	Meaning	Example
1XX	Information about call status	180 Ringing
2XX	Success	200 OK
3XX	Redirection to another server	301 Moved temporarily
4XX	Client did something wrong	401 Unauthorised
5XX	Server did something wrong	500 Internal server error
6XX	Global failure (do not resend same request)	606 Unacceptable

In response to a request, a server sends an SIP response which gives a response code indicating how the request was processed. Response codes are divided into six categories depending on the general form of behaviour expected. These categories are shown in Table 6.2.

The normal progress of an SIP call involves sending an Invite request, getting a 180 Ringing response, followed by a 200 OK response when the callee answers, then sending an Ack request to confirm the connected call. After either party hangs up, a Bye request is sent, which elicits a 200 OK response, which in turn causes a final Ack request to be sent. This whole process in illustrated in Figure 6.5.

The Cancel method is used when a call is made to more than one destination at the same time. For example, a proxy server may respond indicating that someone might be at one of the server locations. My client can either call these one-by-one, or call all of them simultaneously. If doing the latter, then when the callee answers at one of these locations, my client sends a Cancel request to all the other locations to stop the telephone (or whatever it is) ringing there.

6.6.2   SIP reliability

SIP can run over both TCP and UDP. Clearly, UDP is an unreliable protocol, and so in this case SIP must provide its own reliability, which it does by retransmission. So why run SIP over UDP when TCP provides reliability for free?

In truth, this reliability is not 'for free'. When you use TCP, you use a general-purpose reliable transport protocol, and you get TCP's concept of what reasonable retransmission timeouts are. TCP is also totally reliable: once data are put into a TCP connection, they will eventually come out the other end unless the connection is terminated. Sometimes this is not what we want, because old data have been superseded by new data, and if the old data have not got there yet, we no longer want them to be delivered. In short, UDP allows the SIP applications to control the timing and reliability, and so it gives improved performance to this kind of signalling protocol.

In addition, when SIP uses UDP, a proxy server may be stateless – an SIP request can be relayed without leaving behind state in the proxy because any response the request later generates contains (in its *via* fields) all the information needed for the proxy to get these responses back to the caller's client application. This allows very large proxy servers to be built – if these servers used TCP, they would have to maintain TCP connection state for all calls, and this would make very large proxy servers a difficult proposition.

Why then support TCP at all? The primary reason is that many firewalls do not allow UDP traffic to pass whereas it is relatively simple to configure them to pass SIP traffic to an internal server which may then open a hole in the firewall for the relevant RTP traffic. Eventually, though, we expect firewalls to be SIP proxies, and we envisage that SIP over TCP will not be widely used.

6.6.3   SIP: in summary

SIP is a very flexible, lightweight protocol for making multimedia calls. We have talked mostly about telephone-style calls because they are the most familiar to most people, but SIP really comes into its own with user mobility and heterogeneous multimedia terminals.

It is not yet clear whether SIP will see widespread deployment, or whether the ITU's H.323 protocol, which performs a similar task but is more heavyweight and less flexible, ends up becoming the *de facto* standard. Hybrids of the two are also possible. Time and the market will decide.

6.7   SUMMARY

In this chapter we have looked at the protocols associated with *sessions* in the Mbone. These currently include session description and announcement/ advertisement, as well as invitation protocols. These can be seen in some senses as analogous with the telephony work on *call control* protocols, although they have some other functional elements and interact with call routing, multicast address assignment and possibly even with signalling (for example, RSVP) more directly than one would typically admit to in ITU protocol designs.

CHAPTER SEVEN

Conference Control

7.1 INTRODUCTION

In this chapter we look at two starkly contrasting approaches to multimedia conference control.

The ITU has devised a sophisticated system for controlling *tightly coupled* conferences based around its H.261 video codec systems and ISDN networks, incorporating the T.120 protocols, using multipoint control units (MCUs) and a multicast communication service. In its original design, the scheme depended on a centralised model of control, and on the reliable and constant bit rate nature of ISDN networks. More recently, it has evolved to include packet networks and a more loosely coupled and distributed approach to conference control that owes a lot to input from researchers working in the ITU and IETF working groups.

The IETF has evolved an altogether more *loosely coupled* approach, based around the use of IP multicast. This is used for local system control (for example, multicasting packets with a TTL of 0 to control a constellation of processes associated with the same session within a single system) through to wide area multicast use for session formation (the session directory and invitation protocols, the RTCP quality reports and so on) and conference control, for example using a system like CCCP to build various types of control application such as floor management. This is usually claimed to scale to large numbers of participants rather better than the MCU-based approaches.

At the end of the chapter we also take a look at interworking between the Internet and ISDN approaches.

7.2 ROADMAP

Controlling a multi-party session is a complex task, and there are various axes on which one can design a system to achieve this task:

1 *Distributed versus centralised*: The various control functions (membership, speaker, etc.) could be located at a given node, or they can be devolved to all participants.

2   *Tight versus loose*: The control functions may enforce exact behaviour (for example, sequence of speakers, or other constraint on concurrent actions), or may leave such decisions (partly or wholly) to human participants.

3   *Homogeneous versus heterogeneous*: A system may allow users to participate when they have limited or different functionality from each other, or may require a common minimum set of functionality for media and control of all participants, including data delivery mechanisms (for example, unicast versus multipoint, or multicast; reservations; floor control, and so on).

The rest of this chapter looks at the two main standards arena proposals in the area of conference control from these perspectives.

7.3 ITU MODEL H.320/T.GCC

This design is based around the starting point of person-to-person video telephony, across the POTS (plain old telephone system) or its digital successor, ISDN (integrated services digital network). The public network operators (PNOs, or telcos or PTTs), have a network already, and it is based on a circuit model. You place a call using a signalling protocol with several stages – call request, call indication, call proceeding, call complete and so on. Once the call has been made, the resources are in place for the duration of the call. You are guaranteed (through expensive engineering, and you pay) that your bits will get to the destination with constant rate and constant delay, plus or minus a few bit times in a million.

To achieve this, the provider has a complex arrangement of global clocks and an over-resourced backbone network. To match video traffic to such a service, the output from a video compression algorithm has to be padded out to a constant bit rate (i.e. it is constant rate, not constant quality). The assumption is that you have a special-purpose box that you plug cameras and microphones into (a codec) and it plugs into the telephone or ISDN line or leased line, and you conference with your equivalent at the far end of the call.

In such a system, we can ask: how is multisite conferencing achieved?

7.3.1 Multisite circuit-based conferencing – MCUs

In the absence of a shared multiplexed network, the design space for multisite conferencing is quite limited. There are two ways you could set up a multisite conference. Firstly, have multiple codecs at each site, and multiple circuits, one from each site to all the others. This would involve $n(n - 1)$ circuits in all, and n codecs at each site to decode the incoming video and audio. Alternatively, one could design and use a special-purpose multipoint control unit which mixes audio signals and chooses which video signal from which site is propagated to all the others.

With this latter approach, each site has a single codec, and makes a call to the MCU site. The MCU has a limit on the number of inbound calls that it can take, and in any case needs at least n circuits, one per site. Typically, MCUs operate four to six codecs/calls. To build a conference with more than this many sites, you have multiple MCUs, and there is a protocol between the MCUs so that one builds a

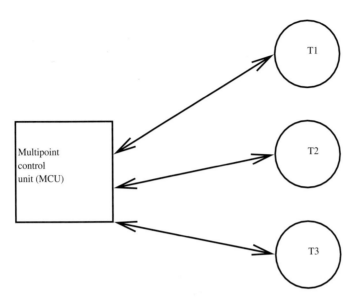

Figure 7.1   Multipoint control unit.

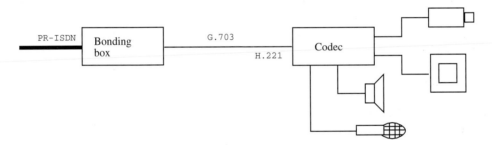

Figure 7.2   B-ISDN channel bonding.

hierarchy of them (a tree). In essence, this must reproduce some of the funcitonality of routing in the multicast distribution schemes of the Mbone. Currently, however, such systems are manually configured.

To select which site's video is seen at all the others, a floor control protocol is required, since the codec for circuit-based video can usually decode only one signal. Floor control protocols distribute information through a control channel to the conference sites concerning who is speaking, who wishes to speak and who can select who speaks next. They may be triggered by who is speaking, simply by automatic detection of audio activity above some threshold level for some minimum threshold period, or on a chairman approach, i.e. through human intervention. Thus ISDN-based conferencing systems must include a data channel between the terminals to carry this control protocol, and have a user interface to allow users to exercise this protocol. Figure 7.1 illustrates the use of an MCU to link three sites for a circuit-based conference.

Should greater than basic rate ISDN be needed, the channels can be combined via a device that synchronises a set of parallel ISDN channels together, as shown in Figure 7.2. This was once known as a 'bonding' box, and is neccessary because separate channels are not guaranteed to be routed over the same path through a circuit switched digital telephone network, so may incur different delays. Thus if data are striped over these different channels, it is necessary to calibrate the delay offset of the bits at the receiver end so that the original data order can be recovered.

7.3.2 Distributed multisite circuit-based conferencing

In the ITU standards, a conference refers to 'a group of geographically dispersed nodes that are joined together and that are capable of exchanging audiographic and audiovisual information across various communication networks'.

Participants taking part in a conference may have access to various types of media handling capabilities such as audio only (telephony), audio and data (audiographics), audio and video (audiovisual), and audio, video and data (multimedia).

The F, H and T series recommendations provide a framework for the interworking of audio, video and graphics terminals on a point-to-point basis through existing telecommunications networks. They also provide the capability for three or more terminals in the same conference to be interconnected by means of an MCU.

This recommendation provides a high-level framework for conference management and control of audiographics and audiovisual terminals, and MCUs. It co-exists with companion recommendations T.122 and T.125 (MCS) and T.123 (AVPS) to provide a mechanism for conference establishment and control. T.GCC also provides access to certain MCS functions and primitives, including tokens for conference conductorship. T.GCC, T.122, T.123, and T.125 form the minimum set of recommendations to develop a fully functional terminal or MCU.

Generic conference control (GCC) functional components are: conference establishment and termination, maintenance, the conference roster, managing the application roster, remote actuation, conference conductorship, bandwidth control and application registry services. The service definitions for the primitives associated with these functional components are given later, as are the corresponding protocol definitions. Figure 7.3 shows an example of how the GCC components fit together.

The top GCC server contains application registry information for the conference. Each node participating in a GCC conference consists of an MCS layer, a GCC layer, a node controller and may also include one or more client applications. The relationship between these components within a single node is illustrated in Figure 7.3.

The node controller is the controlling entity at a node, dealing with the aspects of a conference which apply to the entire node. The node controller interacts with the GCC but may not interact directly with the MCS. Client applications also interact with the GCC, and may or may not interact with the MCS directly. The services provided by the GCC to client applications are primarily to enable peer client applications to communicate directly, via the MCS.

Communication between client applications or between client applications and the node controller may take place, but is a local implementation matter not covered by this recommendation. The practical distinction between this node controller and the client applications is also a local matter not covered by this recommendation.

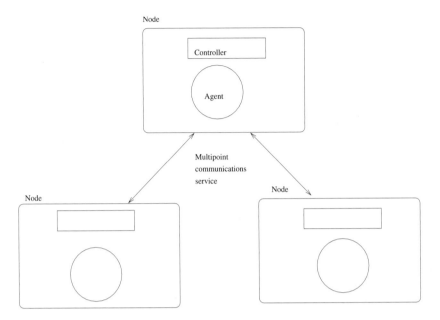

Figure 7.3   ITU-based generic conference control.

The generic conference control service includes the set of primitives as shown in Table 7.1.

7.3.3   Services provided by the MCS layer

The MCS protocol supports the services defined in ITU-T Recommendation T.122. Information is transferred to and from the MCS. Basically, it provides a reliable transport service along the lines of RMP (Montgomery, 1997) or other simulations of multiple simultaneous TCP (Jacobson, 1988) type connections from a single source to multiple sinks.

Regarding services assumed from the 'conventional unicast' transport layer, the standard states that 'the MCS protocol assumes the use of a subset of the connection-oriented transport service defined in CCITT Recommendation X.214'. (See Table 7.2.)

7.3.4   Distributed ITU multisite hybrid packet and circuit conferencing

The set of standards that go together to make up the full range of ITU conferencing control facilities is very complex. A basic list of what has to be implemented is listed in Table 7.3.

H.323 defines the overall structure of the ITU system for conferencing terminals including terminals, gateways (to non-packet nets or to QoS guaranteeing packet nets:), multipoint controllers, multipoint processors and multipoint control units.

Table 7.1 Conference control primitives.

Conference roster	Application roster	Remote actuation	Conference conductorship
GCC-Conference-Join	GCC-Application-Enrol	GCC-Action-List-Announce	GCC-Conductor-Assign
GCC-Conference-Query	GCC-Application-Attach	GCC-Action-List-Inquire	GCC-Conductor-Release
GCC-Conference-Create	GCC-Application-User-ID	GCC-Action-Actuate	GCC-Conductor-Please
GCC-Conference-Add	GCC-Application-Roster-Report		GCC-Conductor-Give
GCC-Conference-Invite	GCC-Application-Roster-Inquire		GCC-Conductor-Inquire
GCC-Conference-Lock			
GCC-Conference-Unlock			
GCC-Conference-Disconnect			
GCC-Conference-Terminate			
GCC-Conference-Eject-User			
GCC-Conference-Transfer			
GCC-Conference-Time-Remaining			
GCC-Conference-Time-Inquire			
GCC-Conference-Extend			
GCC-Conference-Ping			

Note: The Conference roster column also contains GCC-Conference-Announce-Presence and GCC-Conference-Roster-Inquire.

Table 7.2 Multicast communications service.

MCS-CONNECT-F-PROVIDER
MCS-DISCONNECT-PROVIDER
MCS-ATTACH-USER
MCS-DETACH-USER
MCS-CHANNEL-JOIN
MCS-CHANNEL-LEAVE
MCS-CHANNEL-CONVENE
MCS-CHANNEL-DISBAND
MCS-CHANNEL-EXPEL
MCS-SEND-DATA
MCS-TOKEN-GRAB
MCS-TOKEN-GIVE
MCS-TOKEN-PLEASE
MCS-TOKEN-RELEASE
MCS-TOKEN-TEST

Table 7.3 ITU conferencing standards.

Document	What it defines
H.221,222,223	Multiplexing video and audio
T.120	Telematics (e.g. whiteboard) transmission protocols
H.225	Media stream packetisation and synchronisation for non-guaranteed QoS LANs
H.245	Control protocol for multimedia communication
H.310	Overall broadband systems for audiovisual terminals
H.320	N-ISDN terminals
H.321	B-ISDN version of H.320
H.322	H.320 for LANs with QoS (new IEEE 802 standards)
H.323	H.320 for LANs without QoS (i.e. Internet)

It rests on a family of other protocols which do the actual work, i.e. it is a framework. Interoperability with H.324, H.322 (QoS LAN), H.320 (ISDN) and H.321 (B-ISDN) is via the gateways.

Multipoint controllers serve functions that are based on IGMP and other group management functions up to the H.232 application level. Multipoint processors serve functions of mixing, multiplexing and basically getting between unicast sources and multicast delivery. Multipoint control units may incorporate some or all these functions as well as some conference control functions which are also present in all H.323 terminals and gateways.

H.323 terminals would typically be TCP/IP hosts (microcomputers) with RTP/UDP stacks to carry H.261 (or H.263 or other coded video) and G.711 (or 722, 723, 728, 729) coded audio – in the ITU view, the T.120 stack is used for conferencing 'data' applications. To carry out tasks of assigning control and data flows to the right port/address (TSAP in ISO/ITU parlance), the H.225 protocol is used.

On ISDN, H.221 (or similar) is used to multiplex audio and video (and data) onto a virtual circuit. In a packet LAN, we may want separate recovery mechanisms and different levels of reliability for data and video/audio stream (and conference control) so H.221, with its rigid, TDM-like bit-level multiplexing is inappropriate. Instead, H.225 is provided. It makes use of underlying transport as much as possible, i.e. again, like H.323, of which it is part, it is mainly a framework. It makes use of RTP/UDP (and IGMP/IP multicast) as well as TCP. An important part of H.225 is registration, admissions and services (RAS). This serves some of the functions of DNS (as described in Chapter 1) and some of the functions of SAP/SDP/SIP (as described in Chapter 6). RAS messages are used to tell gatekeepers about H.323 terminals. RAS interacts, if needed, with Q.931 signalling protocols to set up calls. Once a call is set up, a terminal will have a TCP connection to proceed with H.245 messages to carry out next-level functions. For media, H.225 selects appropriate TSAP IDs (i.e. UDP ports and multicast addresses) to use.

So H.225 uses Q.931 first, i.e. call establishment and clearing via Alerting, Proceeding, Connect, Connect Acknowledge, Progress, Setup, Setup Acknowledge, and Disconnect, Release, Release Complete messages. Q.932 can be used to get more IN-like facilities, for example, Hold, Hold Acknowledge, Hold Reject, Retrieve, Retrieve Acknowledge, Retrieve Reject. On a packet LAN, clearly Q.931 and so on are not carried on a separate signalling channel (for example, on N-ISDN or B-ISDN there is an agreed circuit for signalling messages – the D channel in narrowband ISDN gives a free 14 kbps or so for this). On a packet LAN, messages must go on the LAN, and must be reliable, so TCP is used to a well known port. H.225 defines what the fields in the Q.931 messages (in the TCP data packets) carry, for example called and calling party addresses. Again, on the LAN, if an H.323 terminal is being called (and not an H.321 ISDN terminal the other side of a gateway for example) then there is no called address.

User-to-user data in the Q.931 messages (in the TCP data messages on IP on the LAN) can carry lots of information, for example, arbitrary 'keypad' data (can use a telephone-style interface).

More importantly, the user-to-user field is used to carry complex messages encoded in ASN.1 to carry higher-level (H.323, H.245) information. This set up carries protocol ID H.245 transport address, source address and information active MC (which is an end-point under control from an MC) conference ID, conference goal (create, join, invite, etc.), call type (point-to-point, multicast, bandwidth). Further messages that are conveyed, according to the H.225 specification, include RAS messages, again specified in ASN.1 (encoded in bit error rate, BER) and carried in the user-to-user part of Q.931 messages over the TCP connection that was set up for this.

RAS message types include: Gatekeeper Request, Confirm, Reject Registration; Request, Confirm, Reject Unregistration; Request, Confirm, Reject Admission Request; Confirm, Reject, Bandwidth, Disengage Location Information and so on. As can be seen, then, these are concerned mainly with support for connecting with gateways that provide interworking between packet LANs and conferencing systems the other side of the gateway. Once all this is done we can carry out some conferencing – this requires video and audio, and conference control. The latter in H.323 is the job of H.245.

H.245 uses other protocols too (for example, H.235 for security specifications). It is used to select between multiplexing layers (H.220, 222, 223 and 225) and to provide transport procedures – it provides analogous (for audiovisual, not data) services to T.120.

So, because of the possible misunderstandings amongst an arbitrary set of peers on a packet net, H.245 provides master/slave determination. It then provides capability exchange, i.e. what is each system able to send/receive (not only in qualitative terms but also in absolute and relative quantitative ones (for example, 'if I can receive three video of such and such a resolution, I can only mix two audio of such a coding').

In the IETF multicast toolset, this could be done on the LAN with the conference bus, which is described later in this chapter, or it could be done with client SAP advertisements or capabilities in svrloc or even partly DHCP.

H.245 provides logical channel selection (i.e. pick a port). Then it provides RTT estimation, channel maintenance, and then a set of commands and indications – these are really the core conference control facilities (media control facilities and so on), as well as audio/video modes (activity on/off messages, silence suppression on/off commands and so on).

Thus, finally, we descend to the end users' requirements, which include H.243 password and other access control, chair token control, terminal control messages, conference ID info, facilities for exchanging certificates, ability to make a terminal the broadcaster, send this source, request all identifiers, remote MC control and so forth.

7.3.5   Multicast Internet-based MCS

The ITU group defining these protocols has started to look at how the MCS might be implemented on top of a reliable multicast transport protocol with the Internet, instead of on top of ISDN. This is a very promising direction for scaling to larger H.320-style conferences.

At the same time, there is a definition for the use of RTP for dissemination of media from an MCU onto a LAN. The combination of these two approaches brings much closer together the ITU approach to that of the Mbone. There are several further stages before there is complete unification – largely in the area of supporting loosely coupled and anonymous sessions, and in supporting heterogeneity (varying receiver capabilities) in the ITU H.320 approach.

7.4   MMCC: A CENTRALISED INTERNET MODEL

It has been argued that the problem with the Internet model of multimedia conferencing is that it does not support simple telephone calls or secure closed, 'tightly managed' conferences. However, it is easy to add this functionality after one has built a scalable system such as the Mbone provides, rather than limiting the system in the first place. For example, the management of keys can provide a closed group very simply. If one is concerned about traffic analysis, then the use of secure management of IP group address usage would achieve the effect of limiting where multicast traffic propagated. Finally, a telephone-style signalling protocol can be provided easily to 'launch' the applications using the appropriate keys and addresses, simply by giving the users a nice GUI to a distributed calling protocol system.

Currently, the IETF working group on conference control is liaising with the T.120 standards work in the ITU and has made some statements about partial progress.

7.5 CCCP: DISTRIBUTED INTERNET MODEL

In this section we will discuss some of the lessons that we have garnered from previous work involving computer-based multimedia conferencing, and use these as a basis for developing an architecture for the next generation of conference control applications, suitable for conferencing over wide area networks. We show that a simple protocol acting over a conference-specific communications channel, named the conference control channel, or CCC, will perform all tasks within the scope of conference control.

The previous generation of conferencing tools, such as CAR, MMConf, etherphone and the Touring Machine (respectively, Kirstein *et al.*, 1993; Crowley, 1990; Schooler, 1993; Arango *et al.*, 1992a) were based on centralised architectures, where a central application on a central machine acted as the repository for all information relating to the conference. Although simple to understand and to implement, this model proved to have a number of disadvantages, the most important of which was the disregard for the failure modes arising from conferencing over the wide area.

An alternative approach to the centralised model is the loosely coupled model promoted by Jacobson and exemplified by the vat (Casner and Deering, 1992; Jacobson and McCanne, 1992) and wb (McCanne and Jacobson, 1995) applications. In the 'loose session model', the network is regarded as inherently unreliable. Our observations of the Mbone show that humans can cope with a degree of inconsistency that arises from partitioned networks and lost messages, as long as the distributed state tends to converge in time. This model makes fewer demands on the network and recognises explicitly the possibility of failure modes.

We have taken these and the other lessons we have derived from experience with conferencing tools, and derived two important aims that any conference control architecture should meet:

1   The conference architecture should be flexible enough so that any mode of operation of the conference can be used and any application can be brought into use. The architecture should impose the minimum constraints on how an application is designed and implemented.

2   The architecture should be scalable, so that 'reasonable' performance is achieved across conferences involving people in the same room, through to conferences spanning continents with different degrees of connectivity, and large numbers of participants. To support this aim, it is necessary explicitly to recognise the failure modes that can occur, and examine how they will affect the conference, and then attempt to design the architecture to minimise their impact.

We model a conference as composed of a (possibly unknown) number of people at geographically distributed sites, using a variety of applications. These applications can be at a single site and have no communication with other applications or instantiations of the same application across multiple sites. If an application shares information across remote sites, we distinguish between the cases when the participating processes are tightly coupled[1] – the application cannot run unless all processes are available and contactable – and when the participating processes are loosely coupled, in that the processes can run when some of the sites become unavailable. A tightly coupled application is considered to be a single instantiation spread over a number of sites, whilst loosely coupled and independent applications have a number of unique instantiations, although they may use the same application-specific information (such as which multicast address to use).

The tasks of conference control break down in the following way:

1 *Application control*: Applications as defined above need to be started with the correct initial state, and the knowledge of their existence must be propagated across all participating sites. Control over the starting and stopping can either be local or remote.

2 *Membership control*: Who is currently in the conference and has access to what applications.

3 *Floor management*: Who or what has control over the input to particular applications.

4 *Network management*: Requests to set up and tear down media connections between end-points (no matter whether they be analogue through a video switch, a request to set up an ATM virtual circuit, or using RSVP (Zhang *et al.*, 1993) over the Internet), and requests from the network to change bandwidth usage because of congestion.

5 *Meta-conference management*: How to initiate and finish conferences, how to advertise their availability, and how to invite people to join.

We maintain that the problem of meta-conference management is outside the bounds of the conference control architecture and should be addressed using tools such as session directory, traditional directory services or through external mechanisms such as email. The conference control system is intended (1) to maintain consistency of state amongst the participants as far as is practical and not to address the social issues of how to bring people together and (2) to co-ordinate initial information such as encryption keys.

We then take these tasks as the basis for defining a set of simple protocols that work over a communication channel. We define a simple class hierarchy, with an application type as the parent class and subclasses of network manager, member and floor manager, and define generic protocols that are used to talk among these classes and the application class, and an interapplication announcement protocol. We derive the necessary characteristics of the protocol messages as reliable/unreliable and confirmed/unconfirmed (where unconfirmed indicates whether responses saying 'I heard you' come back, rather than indications of reliability).

It is easily seen that both tightly and loosely coupled models of conferencing can be encompassed if the communication channel is secure.

We have abstracted a messaging channel, using a simple distributed interprocess communication system, providing confirmed/unconfirmed and reliable/unreliable semantics. The naming of sources and destinations is based upon application-level naming, allowing wildcarding of fields such as instantiations (thus allowing messages to be sent to all instantiations of a particular type of application).

Finally, we briefly describe the design of the high-level components of the messaging channel (named variously the CCC or the triple-C). Mapping of the application-level names to network-level entities is performed using a distributed naming service based upon multicast once again and drawing upon the extensive experience already gained in the distributed operating systems field in designing highly available name services.

7.5.1 Requirements

Multicast Internet conferencing

Since early 1992, a multicast virtual network has been constructed over the Internet. This multicast backbone or Mbone (Macedonia and Brutzman, 1994) has been used for a number of applications including multimedia (audio, video and shared workspace) conferencing. The applications involved include vat (LBL's visual audio tool), ivs (INRIA videoconferencing system (Bolot *et al.*, 1994)), nv (Xerox's network video tool (Frederick, 1994)) and wb (LBL's shared whiteboard) amongst others. These applications have a number of things in common:

1 They are all based on IP multicast.
2 They all report who is present in a conference by occasional multicasting of session information.
3 The different media are represented by separate applications.[2]
4 There is no conference control, other than each site deciding when and at what rate it sends.

These applications are designed so that conferencing will scale effectively to large numbers of conferees. At the time of writing, they have been used to provide audio, video and shared whiteboard to conferences with about 500 participants. Without multicast,[3] this is clearly not possible. It is also clear that, with unreliable networks these applications cannot achieve complete consistency between all participants, and so they do not attempt to do so – the conference control they support usually consists of:

1 Periodic (unreliable) multicast reports of receivers.
2 The ability to locally mute a sender if you do not wish to hear or see them. However, in some cases stopping the transmission at the sender is actually what is required.

Thus any form of conference control that is to work with these applications should at least provide these basic facilities, and should also have scaling properties that are *no worse than the media applications themselves.*

The domains that these applications have been applied to vary immensely. The same tools are used for small (say 20 participants), highly interactive conferences as for large (500 participants) dissemination of seminars, and the application developers are working towards being able to use these applications for 'broadcasts' that scale towards millions of receivers.

It should be clear that any proposed conference control scheme should not restrict the applicability of the applications it controls, and therefore should not impose any single conference control policy. For example, we would like to be able to use the same audio encoding engine (such as vat), irrespective of the size of the conference or the conference control scheme imposed. This leads us to the conclusion that

*the media applications (audio, video, whiteboard, etc.) should not provide any con-
ference control facilities themselves, but should provide the handles for external conference control and whatever policy is suitable for the conference in question.*

Computer-based multimedia conferencing requirements

Computer-based multimedia conferencing has the somewhat different requirements
from POTS- or ISDN-based video conferencing which have made use of custom
terminals. It is also a requirement that such systems interwork with ISDN- and
POTS-based conferencing systems. All told:

1　Multicast-based applications running on workstations/microcomputers where
possible.
2　Hardware codecs and the need to multiplex their output.
3　Sites connecting into conferences from ISDN.
4　Interconnecting all the above.

These requirements have dictated that we build a number of conference management and multiplexing centres to provide the necessary format conversion and
multiplexing to work among the multicast workstation-based domain and unicast
(whether IP or ISDN) hardware-based domain.

Traditionally, such a multiplexing centre would employ a centralised conference
control system. However, this is not scalable and we wish the users of such systems
to participate in large, multicast-based conferences. We also do not wish to change
the multicast media applications when they switch from an entirely multicast-based
conference to one using a central system for some participants.

It is inevitable that translators, multiplexors, format converters and so forth will
form some part of future conferences, and that large conferences will be primarily
multicast based.

Where current systems fail

The sort of conference control system we are addressing here cannot be the
following:

1　*Centralised*: This will not scale.
2　*Fixed policy*: This would restrict the applicability. The important point here is that
only the users can know what are the appropriate policies a meeting may need.
3　*Application based*: It is very likely that separate applications will be used for
different media for the foreseeable future. We need to be able to switch media
applications where appropriate. Basing the conference control in the applications
prevents our changing policy simply for all applications.
4　*Heterogeneous*: Most existing systems have been fairly homogeneous. An
increasing requirement is for different systems to interwork. There needs to be some
basis for this interworking, at both the media datastream level and at the
conference control level.

5 *Difficult to get right*: Writing distributed group applications that interwork and
   tolerate network failures is difficult to get right. Generally, applications writers
   either start from scratch, which means reimplementing stock algorithms, or base
   their applications on a scheme that promises to do everything but in practice turns
   out to be too inflexible.

7.5.2 Specific requirements

Modularity

Conference control mechanisms and conference control applications should be
separated. The mechanism to control applications (mute, unmute, change video
quality, start sending, stop sending, etc.) should not be tied to any one conference
control application in order to allow different conference control policies to be
chosen depending on the conference domain. This suggests that a modular approach
be taken with, for example, specific floor control modules being added when required
(or possibly choosing a conference manager tool from a selection of them according
to the conference).

A unified user interface

A general requirement of conferencing systems, at least for small conferences, is that
the participants need to know who is in the conference and who is active. Vat is a
significant improvement over telephone audio conferences, in part because
participants can see who is listening and who is speaking. Similarly, if the whiteboard
program wb is being used effectively, the participants can see who is drawing at any
time from the activity window. However, a participant in a conference using, say,
vat (audio), ivs (video) and wb (whiteboard) has three separate sets of session
information, and three places to look to see who is active.

   Clearly, any conference interface should provide a single set of session and
activity information. A useful feature of these applications is the ability to 'mute'
(or hide or whatever) the local play-out of a remote participant. Again, this should
be possible from a single interface. Thus the conference control scheme should provide local interapplication communication, allowing the display of session
information, and the selective muting of participants.

   Taking this to its logical conclusion, the applications should provide only
media-specific features (such as volume or brightness controls), and all the rest
of the conference control features should be provided through a conference control
application.

Flexible floor control policies

Conferences come in all shapes and sizes. For some, no floor control, with everyone
sending audio when they wish, and sending video continuously is fine. For others,
this is not satisfactory owing to insufficient available bandwidth or a number of

other reasons. It should be possible to provide floor control functionality, but the providers of audio, video and workspace applications should not specify which policy is to be used. Many different floor control policies can be envisaged. A few example scenarios are:

- *Explicit chaired conference*: A chairperson decides when someone can send audio and video. Some mechanism equivalent to hand-raising as a request to speak is needed. Granting the floor starts video transmission and enables the audio device. In essence, this is a schoolroom-type scenario requiring no expertise from end users.

- *Audio-triggered conferencing*: This has no chairperson and no explicit floor control. When someone wants to speak, they do so using 'push to talk'. Their video application automatically increases its data rate from, for example, 10 kbps to 256 kbps as they start to talk. Twenty seconds after they stop speaking it returns to 10 kbps.

- *Audio-triggered conferencing with a conference management and multiplexing centre*: In essence, CMMC (Kirstein *et al.*, 1993) is one or more points where multiple streams are multiplexed together for the benefit of people on unicast links, ISDN and hardware codecs. The CMMC can mix four streams for decoding by participants with hardware codecs. The four streams are those of the last four people to speak, with only the current speaker transmitting at a high data rate. Everyone else stops sending video automatically.

- *A background Mbone engineering conference that has been idle for three hours*: All the applications are iconised, as the participant is doing something else. Someone starts drawing on the whiteboard, and the audio application plays an audio icon to notify the participant.

Scaling from tightly coupled to loosely coupled conferences

CCCP originated in part as a result of experience gained from the centralised multimedia conference control system. The centralised system is intended for use over ISDN. As described earlier in this chapter, the functionality such systems provide can be summarised by listing the basic primitives:

- Create conference
- Join/leave conference
- List members of conference
- Include/exclude application in conference
- Take floor

In addition, there were a number of asynchronous notification events:

- Floor change
- Participant joining/leaving
- Application included/excluded

The application model was modelled around applications that could replicate either themselves or their display onto remote machines if they were given a list of addresses or displays, hence the include/exclude functionality. However, these are the basic primitives required to support a tightly coupled conference, although for some uses others may be added.

Any conference control system that claims to be fairly generic must be able to support these primitives with reasonable reliability. (Absolute consistency is not really a feasible option in a multiway conference.)

Loosely coupled conferences put fewer constraints on the protocols used, but must scale to much larger numbers, and must be very tolerant of loss and network segmentation.

Taking the modular approach described above, we would expect to change conference controllers when moving from one regime to another, but we do not wish to change the media applications too.[4]

7.5.3 Conference control channel (CCC)

To bind the conference constituents together, a common communication channel is required which offers facilities and services for the applications to send to each other. This is akin to the inter-process communication facilities offered by the operating system. The conference communication channel should offer the necessary primitives upon which heterogeneous applications can talk to each other.

The first cut would appear to be a messaging service which can support one-to-many communication with various levels of confirmation and reliability. We can then build the appropriate application protocols on top of this abstraction to allow the common functionality of conferences.

We need an abstraction to manage a loosely coupled distributed system, which can scale to as many parties as we want. In order to scale we need the underlying communication to use multicast. Many people have suggested that one way of thinking about multicast is as a multifrequency radio in which we tune into the channels in which we are interested. We extend this model to build an inter-process communications model, on which we can build specific conference management protocols. Thus we define an application control channel.

What do we actually want from the system?

1 We want to ask for services.

2 We want to send requests to specific entities, or groups of entities and receive responses from some subset of them, with notifications sent out to others.

CCCP originates in the observation that *in a reliable network*, conference control would behave like an ethernet or bus: addressed messages would be put on the bus, and the relevant applications will receive the message, and if necessary respond. In the Internet, this model maps directly onto IP multicast. This is illustrated in Figure 7.4. In fact, the IP multicast groups concept is extremely close to what is required. In CCCP, applications have a tuple as their address: (instantiation, application type, address). In actual fact, an application can have a number of tuples as its address, depending on its multiple functions. Examples of the use of this would be:

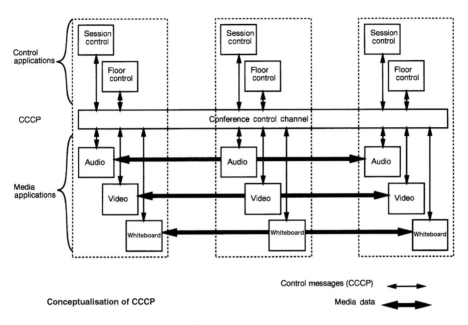

Figure 7.4 CCCP conceptual design.

```
Destination Tuple   Message
- - - - - - - - -   - - - -
(1, audio, localhost)   <start sending>
(*, activity_management, localhost) <receiving audio from host:> ADDRESS
(*, session_management, *)   <I am:> NAME
(*, session_management, *)   <I have media:> {application list}
(*, session_management, *)   <Participant list:> {participant list}
(*, floor_control, *)   <REQUEST FLOOR>
(*, floor_control, *)   <I HAVE FLOOR>
```

and so on. The actual messages carried depend on the application type, and thus the protocol is easily extended by adding new application types.

In keeping with the underlying multicast message reception paradigm, a CCC application needs to register its interest in messages before it will receive them. Where possible, a CCC system uses the underlying multicast delivery to optimise where messages are filtered.

7.5.4 CCC names

Our model of the CCC is a broadcast bus, where the receivers filter the messages according to what information and which protocols they need to receive and participate in. Using this model, we based our naming scheme upon the attributes of an application that could be used in deciding whether to receive a message. We thus build a name tuple from three parts:

`(instantiation, type, address)`

An application registers itself with its CCC library, specifying one or more tuples that it considers describe itself. Note that there is no conference identifier currently specified as part of the tuple, but this is liable to change, since a conference identifier may be useful in unifying conference management and conference meta-management, and considerably simplifies the design of applications which may be part of multiple conferences simultaneously. In the current prototype design, a control group address or control host address or address list is specified at start-up; meta-conferencing (i.e. allocation and discovery of conference addresses) is outside the scope of the CCC itself. The parts of the tuple are described below.

Address

In our model of a conference, applications are associated with a machine and possibly a user at a particular machine. Thus we use a representation of the user or the machine as a field in the tuple, to allow us to specify applications by location. The *address* field will normally be registered as one of the following:

- `hostname`
- `username@hostname`

When the application is associated with a user, such as a shared whiteboard, the `username@hostname` form is used, whereas applications which are not associated with a particular user, such as a video switch controller, register simply as `hostname`. For simplicity, we use the domain naming scheme in our current implementation, although this does not preclude other identifiable naming schemes. Note that the hostname is actually shorthand for `no-user@hostname`, so that when other applications wish to send a message to a destination group (a single application is a group of size 1), they can specify the *address* field as one of the following:

- `username@hostname`
- `hostname`
- `*@hostname` (note that the hostname is actually shorthand for `no-user@hostname`, so that this matches all applications on the given host)
- `*` (this is used to address applications regardless of location)

The CCC library is responsible for ensuring a suitable multicast group (or other means) is chosen so that all possible matching applications are potentially reachable (though depending on the reliability mode, it does not necessarily ensure the message gets to them all).

It should be noted that in any tuple containing a wildcard (*) in the address, specifying the instantiation (as described below) does not guarantee a unique receiver, and so normally the instantiation should be wildcarded too.

Type

The next attribute we use in naming applications is based on hierarchical typing of the application and of the management protocols. The type field is descriptive both of the protocol that is being used and of the state of the application within the protocol at a particular time. For example, a particular application such as vat may use a private protocol to communicate between instantiations of the application, so a vat type is defined, and only applications which believe they can understand the vat protocol and are interested in it would register themselves as being of type vat. An alternative way of using the type field is to embed the finite state machine corresponding to the protocol within the type field – thus a floor management protocol could use types `floor.management.holder` and `floor.management.requester` in a simple floor control protocol, that can cope with multiple requests at once. A final way of using the type field is to allow extensions to existing protocols in a transparent fashion, by simply extending the type field by using a version number. Some examples of these techniques can be found in section 7.5.7.

Some base types are needed to ensure that common applications can communicate with each other. As a first pass, the following types have been suggested:

- `audio.send`: The application is interested in messages about sending audio.
- `audio.recv`: The application is interested in messages about receiving audio.
- `video.send`: The application is interested in messages about sending video.
- `video.recv`: The application is interested in messages about receiving video.
- `workspace`: The application is a shared workspace application, such as a whiteboard.
- `session.remote`: The application is interested in knowing the existence of remote applications (exactly which ones depends on the conference and the session manager).
- `session.local`: The application is interested in knowing of the existence of local applications.
- `media-ctrl`: The application is interested in being informed of any change in conference media state (such as unmuting of a microphone).
- `floor.manager`: The application is a floor manager.
- `floor.slave`: The application is interested in being notified of any change in floor, but not (necessarily) in the negotiation process.

It should be noted that types can be hierarchical, so (for example) any message addressed to audio would address both `audio.send` and `audio.recv` applications. It should also be noted that an application expressing an interest in a type does not necessarily mean that the application has to be able to respond to all the functions that can be addresses to that type. Also, (if required) the CCC library will acknowledge receipt on behalf of the application.

Examples of the types that existing applications would register under are:

- vat – `vat, audio.send, audio.recv`
- ivs – `ivs, video.send, video.recv`
- nv – `nv, video.send, video.recv`
- wb – `wb, workspace`
- A conference manager: `confman, session.local, session.remote, media-ctrl, floor.slave`
- A floor control agent: `flooragent, floor.manager, floor.slave`

In the current implementation, the type field is text based, so that debugging is simpler, and we can extend the type hierarchy without difficulty.

Instantiation

The instantiation field is purely to enable a message to be addressed to a unique application. When an application registers, it does not specify the instantiation – rather this is returned by the CCC library such that it is unique for the specified *type* at the specified *address*. It is not guaranteed to be globally unique – global uniqueness is only guaranteed by the triple of (instantiation, type, address) with no wildcards in any field. When an application sends a message, it uses one of its unique triples as the source address. Which one it chooses should depend on to whom the message was addressed.

7.5.5 Reliability

CCCP would be of very little use if it were merely the simple protocol described above owing to the inherent unreliable nature of the Internet. Techniques for increasing the end-to-end reliability are well known and varied, and so will not be discussed here. However, it should be stressed that most (but not all) of the CCCP messages will be addressed to groups. Thus a number of enhanced reliability modes may be desired:

- *None*: Send and forget. (An example is session management messages in a loosely coupled system.)
- *At least one*: The sending application wants to be sure that at least one member of the destination group received the message. (An example is a request floor message which would not be acknowledged by anyone except the current floor holder.)
- *n out of m*: The sending application wants to be sure that at least *n* members of the destination group received the message. For this to be useful, the application must have a fairly good idea of the destination group size. (An example may be joining of a semi-tightly coupled conference.)
- *All*: The sending application wants to be sure that all members of the destination group received the message. (An example may be 'join conference' in a very tightly coupled conference.)

It makes little sense for applications requiring conference control to reimplement the schemes they require. As there are a limited number of these messages, it makes sense to implement CCCP in a library, so an application can send a CCCP message with a requested reliability without the application writer having to concern themselves with how CCCP sends the message(s). The underlying mechanism can then be optimised later for conditions that were not initially foreseen, without requiring a rewrite of the application software.

There are a number of 'reliable' multicast schemes available, such as Montgomery (1997) and Birman (1991), which can be used to build consensus and agreement protocols in asynchronous distributed systems. However, the use of full agreement protocols is seen to be currently limited to tightly coupled conferences, in which the membership is known, and the first design of the CCC library will not include reliable multicast support, although it may be added later as additional functionality. Unlike distribute databases, or other automated systems that might exploit causal ordered multicast discussed in Chapters 2 and 3, communications systems for humans can exploit the user's tolerance for inconsistency.

We believe that sending a message with reliability 'all' to an unknown group is undesirable. Even if CCCP can track or obtain the group membership transparently to the application through the existence of a distributed nameserver, we believe that the application should know explicitly to whom it is addressing the message. It does not appear to be meaningful to need a message to get to all the members of a group if we cannot find out who all those members are, as, if the message fails to get to some members, the application cannot sensibly cope with the failure. Thus we intend to support the 'all' reliability mode only to an explicit list of fully qualified destinations (i.e. no wildcards). Applications such as joining a secure (and therefore externally anonymous) conference which requires voting can always send a message to the group with 'at least one' reliability, and then an existing group member initiates a reliable vote and returns the result to the new member.

7.5.6 Ordering

Loss is not the only reliability issue. Messages from a single source may be reordered or duplicated and, owing to differing delays, messages from different sources may arrive in 'incorrect' order.

Single-source reordering

There are many possible schemes to address reordering of messages from a single source, almost all of which require a sequence number or a timestamp. A few examples are:

1 Ignore the problem. A suitable example is for session messages reporting presence in a conference.

2 Deal with messages immediately. Discard any packets that are older than the latest seen. Quite a number of applications may be able to operate effectively in this manner. However, some networks can cause very severe reordering, and it is questionable whether this is desirable.

3 Using the timestamp in a message and the local clock, estimate the perceived delay from the packet being sourced that allows (say) 90% of packets to arrive. When a packet arrives out of order, buffer it for this delay minus the perceived trip time to give the missing packet(s) time to arrive. If a packet arrives after this timeout, discard it. A similar adaptive play-out buffer is used in vat for removal of audio jitter. This is useful where ordering of requests is necessary and where packet loss can be tolerated, but where delay should be bounded.

4 Similar to the above, specify a fixed maximum delay above minimum perceived trip time before deciding that a packet really has been lost. If a packet arrives after this time, discard it.

5   A combination of points 3 and 4. Some delay patterns may be so odd that they upset the running estimate in 3. Many conference control functions fall into this category, i.e. time bounded, but tolerant of loss.

6   Use a sliding window protocol with retransmissions as used in TCP. This is useful only where loss cannot be tolerated and where delay can be unbounded. Very tightly coupled conferences may fall into this category but will be very intolerant of failure. It should probably be used only along with application-level timeouts in the transmitting application.

It should be noted that all except item 1 require state to be held in a receiver for every source. As not every message from a particular source will be received at a particular receiver owing to CCCP's multiple destination group model, receiver-based mechanisms requiring knowing whether a packet has been lost will not work unless the source and receiver use a different sequence space for every (source, destination group) pair. If we wish to avoid this (and I think we usually do), we must use mechanisms that do not require knowing whether a packet has been lost.

Thus the above list of mechanisms becomes:

1   Have CCCP ignore the problem. Let the application sort it out.

2   Have CCCP deal pass messages to the application immediately. Discard any packets that are older than the latest seen.

3   As above, estimate the perceived delay within which (say) 90% of packets from a particular source arrive, but delay *all* packets from this source by the perceived delay minus the perceived trip time.

4   As above, calculate the minimum perceived trip time. Add a fixed delay to this, and buffer *all* packets for this time minus their perceived trip time.

5   A combination of points 3 and 4, buffering *all* packets by the smaller of the two amounts.

6   Acknowledge every packet explicitly. Do not use a sliding window.

Note that just because CCCP cannot provide more elaborate mechanisms, this does not mean an application itself (with some semantic knowledge) cannot build a more elaborate mechanism on top of any of 1–5. However, it does mean that *message timestamps and sequence numbers must be available at the application level.*

Multiple source ordering

In general, we do not believe that CCCP can or should attempt to provide ordering of messages to the application that originate at different sites. CCCP cannot predict that a message will be sent by, and therefore arrive from, a particular source, so it cannot know that it should delay another message that was sent at a later time. The only full synchronisation mechanism that can work is an adaptation of items 3–5 above, which delays all packets by a fixed amount depending on the trip time, and discards them if they arrive after this time if another packet has been passed to the user in the meantime. However, unlike the single source reordering case, this requires that clocks are synchronised at each site.

CCCP does not intend to provide clock synchronisation and global ordering facilities. If applications require this, they must do so themselves. However, for most applications, a better bet is to design the application protocol to tolerate temporary inconsistencies, and to ensure that these inconsistencies are resolved in a finite number of exchanges. An example is the algorithm she for managing shared teleconferencing state (Shenker *et al.*, 1994).

For algorithms that do require global ordering and clock synchronisation, CCCP will pass the sequence numbers and timestamps of messages through to the application. It is then up to the application to implement the desired global-ordering algorithm and/or clock synchronisation scheme using one of the available protocols and algorithms such as NTP (lam),(fel),(bir).

7.5.7   A few examples

Before we describe what should comprise CCCP, we will present a few simple examples of CCCP in action. There are a number of ways each of these could be done – this section is *not* meant to imply that these are the best ways of implementing the examples over CCCP.

Unifying user interfaces: session messages in a 'small' conference

We illustrate how services and applications are unified using CCCP in Figures 7.5 and 7.6.

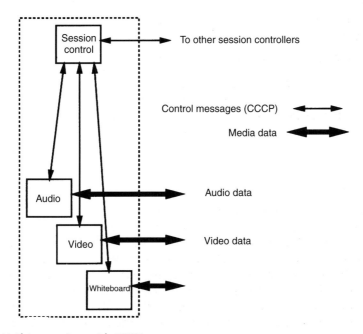

Figure 7.5   Unifying services with CCCP.

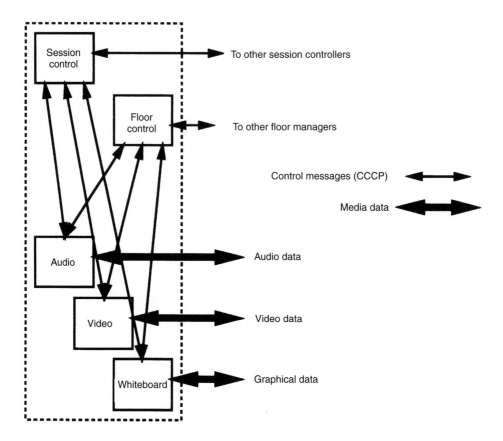

Figure 7.6   Unifying floor control with CCCP.

Applications include:

- An audio tool (at), registers as types `at, audio.send, audio.recv`
- A video tool (vt), registers as types `vt, video.send, video.recv`
- A whiteboard (wb), registers as types `wb, workspace`
- A session manager (sm), registers as types `sm, session.local, session.remote`

The local hostname is x. There are a number of remote hosts, one of which is called y. A typical exchange of messages may be as follows:

From	To	Message

the following will be sent periodically:

```
(1,audio.recv,x)   (*,sm.local,x)     KEEPALIVE
(1,video.recv,x)   (*,sm.local,x)     KEEPALIVE
(1,wb,x)           (*,sm.local,x)     KEEPALIVE
```

the following will be sent periodically with interval

```
(1,sm,x)                (*,sm.remote,*)   I_HAVE_MEDIA text_user_name
                                          audio.recv video.recv wb
```

an audio speech burst arrives at the audio application from y

```
(1,audio.recv,x)   (*,sm.local,x)     MEDIA_STARTED audio y
```

session manager highlights the name of the person who is speaking
speech burst finishes
```
(1,audio.recv,x)   (*,sm.local,x)      MEDIA_STOPPED audio y
```
session manager de-highlights the name of the person who was speaking
video starts from z
```
(1,video.recv,x)   (*,sm.local,x)      MEDIA_STARTED video z
```
periodical reports:
```
(1,audio.recv,x)   (*,sm.local,x)      KEEPALIVE
(1,video.recv,x)   (*,sm.local,x)      MEDIA_ACTIVE video z
(1,wb,x)           (*,sm.local,x)      KEEPALIVE
```
someone restarts the session manager:
```
(1,sm,x)           (*,*,x)             WHOS_THERE
(1,audio.recv,x)   (*,sm.local,x)      KEEPALIVE
(1,video.recv,x)   (*,sm.local,x)      MEDIA_ACTIVE video z
(1,wb,x)           (*,sm.local,x)      KEEPALIVE
```
and so on

A voice-controlled video conference

In this example, the desired behaviour is for participants to be able to speak when they wish. A user's video application should start sending video when their audio application starts sending audio. No two video applications should aim to be sending at the same time, although some transient overlap can be tolerated.

Applications include:

- An audio tool (at), registers as types `at`, `audio.send`, `audio.recv`
- A video tool (vt), registers as types `vt`, `video.send`, `video.recv`
- A session manager (sm), registers as types `sm`, `session.local`, `session.remote`
- A floor manager (fm), registers as types `fm`, `floor.master`

There are hosts x and y, amongst others. It is assumed that session control messages are being sent, as in the example above. A typical exchange of messages may be as follows:

From   **To**   **Message**
the user at x starts speaking; silence suppression cuts out, and the audio tool starts sending audio data:
```
(1, audio.send, x) (*,sm.local,x),    MEDIA_STARTED audio x
                   (*,floor.master,x)
```
this causes the sm to highlight the 'you are sending audio' icon
it also causes the floor manager to report to the other floor managers:
```
(1, floor.master,x)(*, floor.master, *) MEDIA_STARTED audio x
```
and it also requests the local video tool to send video:
```
(1, floor.master,x)(*, video.send, x) START_SENDING video
```
this causes the video tool to start sending
```
(1, video.send, x) (*, sm.local, x),  MEDIA_STARTED video x
                   (*,floor.master, x)
```
which, in turn, causes the sm to highlight the 'you are sending video' icon

the user at x stops speaking; silence suppression cuts in, and the audio tool stops sending audio data

```
(1, audio.send, x) (*,sm.local,x),   MEDIA_STOPPED audio x
                    (*,floor.master,x)
```

this causes the sm to de-highlight the 'you are sending audio' icon
the session manager starts a timeout procedure before it will stop sending video

a user at y starts sending audio and video data.
the local audio and video tools report this to the session manager:

```
(1,audio.recv,x)   (*,sm.local,x)     MEDIA_STARTED audio y
(1,video.recv,x)   (*,sm.local,x)     MEDIA_STARTED video y
```

as in previous example, sm highlights sender's name
Also y's floor manager reports what's happening:

```
(1, floor.master, y)(*, floor.master,*) MEDIA_STARTED audio y
(1, floor.master, y)(*, floor.master,*) MEDIA_STARTED video y
```

the local floor manager tells the local video tool to stop sending

```
(1, floor.master,x) (*, video.send, x)  STOP_SENDING video
```

this causes the video tool at x to stop sending

```
(1, audio.send, x) (*,sm.local,x),   MEDIA_STOPPED video x
                   (*,floor.master,x)
```

and so on

7.5.8 CCCP messages

The message format is:

```
(SRC triple){list of (DST triple)s} FUNCTION parameter list
```

7.5.9 More complex needs

Dynamic type-group membership

Many potential applications need to be able to contact a server or a token-holder reliably without necessarily knowing the location of that server. An example may be a request for the floor in a conference with one roaming floor-holder. The application requires that the message gets to the floor-holder if it is at all possible, which may require retransmission and will require acknowledgement from the remote server, but the application writer should not have to write the retransmission code for each new application. CCCP supports 'at least one' reliability, but to address such a 'Request Floor' message to all floor managers is meaningless. By supporting dynamic type-groups, CCCP can let the application writer address a message to a group which is expected to have only one (or a very small number) of members, but whose membership is changing constantly.

  In the example described, the application requiring the floor sends:

```
SRC Tuple               DEST Tuple                  Message
- - - - -               - - - - - -                 - - - -

(1, floor.master, x)  (*, floor.master.holder, *)  REQUEST_FLOOR
```

with 'at least one' reliability. Retransmissions continue until the message is acknowledged or a timeout occurs.

When the floor-holder receives this message, it can then send either a Grant Floor or a Deny Floor message:

```
SRC Tuple              DEST Tuple              Message
- - - - -              - - - - - -             - - - -
(1, floor.master, y)   (1, floor.master, x)    GRANT_FLOOR
```

This message is sent reliably (i.e. retransmitted by CCCP until an ACK is received).

On receiving the 'Grant Floor' message, the floor manager at x expresses an interest in the type-group floor.master.holder. On sending the Grant Floor message, the floor manager at y also removes its interest in the type-group floor.master.holder to prevent spurious Acking of other Request Floor messages. However, if the 'Grant Floor' message retransmissions timeout, it should re-express an interest.

See Chapter 6 on the naming service for more details of how dynamic type-groups work.

Need to know

When an application sends a message, it is up to the sending application to choose the reliability mode for the message. For example, in a large, loosely coupled conference, multicasting a floor change announcement is to use an unreliable mode. However, there may be a number of applications that really do require to see that information. In the floor control example, the existing floor-holding applications need to see the floor change announcements. We propose allowing a receiving application to modify the reliability with which other applications send specific messages by allowing messages of the form:

```
(SRC triple)(*, floor.manager, *) NEED_TO_KNOW (*, floor.slave, *) [list of fns]
```

In this case the application specified by the source triple is telling all floor manager applications that when they send one of the specified functions to (*, floor.slave, *), this application would like reliable delivery of the message.

Need To Know messages should be sent periodically, and will timeout if one has not been received in a set amount of time. Need To Know requests will also timeout at a particular application if that application ever fails to reliably deliver a message to the specified address. Clearly, Need To Know messages should be used sparingly, as they adversely affect the scaling properties of the CCC. However, there are a number of cases where they can be useful. The same effect could be achieved by declaring another type (for example floor.holder, which may be desirable in some cases), but Need To Know also has the benefit that it can be used to modify the behaviour of existing applications without a requirement to access the source code.

7.5.10 The naming service

CCC can be run on the bus model, passing all messages around a single multicast group per conference. This will scale reasonably, since it scales with the number of participants in the conference. Name resolution occurs at each host, matching

the destination naming tuple in the message against the list of tuples that are registered at this particular host. However, it does not scale indefinitely, because the load
on each host and the network increases with the complexity of the conference and the
number of messages. To improve scaling, the communications should be optimised
so that messages are propagated only to the machines that are interested. Thus
we need a service that maps the naming tuples to locations, so that intelligent mapping of message paths to locations can be performed (also known as intelligent
routing and placement of multicast groups). This name location service (or naming
service as it is more generally known) has a number of properties that differentiate
it from other naming services such as X.500 and the DNS. They are:

1   Dynamic and frequent updates.

2   Fast propagation of changes.

3   Ability to fall back to broadcast to interested parties when uncertain about the
    consistency of a refined addressing group, since names are unique per conference
    and are included in each message.

The last property is important since it allows a relaxed approach to maintenance of
consistency amongst the naming servers, saving greatly in the messages and complexity of the internals of the service.

   We intend to implement a nameserver suitable for loosely coupled conferences as
the default in the CCC library. However, CCCP will also allow the use of an external
nameserver to supplement or replace the internal nameserver behaviour, which will
allow much greater use of the nameserver to be made in more tightly coupled conferences, for instance by using the nameserver to keep an accurate list of members.

7.5.11   Security

CCCP will implement two levels of security: a very simple host access model similar
to the xhost mechanism in the X window system [xse], and encryption of all CCCP
packets with a key provided.

Host access security

The application is started with an access control string, which is a list of hosts from
which it is prepared to accept commands. It passes this to the CCC library, and
the CCC library then filters all messages whose source is not in the access control
list.

   This very simple level of security is intended primarily to prevent external attacks
such as switching media tools' transmission on or off and thus compromising the
privacy of users.

   Note that the X magic-cookie mechanism is not too useful here, as the cookie
would have to be carried in over CCC packet, which lays it open to attack from
anyone who can capture multicast packets.

Encryption

We recognise that the only way for CCCP to be really secure is to use encryption of all CCC packets, and CCCP will support an encryption scheme. The key distribution problem is considered to be outside the scope of CCCP itself, and CCCP will require the application to pass the key to it. After this, all CCCP messages from this library will be encrypted, and non-encrypted messages will be ignored.

CCCP will allow an encryption key per conference ID, and a key for messages not associated with any conference. Which encryption key to use for outgoing messages is chosen by the CCC library according to the conference ID. Once the application has passed the set of keys to the CCC library, it no longer has to concern itself with encryption.

Encryption and host access can be used simultaneously.

7.5.12 Conference membership discovery

CCCP will support conference membership discovery by providing the necessary functions and types. However, the choice of discovery algorithm, loose or tight control of the conference membership and so forth are not within the scope of CCCP itself. Instead, these algorithms should be implemented in a session manager on top of the CCC.

7.6 USING ISDN TO DO IP ACCESS TO THE MBONE

The session description protocol can be extended to provide Mbone access from unicast sites (behind ISDN or other links into the net).

Components include:

- Session directory servers (SDS)
- Mixers (application-level multicast to unicast traffic forwarder)
- A modified SDP client
- Two new protocols:
  - session lookup protocol (SLP)
  - remote multicast join/leave protocol (RLJMP)

7.6.1 Lookup and control

Somewhere in the Mbone there is a mixer (or several), known to session directories servers around the place. Ideally these mixers will be situated close to the point where the ISDN/unicast feed hits the Mbone. (In RTP, this mixer is known as a translator.)

A session directory server is a daemon that listens to SDP announcements and caches them. On demand, it provides the latest list to clients that query it.

When a client queries an SDS, the sessions reported include the mixer to use for the session with a unicast session address, but the media all have multicast addresses. The choice of mixer is dependent on the locations of the SDS and the client.

A unicast SDP client program runs on a unicast host at a site one or more hops removed from the Mbone (i.e. one incapable of using multicast IP). On demand, the SDP client contacts an SDS to get the current list of sessions, by making a TCP call to a well known port and formulating an HTTP 'Get' request. The returned type contains the list of all sessions. In other words, the SLP is based on HTTP over TCP.

A user then starts the media associated with a particular session by clicking on that entry in the SDP (modified) client. The modified client then sends a remote 'join' request to the mixer address (either configured, or retrieved from the SLP lookup), and starts the media application on the unicast address and port of their choice. The RLJMP 'join' message contains an SDP session description, but with added media fields ('mix-to') with the media tool's unicast address and port. RLJMP messages are text-based SDPv2 messages sent in a TCP connection to the mixer on a well known port and preceded by a line containing the RLJMP command (Join or Leave).

The mixer joins the group and adds the maplet from this group to the 'mix-to' site to its forwarding table. The session directory client on some subnet monitors the receiver program, and when it exits, sends a RLJMP leave message to the mixer.

7.6.2 Mixer operation

The mixer is an application-level program that is table driven. Basically, it is a cousin of the nv to CUSeeMe reflector program (or monstermash program), that receives multicast, and forwards to unicast, and receives on unicast and forwards to multicast based on maplets based on table entries created and deleted by RLJMP messages. Table 7.4 gives an example of a mixer operation.

The mixer may optionally apply priorities to the traffic (in the manner of class-based queuing). For example, a site might be down the end of a 64 kbps ISDN dial-up unicast link to the remote Mbone. A default might be that a mixer prioritises audio, then whiteboard, then video. An implementation hack might be that the forwarding loop of the mixer simply ignores overlimit input queues (this is tricky if people multiplex media on the same port and the same multicast address or we want to treat different sources differently, but will be easy otherwise).

As well as configured defaults at the mixer, we may want to specify priorities. One possibility is to implement an RSVP client in the modified session descriptor client and an RSVP server in the mixer. Easier still might be a mix-to-priority.

To decide on overlimit actions, the mixer also needs to know the bandwidth between it and the unicast client. This can be configured or monitored through spying on RR messages.

Finally, a refinement of the model above might permit a user to specify priorities with respect to sources of traffic (source descriptor fields or source IP address + port if available can be used to decide which class a flow belongs to).

Table 7.4 Mixer operation.

while(1) readmask = setupSelectMaskForThisTimeAround(); select(readmask);
dealWithReadDescriptorsAndUpdateClassUsage(mask);

The bandwidth (shared link) between the mixer and the unicast site is gleaned through some other process (for example, configured through management). Further study is needed on how an overlimit action might trigger demand for more bandwidth, again through some other configured information (basically derived from policies at the mixer and user site concerning costs and so forth).

Soft state

The mixer *must* fail to 'not forwarding' to a unicast site, since the act of forwarding uses possibly expensive bandwidth. This is achieved by timing out maplets in the table. Although the entry can be kept, it is marked as idle after timeout T1, and deleted only after a longer timeout, T2. The entry is refreshed by repeated RLJMP messages from the modified SD client at the unicast site. The refresh time (T3) is (hopefully) shorter than the idle timeout T1. Typical values of T1 will be set long enough not to incur costly control traffic on the link, and T2 short enough to close the link after application failure or abort/hang-up by an abrupt user without incurring costly forwarding of multicast traffic down the unicast link.

Unicast hop

The mixer and session directory server may be co-located. Further, they may be co-located on the unicast router immediately at the end of the unicast hop from the user site to the Mbone. More likely, they are a little way off from this. If the unicast hop is a bandwidth-on-demand circuit, the RLJMP is a way of implicitly controlling whether traffic goes to and from on this hop (keeping any potentially costly call open). T3 can be set high (it is really a resource protection timeout). Example values might be T3 = 3600 s, T2 = 120 s and T1 = 60 s.

7.6.3 Futures

You can connect two Mbones with two UMbone configurations. The simplest example is a small site (for example, a school) with a unicast router and a local Mbone router, and an ISDN link and a unicast router. There might be administrative reasons for not running a tunnel over the link. You can extend this model to allow non-Mbone-application-level gatewaying, for example, an analogue telephone gateway. A touch-tone dial interface to a remote SD client would be the obvious control interface (compare the Internet Phone model in the glorious RFC 1789).

Simplifications

The modified SD server and mixer may be co-located or even the same process. In some cases (for example, no ISDN), the SLP step might not be needed and the user site might simply get session advertisements mixed down to them always. In other cases, the RLJMP step might not be needed if there were few sessions and all could be accommodated.

Implementation

The session directory tool is being modified to accommodate SLP, and to be able to run as a daemon/server without a GUI. The mash program can be extended easily to accommodate RLJMP, and then enhanced through a user space version of CBQ to provide appropriate action when inbound traffic to the mixer exceeds outbound bandwidth.

7.7 SUMMARY

In this chapter we have looked at conference control systems, ranging from centralised, through distributed at the application level, as with MCUs in ISDN-based systems, on to multicast-based ones using a conference control channel or bus as the basic paradigm for messaging between conferencing components. The CCCP protocol was designed to be exemplary. It is probably far too complex to be implemented in its entirety.

For small to medium scale in terms of numbers of participants, the H.320 system's approach is feasible and can be made to work on packet nets by simulating the circuits for control messages by using a reliable multicast protocol. For larger-scale conferences, the Mbone approach and use of multicast scales to large numbers of senders and receivers is workable, but the protocols and standards need to be developed to provide tight control of a set of participants.

We will certainly see interworking units relaying between systems employing these two approaches – indeed, H.323 addresses simple dissemination of media from an H.320-type system onto LAN-based receivers. It is only a matter of time before systems work the other way too.

Notes

1 We define a tightly coupled system as one which attempts to ensure consistency at all sites. By contrast a more loosely coupled system tolerates inconsistencies, though it should attempt to resolve them in time. A very loosely coupled system will not even know the full list of conference members.
2 Actually ivs does support audio, but has also been widely used as a pure video codec with vat as the audio tool.
3 Or broadcast, but that is outside the scope of this book as it does not usually provide a reverse path from receiver to sender.
4 Actually, many shared workspace tools will not scale anyway, but we shall concern ourselves here only with those that will.

PART THREE

Applications and Services

In the preceding chapters we have presented a number of aspects of the Internet that have evolved to permit multicast multimedia applications. In particular, we can identify certain functions of the Internet that have made this evolution quite rapid and effective:

1 'No circuits, thank you' – The use of packet switching allows efficient multiplexing. The fact that these packets contain *both* source and destination (possibly group) addresses allows efficient distribution of control.

2 Scaling – Aggregation of flow information RSVP allows for policy free allocation of resources. Where fine grain allocation is needed, it is possible; but where a best effort (or other emerging default Internet packet delivery service) is sufficient, it can be used for large aggregations of flows.

3 Multicast encourages distribution of control functionality to the edges of the network, where the edge system is a computer, and is more flexibly programable in many case. This makes deployment of new services much more feasible than an approach which rests on intermediate nodes (for example, smart MCU or other application-level device within the network).

4 Soft state and receiver reservation are based on a notion of *optimism* about resource availability – in essence, the average case behaviour is most common, and its 'calls' (or sessions or flows) are typically not blocked. Thus we should incur expensive, and delay-ridden round-trip-time exchanges of call-control or signalling messages only when we really have to.

5 Based on all the above, the idea that a large-scale system is always consistent is clearly not achievable, and given the principles described here (really a logical extension of the Clark end-to-end principles), we should design distributed applications for convergent state and convergent consensus. For multimedia applications with human users, this is particularly attractive because of humans' tolerance of temporary inconsistency in many application usage patterns.

Multicast is a powerful building block. It has led to the evolution of a whole new way of constructing protocols, based around the paradigm[1] shift from sender-based protocol design, to *receiver-based* protocols.

The idea of receiver-based protocols has now been applied in a number of ways:

1 The basic multicast join mechanism is receiver based (IGMP joins do not involve sources, ever).

2   The Internet resource reservation protocol is receiver based.

3   Receiver-based adaption to congestion has been described by McCanne *et al.*
    (1996), using multiple IP multicast groups, and layered coded video with different
    layers sent on different addresses. Congestion avoidance is achieved as with TCP,
    by a control loop based on perceived loss, but without the closed loop feedback
    needed by TCP – receivers simply monitor loss for each level, and leave the
    associated group if congestion is causing too high packet loss, and carry out
    join experiments to probe whether they can start to receive more layers on other
    groups as loss reduces on existing ones.

4   Receiver-driven repair protocols such as that in the scalable reliable multicast
    protocol used in the LBL whiteboard application, and a similar one in nte,
    are seen as having very general application.

It is not yet clear, but if unicast is just a special case of multicast, it may be the case
that the receiver-driven approach is appropriate to *all* types of communication
protocol.

The Mbone and the multicast multimedia applications have seen deployment
without any formal resource reservation system. It is now believed by not a few
researchers that a formal resource reservation protocol *per se* may never be necessary
– a subscription-based approach, combined with measurement-based admission control and queuing in routers that provides simple priority for interactive (for example,
audio *and* Web browsing) traffic may be sufficient, and sufficiently less complex in
management terms that the under-utilisation that this might imply for the network
designer may be acceptable.

When we discussed the Mbone conference control and media delivery models, one
of the claims made was that they scaled well for systems with large numbers of
participants over very large networks (in the face of partial failures). Of course,
this means that there are (at least temporary) inconsistencies that may be perceived
by users. Luckily, humans are quite capable of holding inconsistent views temporarily and waiting for conflicts to resolve, so this is not necessarily a showstopper.
Unreliability and human tolerance work surpassingly well in the experience of many
Mbone users. Ordering and human frailty may be a problem for some classes of user,
though. For example, a distributed auction system would not be feasible using a
scheme that did not constrain bids (and video/audio from bidders) in the correct
order. In a large-scale system, it may be that this is achievable only at a very great
cost. There has been quite a bit of research on reliable, and on ordered reliable,
delivery multicast protocols, and the work at Cornell on Isis and Horus is particularly relevant. The most recent transport level work is that at Berkeley for NASA,
and we have a brief look at that next.

The reliable multicast protocol is a multiservice protocol with the goal of
supporting a range of services on top of the Internet Mbone delivery service.
RMP supports various types of ordering, and organises participants into virtual
topologies to achieve levels of reliability. It remains to be seen whether a single
protocol can carry out the very broad range of services that we have outlined.

An often expressed concern about the Mbone open channel model of conferencing
is that it is not secure. This is in fact simply not the case. Privacy and authentication
are end to end functions, and whether media and media control are unicast or
multicast is not relevant (Ballardie and Crowcroft, 1995). There are only a couple
of consequences of the fact that Mbone conferencing uses multicast:

1 Since this encourages multiway video conferencing, there is a greater need for multi-party key distribution. Typically, this means that an asymmetric key system is needed such as PKC based on RSA or PGP.

2 Traffic analysis and denial of service, two threats to security which are often overlooked, are potentially easier with a multicast network. It transpires that the very techniques used to provide better resource guarantees (RSVP and integrated service IP routers) can prevent the denial of service attack. Traffic analysis may be a little harder to prevent in a multi-provider Internet. Generally, it may be that sites will use random traffic from other sources, and perhaps route their traffic so it appears to source from different entry points to the net (perhaps different rendezvous points or cores in the multicast routing system), to avoid analysis. It remains to be seen if traffic analysis is a serious threat.

Note

1 For once, we believe the use of the word 'paradigm' is justified here, in its normal sense of 'pattern'.

CHAPTER EIGHT

Applications

8.1 INTRODUCTION

In this chapter we have a look at some Internet multimedia applications. We have looked at a number of the building blocks, and have just seen that there are some principles of design for Internet applications that have emerged that are very powerful (Clark and Tennenhouse, 1990):

1   *Application-layer framing*: The notion that an application can best select the 'element of synchronisation', and that this is then suitable as the protocol data unit, or packet size to be used, is pursuasive. It turns out that for multimedia applications and especially for multicast, this greatly simplifies application design.

2   *Integrated layer processing*: This is more a hint to implementors than the previous principle which addresses system design. Layers of protocol software are often slowed down by the very layering that makes their design simple. However, ILP is basically the same idea as that which compiler writers call inlining. Instead of a hierarchy of layers mapping onto an implementation model of a sequence of procedure or function calls, one can observe that much protocol processing is repetitive sequences carried out over a PDU/packet which can be rolled together. Together with ALF (which is a prerequisite for ILP to deploy sensibly), this can be applied, particularly to multimedia units of data sent as RTP/UDP/IP encapsulations.

We do not need to go into the design of audio and video software here. Vic, vat and rat are all well documented elsewhere, and the algorithms for compression, play-out adaptation and mixing have already been described in earlier chapters.

Here we concentrate on the shared applications and the LBL whiteboard, wb, and the UCL network text editor, nte. We take a close look in particular at the distributed repair algorithms.

8.2 ROADMAP

The main aspects of multimedia audio and video applications have already been covered, but the real advantage of the Internet is that other applications oriented around data can be coupled with the audio and video applications. In this chapter we discuss two example applications: a shared editor to illustrate distributed reliable data sharing, and a model for shared virtual reality or games, where reliability can be relaxed further.

The lesson to take away from this chapter is that for each application the designer needs to consider consistency and reliability anew.

8.3 SHARED APPLICATIONS IN THE MBONE

Shared applications that currently exist in the Mbone are what is termed collaboration aware, which is to say that they have been written specifically to be used by multiple simultaneous users, rather than simply being adapted to such use through some kind of wrapper such as a shared windowing system with floor controller.

Wb and nte represent a fairly radical departure from previous shared applications in that they are engineered in the context of very large numbers of users (thousands) and over very long haul networks, where there are very poor guarantees of full connectivity for the duration of a conference that is using the application, and where the capacity and delay from any given source to the group of users of the shared application may be varying by orders of magnitude.

To deal with this, the authors of both of these tools recognise explicitly that consistency of views for all users is a holy grail, and is simply unachievable within finite resources. However, correctness of view should be possible up to some point.

The starting point for solving this is that an application specific reliability is required, and that it is different for wb and nte.

Wb defines a set of operations that each user can carry out on the whiteboard, each of which is idempotent, or can be repeated without danger. The reliability in wb is achieved through retransmission of missing operations. Again, to gain scaling to large numbers of participants, there is a very ingenious scheme to decide who requests a retransmission. Conventional schemes rely on recipients notifying senders of missing packets through negative acknowledgement packets or NACKs. However, a NACK/retransmit-style protocol would not scale as, typically, a loss that is incurred somewhere in the Mbone might be perceived by entire cohorts of receivers when a subsequent operation arrives; an implosion of NACKs from all of them would then result. Wb uses multicast to its own benefit. All messages for all functions are always multicast. They also all contain timestamps, and all participants monitor their closeness to each other. When a recipient wishes to request a repair retransmission, they first throw a die with a number of sides depending on how near they are to the source of the missing message, and wait for the time indicated by the die. If they subsequently see a repair request from one of their cohorts, they suppress the timer that would otherwise have gone off and caused them to make the request.

The wb scheme is self-tuning, and works very well.

Nte is somewhat different in that it is not a whiteboard but a shared document editor (network text editor). Thus the operations by different users cannot be conveniently made idempotent. Nte attempts a stronger ordering than wb, but uses similar schemes to achieve the repair. In the event of a partition of the network, followed by a healed network, nte will offer the users a choice of which branch of the now disjoint edits to follow (or to revert to the pre-partition version of the document).

8.3.1 Background to nte

Since 1992, the multicast backbone (Mbone) on the Internet has been used for a large amount of multi-party multimedia conferencing experimentation. Although several audio and video tools have been developed and used on the platform, only one shared workspace tool has seen significant usage, namely the wb shared whiteboard tool from Van Jacobson of Lawrence Berkeley Laboratory. Although wb is a good shared whiteboard tool, we have often seen it used in circumstances where a shared text editor would have been a better choice of tool.

Wb is not a shared editor – for good reasons it keeps users' drawings and text separate, as this greatly simplifies both its usage and its data consistency problems. We believed that for a relatively simple environment – that of shared text editing – these consistency problems could be solved within a loose consistency framework that had excellent scaling properties similar to those of wb.

Starting from some general guiding principles – those of IP multicast, application-layer framing and lightweight sessions – we set out to develop a scalable shared text editor. In this section we discuss these general guiding principles. In the next subsections, we discuss the more general requirements of a shared text editor. In sections 8.3.2 and 8.3.3 we explore in detail the effects of these requirements, the development of a data model and the constraint the data distribution model places on the operations that can be performed on the data set. In sections 8.3.4 and 8.3.5 we examine some more detailed issues that affect the usability of our shared text editor, and in section 8.3.6 we attempt to generalise from our experiences to see how some of the solutions might be applied elsewhere.

Scalability

Typical usage of a multiway shared editor is envisaged as being in a 'meeting' with a number of people at geographically distributed sites. Although the number of people actually making changes to a document at any time is likely to be small, we wish to avoid placing constraints on the number of people able to participate in such a meeting. In particular, we do not wish the load[1] on any participating component to scale[2] with the number of participants.

Resilience

We wish a shared editor to be resilient to network conditions including packet loss, link failure, and failure of any participating end system. In combination with the scalability requirement, the necessity to tolerate link or end-system failures implies that a distributed, replicated data model is appropriate. Resilience to packet loss can be achieved through redundancy, through retransmission, or through network reservation. Network reservation is not widely available and we will aim to show that it is unnecessary for this sort of application.

Loose consistency

Observations from the MICE project of people using a shared whiteboard in conjunction with an audio tool lead us to conclude that the users of such tools will happily tolerate temporary inconsistencies between the view of a document at one site and the view of it at another, so long as eventual consistency is achieved and so long as the time they have to wait is predictable. This is fortunate as the requirements of resilience and scalability dictate that total consistency of view is not possible unless mechanisms requiring unacceptable delays are employed.

Interactivity

As a general rule, constraints on interactivity between users via a shared application should be kept to a minimum, and imposed only as a policy where the users actually require such constraints rather than imposed by the mechanism of the shared application. Thus, with a shared editor, the mechanism implementing the editor should allow multiple users to edit the document simultaneously. Thus if the sharing mechanism requires a lock to be imposed on a part of the data set, then this lock should be imposed on as small a part of the data set as possible in order to maximise the potential interactivity that can be achieved between users through the editor. However, the imposing of locks of any sort is at odds with the resilience and scalability requirements above, and, because we do not require global consistency at any time, the use of locks should be avoided if suitable alternative solutions are available.

Usage modes

Generally speaking there are two main forms of usage for a shared editor:

1   Collaborative editing of a passage of text
2   Annotation of a passage of text

In practice, when working in groups, we observe that shared editors are also used to a degree as an additional communication channel, but this can be thought of largely as annotation, even though these meta-annotations are not directly associated with existing text. Thus it is important for a shared editor to be able easily to support both these communication modes as transparently as possible.

If we satisfy the interactivity requirement above, it is vitally important, whether annotating or modifying text, that the person making a particular change is easily identifiable, even though several changes may be being made simultaneously.

8.3.2   Design

The basic building block for nte is IP multicast (Deering and Cheriton, 1990; Macedonia and Brutzman, 1994). This provides us with many-to-many communication at constant cost irrespective of the number of receivers. To achieve resilience, we adopt a distributed, replicated data model, with every participant attempting to hold a copy of the entire document being shared. This means that end systems or links can fail, but that the remaining communicating sites still have sufficient data to continue if they desire to do so. Updates to the distributed data model are made using IP multicast, although this means that owing to packet loss, not all sites will receive a particular update – how this is resolved is discussed later.

In designing nte, we attempted to apply the guiding principle of *application-layer framing*, ALF (Clark and Tennenhouse, 1990). Thus the application and its communication model employ the same data units.

Application data units

Our choice of application data units is driven in part by the model for data distribution and our choice of data distribution model is driven in part by the choice of application data units. Although we present the two as separate sections for the sake of readability, it should be clear that the two are closely interrelated.

The guiding factors in determining nte's data model come from the interactivity requirement listed above – many users must be able to work on the same document simultaneously – and the observation of usage modes, particularly the need to be able to keep annotations separate from the primary text being worked on.

These guiding factors led us to choose a hierarchical data model based around blocks of text, each consisting of a number of lines of text. Each block of text is independent of other blocks of text – it can overlap them if required although this does not aid readability. An example of blocks of text used for annotation, with each block in a different font, is given in Figure 8.1.

As it is not expected that most annotations will be modified by multiple users simultaneously, this by itself allows a number of users to be working simultaneously on the document in separate blocks.

However, only allowing multiple people simultaneously to *annotate* a document imposes too great a constraint on the potential usage modes of the editor. Thus we also make each line of a block of a document a separate entity. This allows users to be working on separate lines in the same block without there being a potential conflict.

We could have taken this model further and treated each character of a line as an independent entity. There are, however, a number of reasons why this is undesirable. Firstly, the amount of state that needs to be kept for each separate entity to ensure eventual consistency is significant. In addition, if we choose a line rather than a character as an application data unit (ADU), we do not need to

```
:-) Smiley

:-( Unsmiley

:-o Smiley singing national anthem  Surprised smiley?

:-* Smiley after eating something sour

=:-) Smiley punk-rocker  No, real punks don't smile
                          OK, this is a real punk smiley:
                          =:-(
```

Figure 8.1   An example of blocks of text used for annotation.

receive all the individual changes to the line as a user types – the most recent version of the line is sufficient, which gives us a large degree of redundancy in the face of packet loss. Lastly, there are potential transmission failure modes that with either line ADUs or character ADUs render us with no globally consistent ordering for the ADUs. However, owing to the nature of the changes to text, these are significantly less likely to occur with line ADUs than with character ADUs. We shall discuss these failure modes and also the implications of two users attempting to modify the same line simultaneously later, in the light of the loose consistency model described below.

It is perhaps not immediately obvious that either a line or a block is truly an independent entity. A block of lines is an independent entity because it has no interaction with, or dependency on, other blocks. However, within a block, lines are dependent on the block that contains them as their location is dependent on its position. In addition, a line has a position within a block. This can be represented in a number of ways, the simplest being an absolute line number, or relative links to next and previous lines. However, given that we wish to avoid any form of locking, it is possible that a message conveying the creation of a new line by one user crosses with a message conveying deletion of an earlier line by another user – in this and other similar cases it is clear that an absolute line number is insufficient to place the line uniquely within a block. Positioning a line relative to neighbouring lines is more robust, as even if a line creation crosses with the deletion of the line immediately previous to the new line, the location of the previous line can be retained after its deletion and the location is still unambiguous. Perhaps as importantly, so long as lines are only created or deleted (never moved), relative location of lines means that only changes in the immediate location of the line in question can cause possible confusion, which makes it much easier for the user interface to make the possible confusion obvious to the users involved.

However, although relative location information for lines is more flexible, it is insufficient to be able to display a block of text as it arrives complete with lost packets – such as might happen when a file is loaded into the editor. In such a case, adding additional line numbering allows the parts of the block that have been received to be displayed immediately irrespective of whether there are any missing lines at this stage. Whether this is an important requirement depends on the importance placed on timeliness of display – we took the viewpoint that it is important to be able to display any change as soon as it is received, and so added line numbers to the line ADUs which are ignored after all previous lines in the block have been received.

Given the choice of ADUs as lines and blocks, there is a certain amount of metadata that must be associated with each. Thus a block contains, amongst other things, the following:

- Position of the block on the page
- The line ID of the first line in the block

And a line contains, amongst other things:

- The text of the line
- The block ID of the block this line forms a part of
- The line ID of the previous line
- The line ID of the next line

- The line number of the block (ignored if all previous lines in the block are present)

Thus, although lines and blocks are not completely independent, blocks can be moved without modifying the lines contained in the block, and lines can be created, deleted and edited independently of other lines and blocks. There are, however, a number of desirable operations on lines that cannot be carried out independently – we shall discuss these and their consequences later.

Distributing the data model

The choice of a line as the ADU was made in part because of the simple observation that most consecutive changes are made to a single line – generally because a user continues to type. Thus if the whole line is sent for every character typed the additional overhead (over sending just the changes) is not great, the data transfer is idempotent (assuming a version of the block has already been received), and a great deal of 'natural' redundancy is available – so long as a user continues typing on the same line, lost packets are unimportant. However, this is only the case if we take a loose consistency approach (changes are displayed as soon as they arrive, irrespective of whether other sites have received them).

In order to be able to use this 'natural redundancy' property, it must be possible to identify whether a version of a line that just arrived is more recent than the copy of it we have already. This is necessary for two reasons: firstly to cope with misordered packets from a single source, and secondly to cope with retransmitted information from hosts with out-of-date versions of the data.

Misordered packets could be spotted easily using a sequence number; however out-of-date retransmitted data cannot be identified in this way. If we assume synchronised clocks at all sites, recognising out-of-date information is easy to achieve by timestamping every line with the time of its last modification, and sending these timestamps along with the data. Packets containing a line or block with an out-of-date timestamp can be ignored at a receiver with a later version of the same data. If we wish to take advantage of redundancy by not requiring retransmission of many lost packets, and we have modification timestamps in the packets, then we have no use for a sequence number in the packets. In general, a receiver does not care if it receives all the changes to a line as they happen; rather, it cares only that it receives the final version of a line, and that it receives sufficient changes that users understand what is happening as it happens.

In practice, we cannot assume synchronised clocks, but we can implement our own clock synchronisation protocol in the application. Also, if a receiver sees a retransmission of out-of-date data, it should attempt to update the sender of that data. We shall discuss how this can be achieved scalably under retransmission schemes below.

Clock synchronisation

Given that all changes to a document are multicast, and that all changes are timestamped, we have a simple mechanism for clock synchronisation amongst the members of a group:

1 If a site has not sent any data and receives data from another site, it sets its clock (application clock) to the timestamp in the received message.

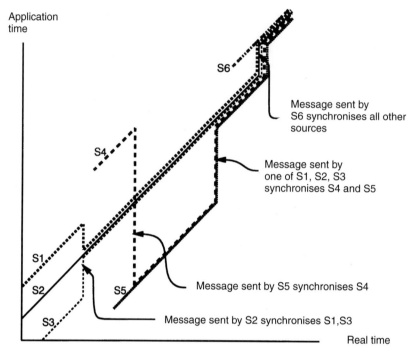

Figure 8.2   An example of application-based clock synchronisation.

2   If a site has not received any data, and needs to send data, it sets its application clock to its own local clock time.

3   If a site then receives a message with a timestamp greater than its current application clock time, it increases its application clock time to match that of the received message.

These simple rules ensure that all sites' application clocks are synchronised sufficiently accurately for our purposes.

Figure 8.2 illustrates this process. Source S2 sends the first message, and S1 and S3 synchronise to the timestamp in the message. Note that S1 can only move its clock backwards because it has no data. Two new sources then join, S4 and S5, and before any of the original sources send a message, S5 does so. As S4 has sent no message (therefore has no data), it now synchronises to S5. The three original sources have data and therefore do not synchronise to S5. One of the three original sources then sends, and both S4 and S5 synchronise to the timestamp in the message. A new source S6 then joins, and sends before anyone else does. As its local clock is ahead, all the existing sources now synchronise to it.

To illustrate this in more detail, consider three sites A, B and C, with three application clocks t_A, t_B, and t_C, and positive transmission delays d_{AB}, d_{AC}, etc. If A sends the first message, we have

$$t_B = t_A - d_{AB}$$

$$t_C = t_A - d_{AC}$$

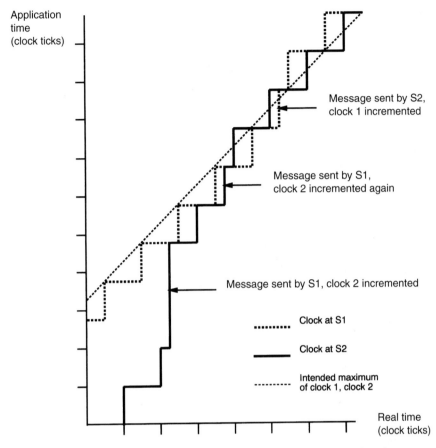

Figure 8.3 Clock synchronisation failure owing to clock granularity being less than transmission delay.

If d_{AB} ever decreases when A sends, then B will increase its clock to match the new delay, and t_A and t_B become closer. If d_{AB} increases, B continues to use t_B. Now consider a message sent by C. This message arrives at B with timestamp $t_A - d_{AC}$ and it arrives at time $t_A - d_{AB} + d_{CB}$. A comparison is made and only if $d_{AC} < d_{AB} - d_{CB}$ is the clock at B increased to be $t_A - d_{AC}$. Thus the clock at B can only get closer to the clock at A when a message is received from C. The process continues so long as messages are sent.

As all messages are timestamped anyway, global clock synchronisation to less than the minimum delay between any two active sites is provided for free, and no explicit clock synchronisation protocol is required. Naturally this assumes that all local clocks run at the same rate. This is a reasonable assumption for almost all of today's workstations. Even if there is a clock in a conference that does not run at the same rate as the rest, this does not cause the application any real problems. The worst that can happen is that all clocks increase whenever a message from the fastest clock is received, and that timestamps bear no relation to real time, and do not get successively more accurate than the first-pass approximation.

There are many algorithms that synchronise the clocks more accurately than the algorithm given above, but for the purposes of consistency control, a necessary feature is that clocks are never decreased, and the algorithm given is simple and sufficient.

Implementation of this algorithm reveals that there is a case where clocks do not stabilise to the fastest clock. This occurs when two sites with a clock tick of length t are connected by a network with a transit delay of less than t, as illustrated in Figure 8.3. This can happen with some Unix workstations with a 20 ms clock resolution connected by a local ethernet. Under these circumstances, the receiver will synchronise to the sender to a resolution of less than t. If the two clocks are not in phase, then the receiver can be ahead of the sender for part of each clock cycle. If their roles as sender and receiver are reversed and the new sender now sends a packet at a point in the clock cycle where its clock is ahead, the old sender then increments its clock to match the new sender. If both sites send alternately, this can result in both clocks being incremented indefinitely. This can be avoided if the clock tick interval is known, by simply ignoring clock differences of less than the clock tick interval. This is not noticeable from the user's point of view as clock tick intervals are generally less than 20 ms.

Towards reliability

Owing to the redundancy inherent in the data distribution model – namely that a user that continues typing will refresh and repair earlier packet losses on the same line of text – nte will often perform acceptably with no mechanism for ensuring reliability. However, there are also many situations where this is not the case, and so we need a mechanism to detect and repair the resulting inconsistencies.

Inconsistencies may result from:

1 Simple packet loss not corrected by subsequent changes (particularly where the last change to a line has been lost, or where a block is the result of loading from a file).

2 Temporary (possibly bidirectional) loss of large numbers of modifications owing to network partition.

3 Late joining of a conference.

4 Effectively simultaneous changes to the same line.

Inconsistency discovery

Discovery of inconsistencies is not a difficult problem. However, unlike the mechanisms used in RMP (Montgomery, 1997) and SRM (Floyd *et al.*, 1995), inconsistencies owing to simple packet loss cannot be discovered simply from the absence of a packet, as we wish most such changes to be repaired by redundancy and therefore do not need to see every packet at a receiver.

Instead we use a mechanism that ensures inconsistencies are resolved, irrespective of the number of packets lost. There are three parts to this inconsistency discovery scheme. Two schemes are based on the session messages that each instance of the application sends periodically to indicate conference membership. These session messages are sent by each site with a rate that is dependent on the total number of sites in the conference. Thus the total session message rate is constant (albeit a low one). To detect inconsistencies, each session message carries two extra pieces of information: the timestamp of the most recent modification seen and a checksum of all the data. If the timestamp given by another site is later than the latest change a receiver has seen, the receiver can request all changes from the missing interval without knowing what those data were. This is most useful when changes have happened during a network partition but all sites were passive when the partition was resolved. However, if a network partition was resolved as a site was transmitting, the receiver may have the most recent changes but not some older ones: hence the checksum is a last resort to discover that a problem has occurred or which data are missing.

The third scheme is a more active one designed to prevent the above schemes from needing to be used where possible. We have a concept of the current site – this an instance of the application at the site which has most recently been active. If more than one site is active, any of those sites can be chosen as current site. The current site periodically multicasts out a summary packet giving the timestamps and IDs of all the most recently changed objects (lines and blocks). If a receiver has a different version (either older or newer) of one of these objects then it is entitled either to request the newer version from the current site, or to send its later version. The current site may change each time a new user modifies the document; however, the rate that these summary packets are sent is a constant while any users are modifying the document – a new current site simply takes over from the previous one. In fact, sometimes more than one site may think it is the current site at any one time.

An alternative to sending explicit summary packets might be for session and data packets to have an additional object ID and its modification timestamp added to them, and for all sites to take turns to report the state of the most recently modified objects. Indeed, depending on the choice of retransmission scheme, this may be preferable, but we have chosen not to use this scheme. We shall discuss why not after we have discussed the choice of retransmission scheme.

Scalable retransmissions

When a receiver discovers there is an inconsistency between its data and those of another site, it cannot just send a message to resolve the inconsistency immediately – if it did so there is a high probability that its message would be synchronised with identical messages from other receivers causing a NACK implosion. Instead we require a mechanism to ensure that approximately one site sends the message. If such a message is an update, it should be multicast as this may update other sites with out-of-date information. In fact, if such a message is a retransmission request, it should also be multicast, as then the reception of the request can be used at other sites to suppress their retransmission requests.

Jacobson uses such a scheme in wb (see Floyd *et al.*, 1995) where a retransmission request is delayed by a period of time dependent on the round-trip time between the receiver and the original source plus a random amount. This scheme requires all participants to calculate a delay (round-trip time) matrix to all other sites, and this is done using timestamps in the session messages.

Wb is more dependent on its retransmission mechanism than is nte, as wb has no natural redundancy, and thus it requires its retransmission scheme to be extremely timely. Nte does not wish its retransmission scheme to be as timely as wb's scheme, as it expects most of its loss to be repaired by the next character to be typed. In fact, in many cases this results in significantly fewer packet exchanges because in a large conference on the current Mbone, the probability of at least one receiver losing a particular packet can be very high. Thus what we require is a retransmission scheme that ensures that genuine inconsistencies are resolved in a bounded length of time, but that temporary inconsistencies owing to loss which will be repaired anyway do not often trigger the retransmission scheme.

Wb's scheme can easily be tailored to do this effectively by adding a 'dead time' to the retransmission timer to allow a window during which the next modification to the line could arrive. If we used wb's randomised time-based scheme, then we would probably opt for not sending summary messages but instead adding ID/timestamp pairs to the session messages as described above. These would then tend to spread the retransmission requests more evenly.

In fact, wb's mechanism had not been described in detail at the time nte was designed and implemented, and a different sender-driven retransmission request scheme was used.

Sliding key triggered retransmissions

When an instance of nte sends a summary packet, it starts upon the process of sending a sequence of keys. When a receiver matches a key sent by the sender, it can immediately send its retransmission request (which can be many objects if necessary) along with the key that was matched. On receiving this request, the sender then starts the retransmission of the missing data.

What causes this to be scalable is the nature of the keys involved. The sender generates a random integer when it creates its summary message. Upon receipt of the summary message, the receiver also generates a random key. Then the sender sends its key along with a key mask which indicates the bits in the sender's key that must be matched in order for the receiver to send a retransmission request. This key/mask pair is sent several times (typically two or three times) and then, if no retransmission request is forthcoming, the number of bits indicated by the mask is reduced by one, and the key/new mask pair is sent again. If no retransmission request is forthcoming by the time the mask indicates no bits need to be matched, then the process is started again with a new random key, a new summary report, and possibly a new current site. If no change has occurred since the previous summary report, the rate of sending sliding keys is reduced to half the rate for the previous round or until it reaches a preset lower rate limit. This process is illustrated in Figure 8.4 and is based on a scheme devised by Wakeman for the solicitation of congestion report messages in multicast-based adaptive video coders (see Bolot *et al.*, 1994).

As the session messages give us a reasonable approximation of the size of the conference at the point when we generate the summary message, the sliding key can be started close to the point where it would be expected to elicit the first response if all receivers need a retransmission. For a typical thousand-way conference, where only one receiver requires a retransmission, with each key/mask pair sent twice per round and an estimated worst case RTT of 250 ms, this results in four (small) packets per second and a maximum delay of five seconds before requesting retransmission. Note that this is a much shorter time than can be achieved by having

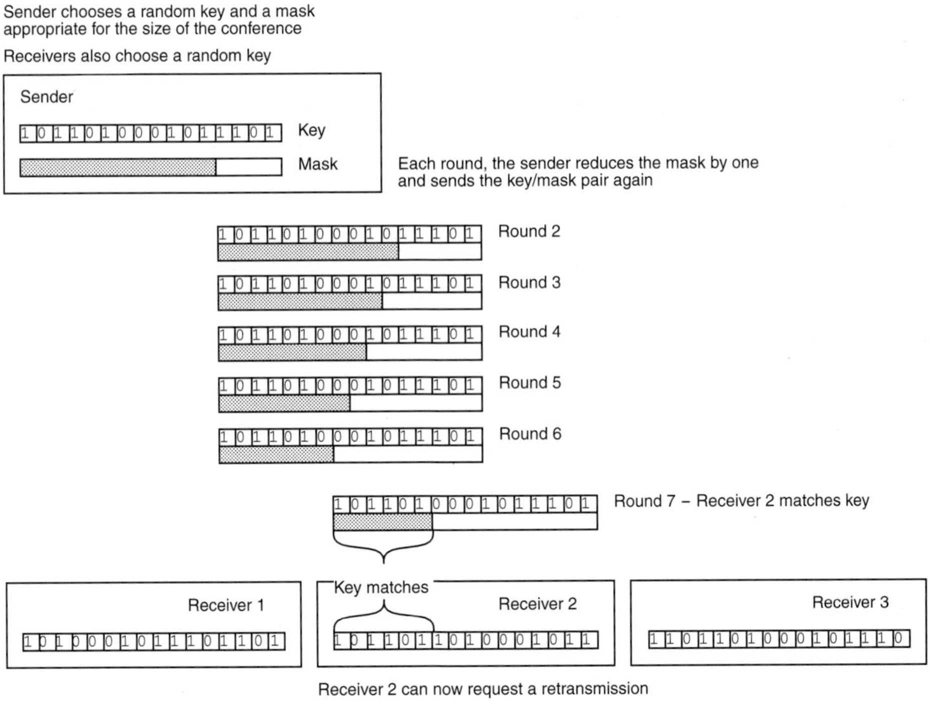

Sender chooses a random key and a mask
appropriate for the size of the conference

Receivers also choose a random key

Figure 8.4   Sliding key triggered retransmission requests.

each receiver randomly choose a delay from a sufficiently large uniform interval to ensure approximately one retransmission request is made. If the conference was smaller, or more sites had suffered loss, this time would be reduced.

8.3.3   Limitations of the data model

We have described a data model and a distribution model which are oriented towards building a scalable distributed shared text editor. However, the data model, and more importantly its distribution model, impose a set of limitations on the functionality of the shared editor, or on the way this functionality is implemented.

Whilst a data model based on blocks and lines allows different blocks or lines to be modified simultaneously without any problem, the lock-free distribution model and the choice of a line as the ADU mean that it is possible for two or more users to attempt to modify the same line effectively simultaneously.

In addition, network partitions can result in more complex inconsistencies arising. We shall show below that a few simple choices can result in all such more complex inconsistencies becoming equivalent to a *detectable* case of effectively simultaneous insertion of lines into the same place, and that this can be resolved as all the alternative information is available at each site.

Effectively simultaneous changes to the same line

By 'effectively simultaneous' we mean changes to the same line where, owing to network delay or to partitioning, two users attempt to change the same line without seeing the effects of the other's changes first. Thus the timestamps of the changes may not be identical.

Effectively simultaneous changes owing to transmission delay

Nte is designed for use in multimedia conferences where there are other channels of communication between users than just nte. Thus two users whose sites are not partitioned from each other attempting to modify the same line effectively simultaneously will see the change made by the later site being substituted for the change made by the earlier site. If such changes do not involve adding a line break to the middle of a line, then no lasting confusion should remain, and at least one of the users will be notified of what is happening. It is to be hoped that at this point the users will talk to each other and decide who should make the change. Even if the users do not have an out-of-band communications channel, they can always create a new block to make meta-comments to resolve the confusion.

It should be noted that although there are circumstances when one site does not even see the *change* made by the other site (for example, site 1 does not see change 2 in Figure 8.5), it is possible for the user interface to flag the fact that another user is attempting to modify the line, so that both users do realise what is happening.

If one of the users adds a line break to the middle of a line, this is mapped into a truncation of the existing line, and the creation of a new line after the existing line with the remainder of the text. The overlapping request, if it happens after the line break insertion but before the receipt of the message (see Figure 8.6), will then reassert the previous line. This will be confusing for users, as suddenly text has been duplicated.

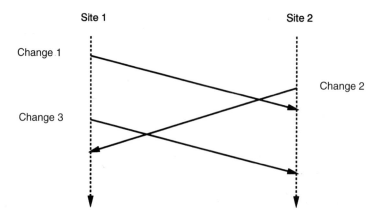

Changes 1 and 3 prevail. Change 2 is seen briefly at site 2 then disappears.
Site 1 never sees change 2 – it is already too old when it arrives at site 1

Figure 8.5 Two users attempting simultaneously to modify the same line.

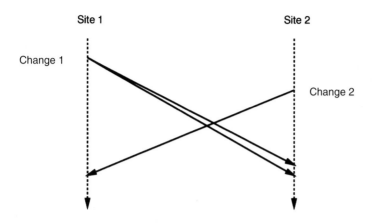

Change 1 results in a line being split in two, creating a modified line and a new line.
Change 2 modifies the original line
In a simple scheme, the new line from change 1 and the modified original from
change 2 remain. This is most likely with a network partition, but could also occur because of
simple transmission delays

Figure 8.6   Undesirable behaviour owing to simultaneously splitting a line and modifying it.

One way to deal with this is to maintain a very short history, and if a remodification of a line we just modified arrives within the expected round-trip time, we reassert (and retransmit with a new timestamp) the old unmodified line, and delete the extra created line. This strategy can be defeated by packet loss, but may reduce confusion in those cases where the problem can be detected. (It should be noted that packet loss can be treated as an abnormally long transmission delay for these purposes.)

An alternative depends on the model we use for deletion. If deletion is an irreversible operation (i.e. deletion overrides modification), then simply deleting the line to be split and inserting two new lines in its place prevents this undesirable behaviour.

Effectively simultaneous changes owing to network partition

Whereas in the case of simultaneous modification owing to transmission delay we could in effect back up with a minimum of confusion to the user (so long as we inform them why we have done so), we cannot do so in the case of simultaneous modification owing to network partitioning.

If only single lines have been modified, there is no real problem, as the later change will be asserted, and although this may not be what the user whose change just got replaced actually wants, at least the document ends up in a consistent state.

However, if the user making the earlier modification adds any new lines (particularly if they do so by inserting a line-break into the middle of a line), then there is a potential for the document to end up in an inconsistent state. We shall show later that we can detect simultaneous insertion. In order to maintain internal consistency, then, we should treat the splitting of a line (by adding a line-break to the middle of an existing line) as deletion of the old line, plus insertion of two new lines.

It is also possible to keep a local copy of the state of any line we have modified at the time we last modified it in order to be able to reassert the state if the conflict resolution was not what we actually wanted. However, it is always possible to envisage ways to defeat such a scheme if it were to be performed automatically, so such a reassertion should be performed only with explicit consent from the user for each step.

We hope that these mechanisms will not be often called upon, but choosing a line as our minimum unit means that there will always be occasions when such mechanisms are called upon. How effective they are depends largely upon how well what has happened is communicated to the user and what options they have to deal with it.

Deletion of lines of text

Deleted lines need to be stored as if they were modified lines, with a marker that they are no longer visible. If they were not stored as actual objects, then they may be reasserted by sites which have missed seeing the deletion event. Unfortunately, it is necessary for deleted line IDs and deletion times to be transmitted and stored at all sites to prevent unintentional reassertion of deleted lines after the deleting site has left the conference.

If an entire block of text has been deleted, sites need only hold the ID and deletion time of the block – the holding of information of lines within the block is unnecessary.

To prevent the reassertion of lines or blocks after deletion when a network partition is resolved, it is even necessary to send deleted block and line IDs and timestamps to new sites joining the conference so that they can continue to suppress reassertion of the deleted line or block after all the other members of this partition have left the conference.

To prevent unnecessary usage of bandwidth and memory, line and block IDs could be reused for new lines and blocks. However, this is dangerous, as a deletion event and the subsequent reuse of the line ID in one partition followed by the modification of the original line in another partition can lead to undesired consequences. It would be possible to consider schemes where a line ID can be reused only in a different block from the one it was previously used in, and thus the line's block ID field can be used for collision detection, but if the site originating the ID is no longer reachable, it is far from obvious who can resolve the conflict without introducing further complications. Thus in nte, we have not attempted to implement any ID reuse system.

The most significant design decision here concerns the effects of network partitioning. If a user at a site in one partition deletes a line, and subsequently another user in the other partition modifies the line, we have two choices when the partition is resolved:

1　Rely only on modification time (i.e. treat deletion as just another modification that can be rectified later if required).

2   Impose an ordering on operations such that deletion is of higher order than normal modification, such that deletion always prevails over modification.

If we treat deletion as modification, then when several neighbouring lines are deleted in one partition, and one of the middle lines is subsequently modified in the other partition, a single line would be reasserted with no surrounding context. There are mechanisms we could employ to deal with this, but they tend to add unnecessary complexity, and generally are less natural to users.

If we treat deletion as a higher-order operation, then a different scenario causes potential problems. A line can be split into two lines in one partition (one modified line and one new one), and subsequently deleted in another partition, leading to only half a line remaining after the split when the partitioning is resolved.

We took the decision that deletion is a higher-order operation, as this provides a mechanism that is independent of causal ordering in a partitioned network, and this causal ordering independence provides a mechanism which we can utilise to achieve internally consistent global consistency.

Thus the problem above where a line is split in two (a 'newline' is added to the middle of the line) can be resolved by deleting the line we wish to split and inserting two new lines in its place. This achieves internal consistency because even if the line split in one partition is modified or deleted in the other partition, the deletion operator overrides the modification operator, and the two new lines then take its place. However, if a line is split in both partitions, then we now get both versions of the line after partition resolution, with no globally consistent view of the line ordering in the block. Thus we have moved the problem to that of effectively simultaneous insertion of lines. However, effectively simultaneous insertion is a detectable situation, as we shall show below.

In fact to achieve inconsistency detection, there is one further requirement with respect to deleted lines: not only must they be kept at all sites to prevent reassertion of the line from a site that missed the deletion, but they must also be kept in their original place in the list of lines at each site. Thus, a line preceding a deleted line must still be transmitted with its *next line* field indicating the deleted line. This is necessary so that simultaneous insertion is a detectable situation.

Moving of sections of text

There are two ways to view the moving of a chunk of text:

1   Deletion and then insertion of the contents of the deleted text.

2   Changing the bordering lines' neighbours (sending modifications of the top and bottom lines of text specifying new neighbours).

Deletion and then reinsertion is wasteful of bandwidth and causes extra state to have to be held (and sent) for the deleted lines. We are sure, however, that no one can have already changed the new lines, assuming deletion is not overriden by modification so that the original lines cannot be re-asserted.

Modifying the context information of the bordering lines and simply resending this information has the possible advantage that someone modifying the moved text in its old position owing to temporary partitioning sees her changes reflected in the new positioning after the partitioning has been resolved. However, it is possible that one or more of the bordering lines are modified in a partitioned site after the move has occurred, and that the resolution of the partition then undoes or partially undoes the move, resulting in a block where no one knows the correct line ordering.

Allowing the possible situation of no one knowing the correct line ordering is extremely undesirable, and so we treat moving as deletion and subsequent reinsertion, despite the additional overheads this entails.

Garbage collection and checkpointing

Treating deletion as a higher-order operation than modification gives us a mechanism for both checkpointing of blocks and of garbage collection of deleted lines. Both of these can be done by deleting a block and then reasserting the same data as a new block and lines. Although this might seem wasteful, it means that for the additional cost of keeping deletion information for a single block, we no longer need to store the deleted lines that used to be in the block. In addition, it means that if there is a network partition that is subsequently resolved, any changes made in the other partition will not be asserted. This has to be implemented carefully, as the users in the other partition may not wish to see their changes simply discarded, but there are times when it is desirable to assert the current state. If both partitions checkpoint the same block, then the block will be duplicated at the time of partition resolution, which may or may not be what is desired.

Effectively simultaneous insertion of lines

Effectively simultaneous modification of a single line always results in a block that is internally consistent and a document that is in a globally consistent state. We have shown that if deletion is treated as a higher-order operation than modification, then combinations of moving, deletion line splitting and so forth can be dealt with, but with one potential side-effect: all these operations can result in effectively simultaneous insertion of lines.

Effectively simultaneous insertion of lines is a slightly harder problem than the problems discussed above because it results in a document that is neither internally consistent (we have two copies of essentially the same line or lines) nor globally consistent (different sites can have different views of the document). This occurs because two (or more) lines each have the same neighbouring lines. The problem can be detected at all sites, because a set of lines is received that should fit in the same place in a block as a set of lines we already have.

At this point the choices we made above (about deletion being a higher-order operation than modification but that deleted lines are retained, and moving of lines being treated as deletion and reinsertion) ensure that if a newly received line has a particular previous line, then there are only three choices for where the next line is:

1   There is no next line. This line is the end of the block.

2   We have seen the next line, and it is later in the block (possibly deleted).

3   We have not seen the next line.

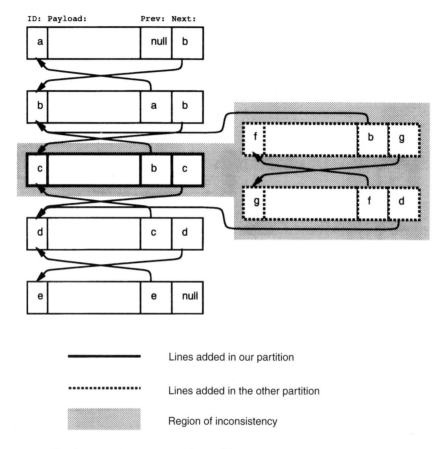

Figure 8.7 Simultaneous insertion is a detectable situation.

If we have not seen the next line, then we know we have a potential inconsistency, and thus we should not display the received line until we have the next line too. We wait until the line's 'next line' arrives and then go through this process again. If the next line is a line we have seen, or the end of the block, then we have enough information to know whether we have a problem or not. We can therefore treat a connected set of one or more new lines as if they were a single line. If the line in our existing block following the 'previous line' of the new data is not the same as the 'next line' of the new data, then we have an inconsistency which must be resolved (see Figure 8.7); otherwise we can unambiguously display the lines.

Now, so long as we keep deleted lines in their original place in the block and do not display them (see Figures 8.8 and 8.9 for examples), and so long as we treat moving as deletion and subsequent insertion, then there is only one way such an inconsistency could occur: alternative new lines were inserted effectively simultaneously. Thus the question comes down to which of the two sets of lines to keep and which to delete. So long as this matter is resolved globally consistently, then global consistency can be restored to the block. In fact, it is not quite as simple as this, because if we delete one version of the lines, we must ensure that the block is globally

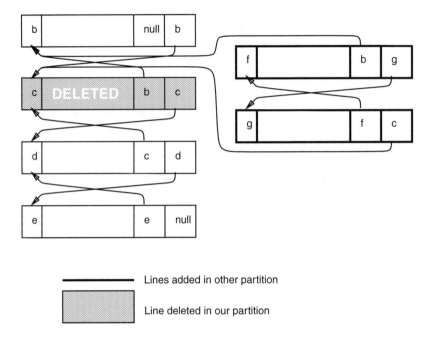

Lines added in other partition

Line deleted in our partition

Partition resolves to a consistent state

Figure 8.8   Simultaneous deletion and insertion – no inconsistency.

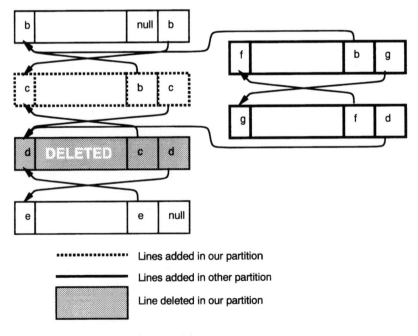

Lines added in our partition

Lines added in other partition

Line deleted in our partition

Partition resolves to an inconsistent state

Figure 8.9   Simultaneous deletion and insertion resulting in inconsistency.

consistent *including the position of the deleted lines* or we may not be able to detect further inconsistencies at all sites. However, we do not care about the order of a set on consecutively deleted lines, so instead of deleting one of the two alternative sets of lines, we must actually delete both alternative sets of lines and reinsert one of them again.

The choice of which alternative set of lines to retain can be made automatically (by the 'current site') or it can be made clear to the users that there is a problem that requires resolution. Either way, if more than one site attempts to resolve the conflict, the cycle is simply repeated again.

Summary of inconsistency avoidance mechanisms

To summarise, the limitations necessary to ensure eventual consistency after the resolution network partitioning are as follows:

1   Simultaneous modification of a single line does not result in eventual inconsistency.

2   Deletion must always override modification, irrespective of the timing of the two operations.

3   Deleted items must be transmitted to and stored at all sites to prevent reassertion.

4   Deleted lines must be kept in their original place in a block, and must remain referenced by their neighbouring lines – this is a precondition for simultaneous insertion detection.

5   Moving of text must be performed by deleting all the original lines containing the text to be moved and inserting the new text in new lines, thus preserving the original line ordering. This includes splitting a single line by adding a line break to the middle of it.

6   If all the above are performed, line ordering within a block is changed only by adding new lines. This makes simultaneous insertion of lines during a network partition a detectable and resolvable situation.

These restrictions will ensure that eventual consistency is achievable, even in the face of continuing modification during a network partitioning. However, they are not always sufficient to ensure that the contents of the document eventually converge on what all of the users actually wish them to be. Although this could be achieved by locking of blocks to ensure that only one person at a time can modify a block, we believe this restriction is unnecessary and would restrict usage of the editor. Indeed, under many circumstances, the usage patterns of the editor are likely to be such that large-scale simultaneous editing of a block during a network partitioning will not happen because the vocal discussion needed to do so will not be possible. If users are concerned about simultaneous editing of a block during a network partition, they should checkpoint the block to ensure no unseen changes can be made to it. For paranoid users, this checkpointing procedure could be automated, although we do not believe this is desirable or necessary.

8.3.4 Usability issues

Much work in the field of computer supported collaborative working (CSCW) has started from a *detailed set* of usability requirements and attempted to engineer a system to support these requirements. In single-user systems this works well, but for near-synchronous shared tools there is a real danger that this results in systems that do not perform well in real-world networks.

We have started with a *high-level* set of usage and performance requirements, and worked through a solution that satisfies these high-level requirements. Such a solution imposes a tight set of constraints on the operations that can be performed on the data set. In designing wb, it appears that Jacobson also pursued this design path, although as the high-level requirements were slightly different, their resulting constraint set is different. There is a danger that, in pursuing this type of path, the resultant system performs well but does not properly support any required task. It is dangerous to attempt to draw general conclusions from a small number of examples, but we believe that both nte and wb have resulted in systems that support the users' tasks well. Furthermore, we believe that engineering a CSCW tool around a set of constraints that ensure good performance is likely to result in a tool that will be used.

Having said that, it is vital that detailed usability requirements are given a great deal of attention when working *within* our constraint set. The detailed requirements we used to design nte include:

1   Nte should be as simple as possible to use. It is not a word processor, and is not intended for single-user usage.

2   It should always be possible to tell who is in the conference.

3   It should always be obvious who is performing any change at any time.

4   WYSIWIS (What You See Is What I See) is *not* a requirement. Different users should be able to edit different parts of the document simultaneously, even if these parts are separated by several screens of text.

5   The primary user operations are:

    (a) block creation

    (b) text addition

    (c) text deletion

    (d) block deletion

    (e) block moving

    (f) cut, copy and paste of text

    (g) search and replace within a block

    (h) setting the font and colour of a block for identification purposes

    (i) using a shared pointer

    (j) loading text from a file

    (k) saving text to a file

6   We expect that no other user operation on the text needs to be supported as it is unnecessary and increases the complexity of the user interface. Other operations should be added only where they aid the above operations.

7   It should be possible to prevent other users from editing a particular block of text
    – a kind of 'annotation only' mode.

8   It should be possible to save the resulting text as either ASCII text or as
    structured text maintaining the block structure.

9   It should be possible to save selected blocks only.

There is little point in discussing all of these detailed design decisions here as most of
them are uninteresting. However, a few are worthy of mention, as they were not
obvious (at least to the author).

8.3.5   Asynchronous events – informing the user

One requirement is that it should always be possible to see who is changing what at
any time. In nte we achieve this by placing a labelled graphical icon at the place
where a change is happening. This is necessary not only because it identifies
who is making a change, but also because it is not always obvious that a change
has been made. For example, single-character changes are not easy for a user to
spot if his attention was focused somewhere else at the time. Thus the appearance
of the icon serves to mark for a few seconds the location of a change, the nature
of the change, and (because the icon is labelled) who made the change.

In nte, all changes are marked in this way. However, when we started to use nte in
group conferences, it became clear that the screen could get very congested, and also
that when a block of text was deleted, users could see from the eraser icon that a
block of text had been deleted and *who* deleted it, but often they could not remember
which text it was that had been deleted. The reason for this was that their attention
was elsewhere, and all they could tell was that something had gone. The solution
was simple: not only display the eraser icon and its label, but also fade the block
away so they can see what is happening as it happens. In practice, this fade need
take no longer than a second to remove the sense of surprise that the users were
feeling when blocks were deleted.

Block locking

As mentioned above, one detailed requirement is to lock a block so that only its
creator can modify it. There are a number of cases where this is important, but
the most likely one is a scenario where a piece of pre-prepared text is included
in the conference for discussion. In this case, comments may be added as
annotations, but the original text most not be modified.

As long as a block has associated with it the metadata of who its creator is, then
locking a block (at least amongst co-operating applications) is simply a case of
marking that block as not editable.

However, given the unreliable nature of the underlying communications protocol,
if a block is created as unlocked, and then subsequently locked, there is no guarantee
that all sites will receive the 'lock' message. Given the scalability and resilience
requirements, we do not even know for certain exactly who is currently in the session.
Thus any site that (temporarily) missed a lock message is free to modify the locked
block until such time as the retransmission scheme succeeds in propagating the lock
message. Given a network partitioning, this could be a significant length of time.

Whilst this circumstance will probably be rare, we would like block locking to be a definite notion: if a user thinks a block is locked, there should be no way that that block can be modified. A similar, though slightly less strong, argument also holds for unlocking blocks.

There are a number of possible ways to ensure that block locking is unambiguous, but many of them infringe our previously stated requirements. The following is in line with our requirements:

1   Allow new blocks to be created as either locked or unlocked. Never allow a block to be changed between the two states.

2   Allow a block to change state from locked to unlocked, or vice versa, only by deleting the block and retransmitting its data as a new block.

In the current version of nte, we have implemented only item 1 above. We do not believe that block locking is frequently required, and when it is, it is most often required on a block whose data have been loaded from a file. Making the decision about whether or not a block should be locked at load time is quite natural. The default for blocks created on-the-fly is for them to be unlocked.

8.3.6   Generalising the models

Nte, its data model, and its underlying protocol were all designed to solve one specific task: shared text editing. We used general design principles: IP multicast, lightweight sessions, and application-layer framing as starting points. However, the application data model is intended only for text. The data distribution model uses the redundancy achieved through treating a line as an ADU combined with the fact that most successive modifications are to the same line to avoid the need for most retransmissions.

However, the restrictions that the data distribution model impose on a data structure consisting of a doubly linked list of application data units can perhaps be generalised somewhat. The imposition of a strict ordering of ADUs, combined with marking deleted ADUs whilst leaving them in position in the ordering, allows the detection of inconsistencies caused by network partitioning in a loose consistency application. It is perhaps not easy to see how this could be applied to other near-synchronous shared applications, so an example is in order.

In nte, the stacking order of blocks of text is a local issue so that overlapping blocks can be simultaneously edited. However, in a shared drawing tool, stacking order must be a global issue, as most drawing tools use overlaying of one object on another to produce a more complicated object. In a shared drawing tool, each drawing object (circle, polygon, rectangle, line, etc.) is the drawing equivalent of a line of text. The concept of a block does not exist as such, instead there is a strict ordering (analogous to line ordering in a block) which is imposed by the stacking order. Thus, the same set of constraints that apply to lines of blocks in nte should be applied to the stacking order of drawing objects in this hypothetical drawing tool.

The retransmission mechanism used in nte is novel, in that its requirements are perhaps atypical of shared applications because of the wish to exploit redundancy. For many applications, scalable reliable multicast (SRM) is a more appropriate choice of retransmission mechanism as, given a stream of packets with sequence numbers, it is likely to be more timely. However, for applications where retransmission is a rare phenomenon owing to redundancy or other relaxed consistency requirements, and where we desire a sender controlled system, nte's retransmission scheme has some possible benefits. Its sliding key messages can carry the latest ID and timestamp, which can be used to ensure that partitions are resolved at the earliest opportunity. Although we do not use the property in nte, sliding key schemes can be used to ration retransmission requests – this might be useful where the reverse path from receivers to senders is bandwidth limited.

8.4 DISTRIBUTED VIRTUAL REALITY

Distributed VR is a relatively new area of research. Virtual reality systems are now largely software components, rather than requiring the dedicated head-up-display input controllers and renderer hardware of the past. Current high-end workstations can now render scenes described in VRML and other languages in near real time.

The introduction of audio and video input and output on desktop machines led to the deployment of software-based multimedia conferencing. We expect to see the deployment of multi-user virtual environments over the Internet shortly.

In this section we present an architecture for distributed virtual reality. We outline the necessary network support and a transport protocol, and the way that distributed VR applications would interact (the API if you like) with each other using these mechanisms.

It is a goal of the architecture to provide policy-free mechanisms for distributed VR application builders. It is not a goal to make it easy to program such applications, since it is all too easy to provide easy-to-program distributed system tools that let the application builder overload the network and at the same time provide suboptimal performance for the user. The architecture provides necessary and sufficient hooks only for distributed VR.

Multicast routing is a mature area of research in the Internet. The system that we now call the Mbone (Macedonia and Brutzman, 1994) has its roots in the research by Cheriton and Deering where they developed the Internet multicast model, including the idea of host groups (Deering, 1989) and the basic service model for IP multicast (Deering and Cheriton, 1990). It is now widely deployed in the network and is available in most common host operating systems and routers.

Some functions in a distributed system can best be performed in intermediate nodes or routers, whilst others can best be performed in end systems or hosts. The end-to-end principle (Saltzer *et al.*, 1984) is used to select where to place a function. The principle is that a function that requires knowledge of the end system in order to be carried out correctly should exist only in the end system; where it appears in the network, it should only be as a performance enhancement.

Two principles behind the design of high performance, low cost protocols that have proved themselves in this environment are *application-layer framing* (ALF) and *integrated layer processing* (ILP) (Clark and Tennenhouse, 1990). These state simply that: the unit of synchronisation and recovery should as far as possible be the same as the unit of communication (packet); and that where possible, modular functionality that is specified in layered form should not be implemented as such, and that new designs' communications systems should factor this in so that processing associated with layered modules can be integrated in one pass.

Combining these principles with the use of multicast for many-to-many communication, a number of further techniques have arisen for protocol design:

1   Multicasting *everything* is a good idea. In applications with relatively high packet rates, the use of multicast for control information as well as for user data is not a high load and can greatly simplify convergence of protocols for correctness, as well as performance and synchronisation.

2   As error rates in modern networks have decreased, end-to-end recovery from packet loss or reordering has been seen to be a more optimal design than hop-by-hop recovery. As we move from one-to-one, through one-to-many and on to many-to-many applications, we can see that the same principle has to be changed. Neither the original sender nor the network can deal with the task of delivering packets in order, and senders cannot know when (or which) receivers are missing packets. It is not a good idea to use a positive-acknowledgement plus timeout-retransmission scheme for multicast applications because of the well known 'implosion' problem (congestive collapse caused by multiple acknowledgements returning to the sender or senders; see Paliwoda and Crowcroft, 1988).

3   Scalable reliable multicast (Floyd *et al.*, 1995) is a technique that has seen wide deployment in LBL's whiteboard application. Wb uses the principles above to provide a reliable delivery. The protocol and repair algorithm are briefly as follows (paraphrased from Floyd *et al.*):

(a)   Messages are sent with a sequence number plus a timestamp. There are three basic types of message: data messages, negative acknowledgements and heartbeat messages.

(b)   All participants keep state for all other participants, which includes the following:

(i)   source address, plus last seen in order sequence number;

(ii)   the estimated distance (delay) from this participant to each of the others.

In addition, participants keep a number of the most recently received messages available.[3]

On detecting a missing packet from a gap in the sequence number space (between last received in order and newly received packet), a receiver prepares to send (multicast) a negative acknowledgement, which acts as a request for a repair from any other participant. However, the receiver defers sending the negative acknowledgement. The time deferred is set so as to cause the set of potential participants sending a negative to (implicitly) conspire so that usually only one (or a small number) of them make the request. To do this, the timer is drawn from a uniform distribution over the range $[c_1 \times d_a, (c_1 + c_2) \times d_a]$, where c_1 and c_2 are constants and d_a is the requesting participant's estimate of the delay to the source. This time is subject to a binary exponential backoff in the usual manner if there is no response.

Participants that receive the request for repair, and wish to try to honour it also dally before sending the repair. Their hiatus is drawn from the distribution $[d_1 \times d_{ab}, (d_1 + d_2) \times d_{ab}]$ to ensure that it is likely that only one (or at least only a few) send the repair.

Repair request messages suppress repair requests from other sites missing the same packet. Repair responses suppress other responses (as well as, hopefully, satisfying the request).

Finally, the delay estimation is based on the same algorithm used in NTP (Mills, 1990). Heartbeat messages are sent by each participant carrying a list of other participants, together with the timestamp from the last message seen from each participant t_1, and the difference, $d = t_3 - d_2$, between its arrival time, t_2, and the heartbeat send time, t_3. On receiving a heartbeat message at t_4, the delay can be estimated as $\frac{1}{2}(t_4 - t_1 - d)$. This can be calculated using a rolling average, and the mean difference kept for safety if required. (As long as paths are reasonably symmetrical and clock rates not too different, this suffices for the repair algorithm above.)

4   Some applications require packets to have a particular inter-arrival rate. So long as the network can support the average rate (i.e. there is no long-term congestion), 'Receiver makes good' is generally a low cost solution to dealing with jitter or partial packet reordering. It is hard to provide a global transmission clock in large, heterogeneous networks. In essence, if timestamped, and a receiver clock does not drift or wander too quickly with respect to a sender clock, a receiver can run an adaptive play-out buffer to restore the play-out times of packets. The size of the play-out buffer is in essence twice the inter-arrival variation in order to ensure a significant percentage of packets arrive within the worst case time. A rolling average of the inter-arrival times (kept in any case if the algorithm described above is in use) is maintained. If the mean delay varies (owing to increased or decreased load on the network, or to route changes) then quiet times can be used to make adjustments.

5   Cheriton (Holbrook et al., 1995) describes a a scheme called log-based receiver repair which was devised for distributed simulations in the DIS (the DISNet is an ARPA-funded program of work whose target is the development of a suite of systems to support the Synthetic Theatre of War demonstration in 1997, from which much of this research stems). This is similar in spirit to the SRM approach, but has separate log servers rather than expecting all applications to participate in the repair algorithm. The upside of this is that a larger history may be kept (and for applications where the entire history is necessary to reconstruct current state, it may be too costly to distribute to all sites). The downside is that a distinguished server type needs a distinguished protocol to maintain replicant servers and so forth.

6   Synchronisation of messages from different sources is generally a bad thing (Floyd et al., 1995). Open loop protocols such as the types we have described above (and many other heartbeat style protocols such as routing update and reachability protocols) are prone to synchronise send times. This can be avoided by careful selection of randomising timers based on unique participant data (own address is a good example).

7   Multicast applications cannot use positive feedback for reliability. Nor can they use positive explicit feedback for congestion or flow control. Instead, implicit and aggregated information may be more effective. One scheme for congestion control and multicast is described by Wakeman in Bolot et al. (1994). It is important to be flexible. Depending on whether group communication can proceed at the speed of the slowest participant (or link to them) or the average, or be completely heterogeneous, we need different schemes for flow and

congestion control. We can separate these also into sender- and receiver-based adaptation, and the next item refers to work in this area. In Wakeman's scheme, the sender elicits responses from a receiver set at a given *distance* by multicasting out a packet with a sliding key, which in essence acts as a selector key to choose some small percentage of recipients to act as samples to report on traffic conditions seen at their point in the network with respect to the sender.

In the LBL work, this idea is generalised. Multicast receivers keep state about all senders. As with SRM, they periodically send heartbeat messages, which contain this state (perhaps spreading the state over a set of heartbeat messages to keep the size of the updates small). This state can be used by senders to estimate the conditions at all points in the network. To keep heartbeat/session traffic to a reasonable level, the rate of the beat is reduced in proportion to the number of participants. Although this means that the rate of samples from any given system is decreased for a larger group, the number of samples stays the same. In fact, as a group gets larger, it is statistically reasonable to assume that it is more evenly and widely distributed, and may give better and better samples concerning traffic conditions throughout the multicast distribution fabric.

8   McCanne *et al.*, in their work on multicast video, have looked at layered media encodings and how they may be mapped onto multiple groups (McCanne *et al.*, 1996). In this work, different levels of quality (or urgency, or interest) are sent to different group addresses. The number of levels, and amount that is sent in each can be adjusted using schemes such as the one described just before. However, receivers can independently adjust the rate of traffic that arrives at them simply by joining (to increase) or leaving (to decrease) one or more groups, corresponding to the appropriate coding levels.

9   Flow and congestion signal actions are generally the same for multicast applications as for unicast. The stable and safe algorithm (Jacobson, 1988) used in TCP since 1988 with a slow start cycle, a congestion control cycle with exponential backoff and linear increase, and a fast retransmit cycle to avoid short-lived congestion can be employed.

The rest of this chapter is structured as follows. In the next section, we outline the structure of a distributed virtual reality system. After that we look at some of the real requirements from distributed VR, from both systems and the human perspectives. Following that we present the transport protocol. Finally we look at further work that needs to be done.

8.4.1   General idea and problems

Virtual reality systems are really glorified renderers combined with simulations, and some fancy display and pointer technology. The software components typically include roughly what you would expect, as illustrated in Figure 8.10.

The performance requirements for distributing VR are surprising. Once a system is up and running, it transpires that objects are introduced/created and destroyed, with relatively low frequency. If a distributed VR system runs the collision detection

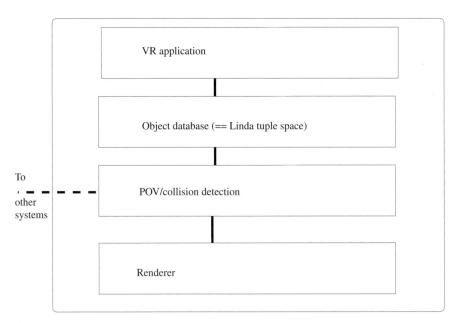

Figure 8.10   Virtual reality software structure.

and rendering at all receivers, it is only point of view (POV) and object locations and attitudes that need updating. Here, though, there may be an extremely stringent latency requirement because of multiple interactions with other objects.

We need three main components to a protocol to distribute this functionality:

1   A virtual world bulk load protocol

2   An object naming system

3   An update protocol

The virtual world bulk load protocol could be based in a number of existing protocols for large-scale information dissemination. We assume that virtual worlds are potentially very large databases (although many VRML examples are not that large, we would anticipate this changing as time progresses and people develop a taste for richer virtual environments). However, it may be possible to use the update protocol that we are devising here too, if it is engineered for high throughput as well as low latency.

The object naming system requires hierarchical naming and wildcarding, as well as a clean mapping from object to multicast group. Such a system has been devised in earlier work, and is partially implemented in the CCCP system (Handley *et al.*, 1995).

The update protocol is what we will concentrate on here. In essence, we propose an extension of SRM, together with the congestion avoidance mechanisms taken from Wakeman and McCanne's work. We propose basing the protocol on RTP, as is described in Parnes' work (Parnes, 1997) since it is likely that eventually VR worlds may include media such as audio and video, and we see no reason to use a different packet header to support point of view and object motion, and new object upload.

We propose that the constants of repair can be adjusted in favour of fast recovery rather than low numbers of repeated requests and repairs, since the load caused by this (given the size of repairs) is relatively small.

The sender application needs to specify the semantics of the operation, and this is conveyed in a single field in the protocol so that receivers can work out whether a repair request is relevant or whether a new update will overwrite the effect anyhow.

8.4.2   Virtual reality operations, user views and network considerations

For a distributed multi-party application, there are a number of constraints which we might try to satisfy:

1   Convergence, or does the interface show a system that reaches eventual consistency?

2   Determinism, or does the system behave according to users' expectations of the underlying model?

3   Multiple modifiers, or does the system allow more than a single user to modify an object (write/update state associated with an object)?

4   Interactivity, or does the system let users lock an object so that they then have exclusive write/update access?

A key point in the design of the system is that when operating over a network with loss, reordering, and different levels of throughput/latency between different senders and recipients, it is clear that it is impossible to satisfy all four of these at any one time. It should be sufficient to relax one of the constraints at one time, but it will be dependent on a particular application and user requirements which constraint is the appropriate one to relax.

Network conditions that pertain to each of these constraints are:

1   *Capacity* – bits per second – may differ between a sender and a set of recipients – a distribution tree rooted at each sender will have paths to recipients, and different parts of the subtree may have different capacity.

2   *Errors/loss* – packet loss may be due to noise on the line, transient outage or temporary congestion. Again, in a multi-party application, this may be different for different receivers.

3   *Availability* – networks can partition. Some senders or recipients may crash, or reboot at different times during a multi-party session.

4   *Delay* – delays over long-haul networks, even without queues, can be significant. Again, they will usually differ from one recipient to the next.

8.4.3   Application model

Initially, we are making the big assumption here, that the model run at each site/host is the same, and that the only differences are POVs and the user at each host. However, it is not necessary for all users at all sites to 'see' all objects. In fact, real estate probably precludes this. This means that certain (large) optimisations are possible in terms of delivering operations/messages to each host.

The set of typical operations between a VR application and the underlying system ranges from moving point of view to moving objects themselves and altering the attitudes.

Taking a more advanced approach, one could consider sending trajectories around and having receivers apply the model world to the object (for example, gravity, wind, friction, etc.).

Messages may be idempotent (describe an absolute position for an object, or position and velocity, and so on), or not (maybe they just say how far the object has moved).

Interactions between users of a distributed VR application are complex. An object must in some senses have an owner. This may be the user at a site (for example, if the object is the POV itself, or the glove/pointer, etc.), or an object currently under the control of a user.

Thus we should associate a set of objects (and users) with a portion of the multicast address space. The idea is that a user is in some *locale* and that only operations relative to that locale need be delivered to their system.

Furthermore, there must be some notion of 'real' virtual world distance. The set of objects in VR in a locale that are 'near' a user are subject to interactions which can reasonably be modelled without having to worry about propagation delay across the net. Beyond some distance, the time to get a message from the originator of the action to the hosts that a set of POVs include this locale may simply be too high to consider. For example, imagine playing catch in a virtual world simulated between two machines on the Net. The time for the ball to reach the ground is less than the time for the message to cross a terrestrial line more than a few thousand miles.

It may be possible to introduce some element of representation of distance into the user interface. Two approaches suggest themselves based on physics models of the real world:

1 *Uncertainty*: As an object gets further away, we can introduce less certainty about its position (note that the SRM protocol above gives us enough information to do this accurately).

2 *Relativity*: We could warp spacetime in the virtual environment to produce a similar effect to gravity – action at a distance could become much slower.

Given this, different VR applications may need to relax a *different* one of the four constraints, possibly at different times. In fact, we can envisage single applications that need to relax different constraints for different *objects* at different times.

8.4.4 Distributed virtual reality multicast protocol (DVRMP)

DVRMP runs on top of RTP (Schulzrinne *et al.*, 1996) and UDP. All DVRMP messages are multicast. As in Parnes' proposal, we use RTP data packets as is, for data. If reliability is needed, the RTP PT field is used to indicate SRM, otherwise it simply conveys normal data. (See Figures 8.11 and 8.12.) The SSRC is the source VR application. The CSRC can be used for input from specific devices.

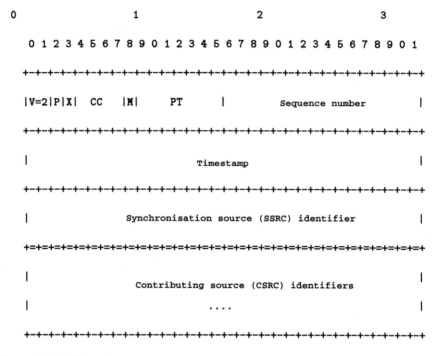

Figure 8.11   RTP header.

We use RTCP as is for session-quality reports, and respect the Parnes protocol for reliability. More than one multicast group is used. Session messages are used within one multicast group to advertise the existence of participants and objects. Objects have owners. At any one time, the owner is the source of the session messages about an object.

Messages can be marked as reliable or not reliable; however, this is not binding on recipients. Recipients can operate the repair algorithm on reliable object messages in the normal way. Other messages are deemed ephemeral and can be lost (or discarded) at will.[4]

8.5 SUMMARY

In this chapter we have looked at two application protocols in some detail: one is a distributed multiuser network text editor; the other is a protocol for distributed virtual reality. Both take advantage of application-layer framing and integrated layer processing to provide simple, scalable and feasible systems.

Notes

1 Load, in terms of messages on any particular link, state or processing power.

SRM RTCP packet

```
 0                   1                   2                   3
 0 1 2 3 4 5 6 7 8 9 0 1 2 3 4 5 6 7 8 9 0 1 2 3 4 5 6 7 8 9 0 1
+-+-+-+-+-+-+-+-+-+-+-+-+-+-+-+-+-+-+-+-+-+-+-+-+-+-+-+-+-+-+-+-+
|V=2|CM | Count |  PT=SRM=205  |             Length             |  Header
+=+=+=+=+=+=+=+=+=+=+=+=+=+=+=+=+=+=+=+=+=+=+=+=+=+=+=+=+=+=+=+=+
```

Heartbeats (CM = 0)

```
 0                   1                   2                   3
 0 1 2 3 4 5 6 7 8 9 0 1 2 3 4 5 6 7 8 9 0 1 2 3 4 5 6 7 8 9 0 1
+-+-+-+-+-+-+-+-+-+-+-+-+-+-+-+-+-+-+-+-+-+-+-+-+-+-+-+-+-+-+-+-+
|         Sequence number       |         Not used             |
+=+=+=+=+=+=+=+=+=+=+=+=+=+=+=+=+=+=+=+=+=+=+=+=+=+=+=+=+=+=+=+=+
```

NACKs/repair requests (CM = 1)

```
 0                   1                   2                   3
 0 1 2 3 4 5 6 7 8 9 0 1 2 3 4 5 6 7 8 9 0 1 2 3 4 5 6 7 8 9 0 1
+-+-+-+-+-+-+-+-+-+-+-+-+-+-+-+-+-+-+-+-+-+-+-+-+-+-+-+-+-+-+-+-+
|                             SSRC                              |
+-+-+-+-+-+-+-+-+-+-+-+-+-+-+-+-+-+-+-+-+-+-+-+-+-+-+-+-+-+-+-+-+
|                       Sequence number                        |
+=+=+=+=+=+=+=+=+=+=+=+=+=+=+=+=+=+=+=+=+=+=+=+=+=+=+=+=+=+=+=+=+
```

Followed by

```
 0                   1                   2                   3
 0 1 2 3 4 5 6 7 8 9 0 1 2 3 4 5 6 7 8 9 0 1 2 3 4 5 6 7 8 9 0 1
+-+-+-+-+-+-+-+-+-+-+-+-+-+-+-+-+-+-+-+-+-+-+-+-+-+-+-+-+-+-+-+-+
```

Figure 8.12 RTP and SRM.

2 We would like components to scale O(1). At the very worst, no component should scale worse than O(n), and even O(n) is not acceptable in some circumstances.

3 This may in fact be a feature of the way that the application is structured in any case. For example, if the application state is the same as the effect of the sequence of messages (as is the case with a whiteboard), then it may be possible to cast a repair in terms of application state, i.e. to reconstruct a message that has the same effect as the missing one.

4 This limits the amount of storage necessary for receivers participating in a possible repair. It is derived from the fact that there are many ways to send descriptions of object locations, velocity, trajectory. Some are coded so that loss of a single message makes it hard to recover, others are largely lists of deltas, and recovery may be reasonably easy, whilst yet others are explicit co-ordinates and only the latest message is relevant.

CHAPTER NINE

Media-on-demand

9.1 INTRODUCTION

It is tempting to think of unifying the interactive multimedia applications that most of this book has been about with the multimedia system that is the World Wide Web. However, the paradigms of use and the protocols are very different. The Web is very much a browser's paradise, whilst the applications we have been concentrating on are much more active. This is shown to a large degree by the design of user interfaces, and attempts to force conferencing applications into the strait-jacket of a Web browser, whilst very tempting, are misguided.

An important aspect of the Web that makes it scalable is that (like DNS) it is largely a 'read only' database. This means that, whilst it might be tempting to think of it as a repository for media, it may not be so suitable for the type of interactive systems we are interested in here.

In this chapter we present the components of a more suitable system for media recording and playback on demand.

9.2 ROADMAP

This chapter falls into two main components: recording and playback. First we look at recording of multicast and multimedia data, then we look at real time retrieval and playback, which is a relatively new area for Internet standardisation.

9.3 RECORDING AND PLAYING BACK MBONE SESSIONS

Experiences of interactive Internet multimedia applications, especially conferencing, indicate that there is a need for a mechanism to record and play back the media of these conferences (Kirstein *et al.*, 1993; Sasse *et al.*, 1994).

When recording, both audio and video streams need to be archived, and possibly the shared workspace too, with the possibility of having stream synchronisation. As some conferences require only a subset of the conferees to be recorded, the record mechanism should allow a selection of the streams to be specified. The retrieval of recorded material needs to be easy for users to access, either for direct playback to the user or for inclusion in another multicast multimedia conference. Users also need to see which conferences have been recorded and are online for access in order to select streams to play. As real time multimedia applications generate vast amounts of data, any recording system must therefore be fully equipped with large storage capabilities.

To meet the above requirements, the objectives of a recording and playback system need to be:

1   The ability to record multicast session data whose source may be any of the conferees.
2   The ability to play back recorded material either directly to one user or into another multicast session.
3   To provide synchronisation between streams from each source.
4   To allow users to create both their own segments of recorded material and their own material for playback.
5   To provide a single point of contact for recording and playback.
6   To supply a large repository of archive space which is accessible to authorised network users who wish to record or play back multimedia data.

In the next section we discuss previous attempts at recording and playback of multimedia conferences and see how they meet the above objectives. Then the design of a system to achieve the above objectives is presented, showing what is actually required for recording, playback and editing of multimedia streams. As the media streams are large, it is pertinent to provide indexes into these streams. Multimedia indexes are a novel approach to accessing such data, and these techniques will be discussed later.

After this, we describe the real time streaming protocol (RTSP), which is becoming the standard for remote control facilities for multimedia servers.

9.4   RECORDING

First we consider multimedia recording and playback systems which are not designed specifically with multimedia conferencing in mind. Most of these aim to be video-on-demand systems (Vin and Rangan, 1993). Some of them aim to produce high-quality, synchronised video with attention paid to playback strategies in order to generate 30 frames per second of media (Rowe and Smith, 1992). The designers of such systems are interested in high-speed disks and storage structures using, for example, RAID disk technology (Tierney and Johnson, 1994; Buddhikot et al., 1994) in order to get high volumes of video data from storage to the user. Other work focuses on designing models for presentation of media (Kato and Mizutori, 1989), and has been extended into the arena of distributed presentation of media (Bates and Bacon, 1995; Little and Ghafoor, 1991; Berra et al., 1990), admission control for multiple users (Rangan et al., 1992), and the mix of both analogue and digital components within the infrastructure (Duval and Olivie, 1993).

9.4.1 Using IP multicast

Within a multimedia conference the media tools utilise the IP multicast mechanism by having every instance of a tool join the same multicast address. For each medium there is a unique address and port pair, on which the tool is started. The addresses used by MICE conferences, for example, are shown in Table 9.1.

Note in Table 9.1 that the address is the same but the port changes. In other conferences both the address and port change. Furthermore, each tool may use more than one port, which is not always advertised. The tools send data to one port and non-core data to another port. The non-core data usually consist of session information such as the user name of the sender or some statistics regarding the quality of the received data. These session messages are sent at low bandwidth as they are secondary to the real data. It is most common for the session message port to be one higher than the advertised port number. So, for the previous examples we would see session messages for audio on port for video on port and for whiteboard on port.

To record data from a multicast conference, the recorder need not be an active part of the conference by executing any of the conference tools, but it must attach to that conference to enable the multicast data to reach the recorder and hence be collected. As data for each medium within a conference will be seen on a different address and port pair, the recorder must accommodate this. The collected data for each medium can then be saved in an archive for later use. In order to play back the recorded data to a multicast conference, a player must join the multicast address for each medium in the conference to enable the data from the archive to be sent into the conference. Again, each medium's data will go to a different address and port pair. In Figure 9.1 we see that, before a recording or playback, the recorder or player, respectively, is independent of the conference, and that the data packets and session messages are on different addresses.

In Figure 9.2 we see that the recorder or player has attached to the conference in order to collect the data from each medium.

9.4.2 Current media tools and protocols

Multicast conferencing tools have been written and improved continuously by their developers over the past three or four years, and new tools are still appearing.

As described in Chapter 5, the media tools send media data inside RTP packets on one multicast address, and session message information inside RTCP packets on another multicast address. For example, the audio tool used by each conference participant sends audio data in small chunks of about 20 ms duration. Each chunk

Table 9.1 Multicast address use in session.

Medium	Address
Audio	224.2.17.11/3456
Video	224.2.17.11/2232
Whiteboard	224.2.17.11/32415

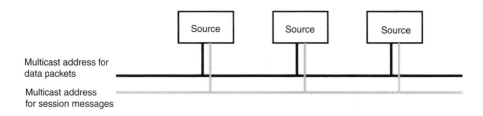

Figure 9.1   The recorder is independent of the conference.

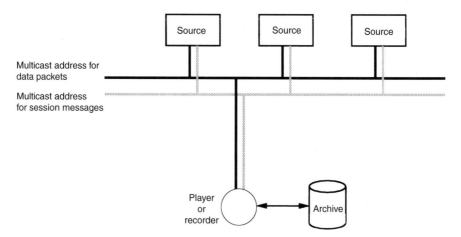

Figure 9.2   The recorder attaches to the conference to record the data.

of audio data is preceded by an RTP header; the RTP header and data are in turn contained in a UDP packet. The RTP header indicates what type of audio encoding, such as PCM, ADPCM or GSM, is contained in each packet so that senders can change the encoding during a conference, for example, to accommodate a new participant or from indications of network congestion. Similarly, the session message data which uses the RTCP format is also contained in a UDP packet.

As all media data and session messages are sent within UDP packets there is no guarantee of packet delivery to the receivers. Owing to the nature of busy packet switched networks, some packets are seriously delayed and others are lost in transit. To accommodate this, most media tools have a play-out mechanism that uses an adaptive play-out buffer (Floyd *et al.*, 1995) in an attempt to hide these effects from the end user. In some circumstances the media tool cannot cope and the media are presented to the user with loss.

Reliable multicast

Many IP multicast tools use a reliable multicast mechanism to maintain consistency between each instance of the tool. Reliable multicast is a mechanism by which data that are multicast from a sender are guaranteed to reach the receivers at some time. The reliability mechanism requires some form of acknowledgement scheme to say which packets did and did not arrive at a receiver, a kind of retransmission scheme to send out lost or late packets, and support within the tools to participate in these schemes.

For media such as video and audio, data arrive so fast that it is better to present then quickly and to tolerate some reduction in quality if packets do not arrive on time or are lost in transmission. This can be done because humans are quite tolerant of loss, particularly for video, and the information content is not reduced drastically if loss does occur. Furthermore, with a reliable transmission scheme, late or lost data could be resent to the receiver at a significant amount of time after the original send time, which would cause the immediacy of any interaction between users to be eliminated. Clearly, this is not suitable for live, interactive conferences. However, this level of reliability is important for shared workspace tools where whole objects need appear with all their data eventually, but where there is no immediacy lost if a packet is retransmitted and arrives at some later time.

Both of the well known shared workspace tools, wb and nte, use a reliable multicast mechanism. The scheme used by wb is described in Floyd *et al.* (1995) and that for nte is described in Handley (1995). Both schemes resend parts of objects that get lost on the network. The RTP protocol is not used because the data are not real time data, but partial object data. In nte, and possibly wb, the RTP timestamp does not have enough resolution to hold all the timing information required. Therefore both nte and wb have their own packet format to support their reliability and retransmission mechanisms. It is unfortunate that the schemes are not described in enough detail to build a new tool that could participate in these schemes.

9.4.3 A multimedia recording server

To allow easy deployment, the interface to playback systems should be made compatible with Web browsers, such as Mosaic or Netscape. This enables the media to be selected and replayed using a GUI, and this approach avoids writing a special playback client but requires the server playback interface to look like a Web server. However, using a naive approach, the user is able to play back the whole conference, but is not able to select their own start-point or end-point.

Many of the problems associated with the delivery of multimedia to end-users are issues of synchronisation. It has become apparent that synchronisation is more complicated than one may think. We have determined that there are at least three kinds of synchronisation that are important for media synchronisation. They are:

1 *Lip synchronisation*, where the movement of the lips as seen on the video and the delivery of the audio persuade the user that the person is really speaking at that time.

2   *Time synchronisation*, where a specification of time, either relative or absolute, goes to the same point in time in each stream of each medium, regardless of the volume of data in the streams.

3   *Inter-packet synchronisation*, where packets are presented to the network, by a player, in such a way that they arrive at the media tools in the same order and inter-packet gap as when they arrived at a recorder. Where more than one stream is being played, some kind of inter-stream multiplexing is required to maintain this synchronisation.

It is desirable to have a unified approach which makes the tasks of recording and playback simple to achieve and overcomes the problems just discussed. By considering the problems of the existing tools, it is apparent that a system that does recording and playback must have:

1   A tool for recording multiple media within the same conference.
2   A tool for playing multiple media into a new conference.
3   User specifiable streams on recording or playback.
4   Synchronisation between the media streams.
5   A single point of contact for accessing the recordings.
6   A large repository of disk space for the recordings.

9.4.4   Server interfaces

Owing to the multiple but specialised functionality required, a server has different interfaces. The main include interfaces for recording, playback and editing and are discussed here, but the design allows the server to have as many specialised interfaces as required.

Recording

The record interface of the server allows a client to start a recording of any of the media used in conference, to specify the duration of the recording, to specify one, many, or all of the source streams, and to add a title and text description of the recording. If more than one medium is selected for a source, then the user may choose to have time-based synchronisation between those streams at the server. This will enable synchronisation within the playback mechanisms.

The server system collects all or some of the streams of media for a conference, and a client allows the user to select which media to record and then instructs the server to record them. The client does not need to be part of the conference. With the server listening to the media tool session messages or observing the source addresses of incoming data for each medium of a conference, the server can decide who is in each conference. Another feature of the server is the ability to allow synchronisation between the incoming streams. In this way, playback can be presented to the user with the media streams for a source being synchronised.

A client connected to the record interface allows the user to select a medium to record, and then instructs the server to record that stream. The server can inform its clients whom it is currently recording in a conference in order to stop more than

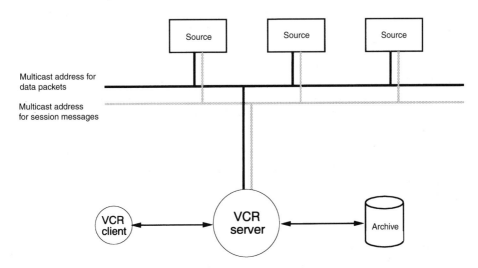

Figure 9.3   Client informs server which collects multicast data.

one client attempting to record the same medium within that conference. It is expected that a new client will be started for each different multicast conference. Figure 9.3 shows that the media tools send and receive data via IP multicast, and that the server under instruction from the client receives that multicast data and records it.

Using this client/server configuration, many sites may have servers which are able to record and play back conferences. These sites may choose to record data for any authorised user on the network, not just for local users. It is not necessary for any special designated site to be the conference recording hub for the whole of the Mbone. With full deployment, there could be a large collection of servers on the Internet. A client can connect to a server anywhere on the network to request a recording.

Playback

The playback interface of the server allows a client to peruse all the online archives, to allow the selection of one or more media and one or more streams for playback, to specify the destination conference for the playback, and to control the media during playback.

For playback, a different client interface is used to access the server. The server presents this client with information showing which conferences have been recorded, which streams are available for playback, and which conferences are currently being played back and on which address.

The playback of the recorded data can be presented to the user in various ways:

1   The user can choose to play a stream or many streams from an old conference into a new conference. In this scenario all members of the conference can see the played-back streams.

2   The user can choose to see a stream or streams presented to his workstation only. In this scenario only the user sees the streams.

3   The user can choose to play back a recording as a presentation to a small group of people.

It would be possible to make the playback interface compatible with Web browsers such as Netscape or Mosaic. This would enable the media to be selected and replayed using a GUI, and avoids writing a special playback client, but requires the server playback interface to look like a Web server by using the HTTP protocol (Fielding *et al.*, 1996). A mechanism similar to this has been successfully deployed by Anders Klemets of KTH in Sweden. The approach suggested here does require the playback interface of the server to look like a Web server.

It may be possible to have a client that combined playback with recording in order to have a GUI that allows both recording and search and access to prerecorded data. This may be desirable if one needed to provide an interface that looked like a traditional tape recorder. In this instance the client would connect to more than one server interface.

In some instances it may be desirable to have a full conference replay. As the server is able to provide synchronisation data for the media streams, during playback it is possible to have all the media streams synchronised. The synchronisation means that the data are presented in near real time rather than at an arbitrary rate which is dependent on the speed of the machine.

Editing

The editing interface will allow the user to make copies of a whole media stream or to select a segment of a media stream in order to create their own personal archives. When editing, the user will be able to create a text description of arbitrary parts of the media to aid playback selection. Further editing tools can be used to combine preselected segments of media, possibly from different conferences, into new presentation material. The new presentations could then be used as lecture material, for summaries of work or for presentations of project work. As these newly created presentations will be independent of one another, multiple uses of one recording is allowed, thus enabling a more flexible use of the whole archive.

A full playback of a video conference can be time consuming and often not what is required. It is envisaged that a set of media editors will be designed to enable each medium to be made presentable for different uses. This will allow for:

- Text annotations to be added at multiple positions in a recording
- The creation of conference summaries
- The elimination of quiet sections
- The creation of lecture material
- The creation of special presentations

The editing functions required are the addition of annotations, the selection of segments and the ability to do postprocessing of the data.

- *Addition of annotations*: The addition of annotations allows users to add metadata to a recording. These annotations can take on many forms, such as text to interface to browsing and selection tools; HTML data or URLs to interface with the World Wide Web; content classification data to interface to search engines; start of video frame or start of speech burst markers to interface to special player, and so

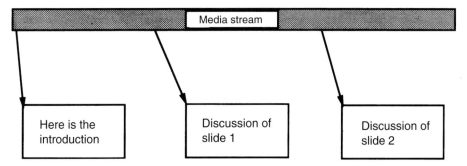

Figure 9.4 Multiple text descriptions for a medium.

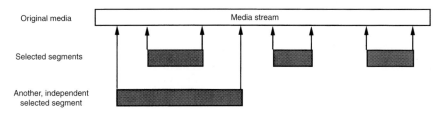

Figure 9.5 Selecting segments from a recording.

on. The addition of text descriptions allows users to specify what is contained in different sections of a recording. These descriptions can be presented via the playback tool, and allow the user to play from a specified point. Figure 9.4 shows a stream with three added text annotations.

- *Segment selection*: The editing process allows segments of a recording to be selected and saved for later use. These segments are independent of the original recording and can be manipulated freely for other uses. Some related techniques to the one suggested here are described by Hampapur *et al.* (1995). Figure 9.5 shows some segments that have been selected from the original media stream. One selection has three small segments, whilst the other has one larger segment. This results in three instances of media for the one recording; the original media, the three small segments, and the larger segment. Each can be used independently of the others.

For each type of medium, and for each different format for that medium, a different segment selection editor may be required. For example:

- For H.261 video, an editor could select on macroblock (MB) or group of block (GOB) boundaries closest to the selection made by the user.

- For audio, the selection boundary could be on either each audio sample or on each talkspurt.

- For shared workspace applications, such as the whiteboard, an editor may not be useful if selections were done on a timeslice basis. Both video and audio are continuous media whereas the whiteboard is a non-continuous medium, such that

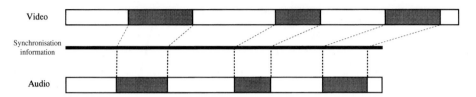

Figure 9.6   The synchronisation of three segments of audio and video.

selecting data from a time period would give a random set of objects. Selection would be useful only on an object-by-object basis and therefore some kind of postprocessing is required.

When using stream synchronisation, the segments of the media should be synchronised such that when one medium segment is selected an equivalent part of some associate medium is also selected. Figure 9.6 shows that the user is able to select segments (shaded) of video and audio which are equivalent with respect to the synchronisation information stored by the server.

9.4.5   Analysis and postprocessing tools

Although the server maintains all the recording information, and has interfaces to allow recording, playback and editing, this functionality is often not enough. For extended use of the data it is beneficial to provide tools for analysis of the media streams held in the server, and tools for postprocessing the media streams in order to modify them.

These tools are different for each kind of processing and each kind of medium. With audio, for example, the tools envisaged are (1) for an analysis to graphically present the temporal aspects of the audio for each user in a conference, and (2) for an analysis to determine the percentage of audio sent by each user in a conference. The analysis data can be used to delete audio from some users in a recording.

With video, for example, it is envisaged that the media streams are postprocessed to generate more intra-frames than exist in the original stream. Having the extra intra-frames enables playback from arbitrary places in the stream. With analogue video a new whole frame is sent to the display every 0.04 seconds. Owing to the way H.261 digital video is compressed using intra-frames and inter-frames, whole new frames are rarely (if ever) sent to the display. These intra- and inter-frames are the differences from the previous image. A whole frame is reconstructed from the differences of the image contained in the intra- and inter-frames.

For shared workspace the postprocessing can reconstruct workspace objects from the stream of sub-objects contained in packets.

This list is not exhaustive, but is meant to give a flavour of the kind of processing required.

9.4.6   **Clients**

The clients of the multimedia server initiate the recording, playback or editing for the user. Each interface uses a TCP stream in order to allow the building of both simple text-based user interfaces, based on the telnet model, or graphical user interfaces based on Windows. Each client can be designed to have a specialised task such as recording or playback only by connecting to the relevant server interface. It is possible to build more complex user interfaces by having the client connect to more than one server interface and provide compound functionality for the user.

Multiple clients can connect to the server, and clients can connect to as many interfaces as they require. There is no limit within the server pertaining to the number of client connections.

9.4.7   **Server storage**

The hardware available for the media include CD and DVD jukeboxes plus some large magnetic disks. The hard disks are used as fast, temporary storage within the server, whereas the CDs are used for mass storage. When recording, media streams are sent from the network to the magnetic disks, and then onto CDs for permanent storage. When replaying data, the media stored on CDs are taken from the CD and sent to the magnetic drives for subsequent playback to the user. To manage this hardware and to present media streams back to the user, some software is needed to select CDs from the CD store and place them into the CD players of the jukebox.

A jukebox is a large collection of CD disks in a box with a few CD drives. These jukeboxes have a huge capacity, going up to terabytes. We have seen that a video stream with a high compression ratio may generate over 1 GB of data an hour, therefore these jukebox devices seem to be ideal for video and audio because of their

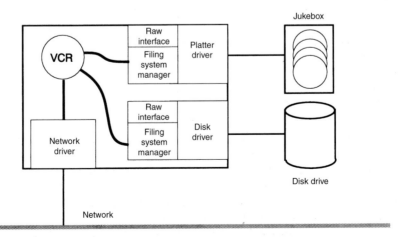

Figure 9.7   Storage devices for multimedia-on-demand servers.

large capacity; however, their throughput could be a limitation. Currently, a high-density CD has a capacity of 650 MB per side. Figure 9.7 shows how the disks, the network and the server software are connected.

Given that an hour of compressed video can be expected to require about 240 MB of storage per source, it is possible to evaluate the amount of storage space needed by an average conference recording. From this figure we can extrapolate to determine how much storage space such a system will require in order to be effective.

In terms of cost, as of January 1999, a 10 GB disk drive costs around £100, and a fully populated jukebox with 144 platters costs about £5000. With a 10 GB disk drive one gets 6 GB for £100, with a jukebox of 144 platters, each with 650 MB per side, giving a total of 172 GB, one gets 2 GB for £100. Clearly there is a factor of three in the cost of owning a jukebox, and to replicate this amount of storage space on magnetic media with just 20 magnetic drives would cost only £20 000. The main benefit of the optical device is that there is no need to buy extra backup devices and media.

Play-out volumes

A real service needs to accommodate a large configuration, with a large optical jukebox, a fast workstation front-end, plus a fast disk cache or just a workstation with a few gigabytes of disk space.

For a larger configuration with a jukebox we can expect to store more low-bandwidth media than high-bandwidth media. A jukebox with 144 platters, each with a total capacity of 1.2 GB has a total storage area of 172 GB. The amount of media which can be stored can be calculated as follows:

- For a video stream which is presented at 2 MBps then 500 seconds of video would use 1 GB. Therefore, in 172 GB we could store 86 000 seconds' worth, which is about 1440 minutes or 24 hours.

- For a video stream which is presented at 128 kBps then 8000 seconds of video would use 1 GB. Therefore, in 172 GB we could store 1 376 000 seconds' worth, which is about 23 000 minutes or 380 hours or 16 days.

- For a video stream which is presented at 32 kBps then 32 000 seconds of video would use 1 GB. Therefore, in 172 GB we could store 5 504 000 seconds' worth, which is about 92 000 minutes or 1530 hours or 64 days.

The most common configuration is expected to be a system in which a workstation with a few gigabytes of disk space can be used as a server. Such a system could still expect to store many hours of audio and video.

The factors to consider for the storage requirements of a large server are related to the total amount of physical data there is, and the volume of data that needs to be recorded or played in either kilobytes per second or megabytes per second. For the amount of physical data we need to consider file size, partition size and disk size as well as file structure; for the volume of data we need to consider disk speed, disk bandwidth, network speed, network bandwidth as well as read/write delay seek times and platter load times.

A full investigation of storage for high bandwidth video-on-demand servers can be found in Chervanak (1994). In this section there is just an overview of the issues that need to be considered for the storage requirements of the server.

Size and structure

For storing large media streams, the use of a database which is amenable to continuous media, or a special video filing system (Anderson *et al.*, 1992) seems pertinent. Using a traditional relational database is not suitable as these RDBMS are optimised for indexed tables of small data items.

Use of raw partitions

Here we consider why a server may choose to use raw partitions on a disk rather than going through the filing system mechanism. The potential reasons for using a raw partition rather than a Unix filing system are:

1 Unix cannot create files greater than 2 GB.
2 Unix generally cannot address disk drives greater than 2 GB, but this limit has been increased under Solaris.
3 When creating a large file the indirection, double indirection and triple indirection to data blocks are an unnecessary overhead.
4 Because video archives are so large we would not get many archives on a maximally large filing system.
5 The overhead of i-nodes, superblocks, etc. is unnecessary.
6 The server may need to map an archive address which may be greater than 2 GB into a disk-specific address; having access to a raw partition will aid this.

It is pertinent to note that many relational database management systems, such as Oracle, use raw partitions to increase performance because the filing system is too much of an overhead.

To fully evaluate the use of raw partitions on any particular architecture would require some tests to be undertaken to determine the speed difference between the data transfer of a huge file representative of a video archive in a filing system and the data transfer of an equivalent amount of data from a raw partition. These tests would confirm if double and triple indirection really are very expensive, or if the caching and read ahead techniques used by the file system make the speed difference between a raw partition and a file system negligible.

Use of a jukebox

There are many approaches to managing the jukebox. Something like a hierarchical storage manager can make many CDs look like one big partition. However, as each high-density CD holds about 650 MB per side, and Unix generally allows a partition to have a maximum size of 2 GB, it takes only three CD sides to make a maximum-sized partition. To store video and audio requires partitions of hundreds of gigabytes.

Current jukebox hardware and software support a range of the features required. However, because some of the other features are not suitable, it may be desirable to write a new jukebox manager. In particular, most jukebox software makes the jukebox look like a collection of NFS disks, with each disk having a Unix file system. For video archiving, a different model is required. There will be far fewer files but their size will be huge.

Speed and delay

In order to fully evaluate a hardware configuration, the speed and delays of the relevant devices need to be considered, in particular their actual performance rather than their nominal manufacturer specifications. Currently, magnetic devices are significantly faster and have significantly lower latency than optical devices.

- *Magnetic drives*: In the video conference recorder, magnetic drives are used as a front-end to the CD jukebox. These magnetic drives have fast access times and high bandwidth in comparison with CD jukeboxes which have slow access times and low bandwidth but very high storage capacity. Currently, high-end disk drives such as 9 GB drives are cheap.

- *Jukeboxes*: Currently, a high-density CD has a capacity of 650 MB per side. As a video stream may be more than 650 MB, the server needs a mechanism to load a stream from many CDs onto the magnetic media. When changing from one CD to another there is a delay. The server mechanism should aim to hide the CD changeover time from the user. If the changeover time were not hidden, the media streams would stop until the new CD was loaded. The magnetic disks provide a buffering mechanism whereby media data can be loaded from CDs onto the magnetic disks and played out to the user with an initial delay. This delay can be large enough to hide the changeover time.

  When changing CDs, the number of CD drives within the jukebox affects the performance of the server. Consider the process of accessing some data on a CD in the two cases:

  - *Two drives*: When using two drives it is possible to read from a CD in one drive and to load another CD into the other drive in advance of its use. When one CD is completely read, then access to another CD is just a case of flipping to the other drive. The CD in the original drive can now be replaced with a new CD. The delay is the time it takes to swap drives.
  - *One drive*: When using one drive, the data are read from the CD until completion. Then there will be a delay whilst the CD in the drive is removed and put back into the jukebox. A new CD has to be chosen from the jukebox and placed into the drive. The delay is relatively large.

  As stated, the use of front-end magnetic disks can hide some of the delay by doing large amounts of buffering.

9.4.8 Indexing techniques

There are various facilities for utilising the data which enhance the basic recorded material, namely the selection of segments, the addition of annotations, and the postprocessing and analysis of data. Furthermore, as the data sets are real time multimedia, they are rather large. To enable the flexible use of the recorded data and to enable access to these large data sets, the concept of the real time multimedia index has been devised.

RTM indexes allow access to the source streams in a multitude of ways. The primary index used is created when a stream is originally recorded. For each source of a medium, the incoming data will be saved together with an entry in this index.

Each index entry contains a reference to the data, the time they arrived at the recorder, and a reference to some metadata, which will initially be empty. At the end of a recording, each source will have a stream of data and a stream of index entries. It is the editing client which allows the user to manipulate these indexes in order to gain the flexibility required. For example, the user can add a text annotation to any part of the recording, and the server will attach this to the source stream in the relevant place in the index by updating the metadata field of an index entry.

These indexes are different but complementary to Rowe *et al.*'s indexes which are used in his continuous media player (Rowe *et al.*, 1994). Their indexes are for content categorisation and are used to aid users in searching particular material in the database. For example, in Rowe's system the user might ask: 'List all videos about dinosaurs', and the system would search the category index for dinosaur. Similar work in the categorisation area has been done by Niblack and Barber (1993), who build indexes based on the colour, texture and shape of the content. Also complementary is the work by Hampapur *et al.* (1995) on video data management systems. Other kinds of index have been used for finding the site at which material is held in a distributed multimedia system.

The index is one of the main design concepts and allows access to the multimedia data in a multitude of ways. When a stream is originally recorded an index is created. This is called the primary index and is used for access to the stream of data. For each source of a medium, every component of the incoming data will be saved together with an entry in the primary index.

An important fact of indexes is that the kind of data being indexed are not important nor is the size of the data or their frequency. Implementors can write specialised recorders and players for each specific data kind, all of which utilise, but are independent of, the index itself.

Index approach and implementation

An index has a name together with four structural components:

- The data
- The index elements
- Some annotations associated with the data
- Some header information

Each index has a header file that contains information such as where to find the data, where to find the index elements, where to find the annotations, the type of the data being indexed.

Each index entry contains a reference to the data, the time they arrived at the recorder and a reference to some metadata annotations, which will initially be empty. At the end of a recording, each source will have a stream of data and a stream of index entries (called the index track) – this is shown in Figure 9.8.

Each annotation in the annotation list is an attribute/value pair, where the attribute is a name and the value is any data, either text or binary, that is associated with the particular index element. Each element of the attribute list contains the following data:

- The total number of bytes in the attribute

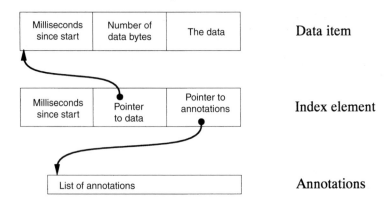

Figure 9.8   Structure of an index element.

Total no. of bytes in this attribute	Attribute status	No. of bytes in name	The name	No. of bytes in value	The value data	*next one ...*

Figure 9.9   Structure of an attribute element.

- Some status information, such as 'active' or 'inactive' for the attribute
- The number of bytes in the name
- The name of this attribute
- The number of bytes in the value
- The value of this attribute

This structure is shown in Figure 9.9.

Using indexes for annotations

After a recording has been completed it can then be manipulated using the editing tools. In Figure 9.10 we show an example where there are three text annotations for a stream of a recording. The text annotations are linked into the recording by the metadata annotations of an index entry. The primary index provides a simple and fast access mechanism to any part of a recording.

Any kind of annotation can be added to any point of a recording, and any index element can have multiple annotations for each index element. The annotations are independent of one another, and can be added at arbitrary times. Because no meaning is imposed on the annotations by the indexing mechanism itself, their use is application specific. The annotations could have values which are text, HTML, URLs, PostScript, references to other indexing systems, and many more.

Using indexes for segment selection

To select segments of a medium it is necessary to access the medium by the selection boundaries. Determining these boundaries for each medium can be problematic, and, in general, segment selection is a difficult task. When a separate index track

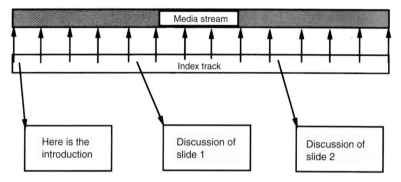

Figure 9.10   The data for a source and its index.

exists, it becomes possible to create multiple segments of a medium for playback by choosing a region of just the index elements. The segment of the index can be copied as it contains references to the real data without copying the original media data. Therefore, when editing, rather than changing the original data for a medium to create new segments, a copy of the index can be created. This means that the original data are left untouched and available for use by other users, and the amount of space used is reduced because copying a segment of an index requires far less space than copying a segment of the medium. The issue of boundaries is eliminated because there are only index elements to view. Using this technique, arbitrary and overlapping segments of edited material can be created. These new segments are independent of one another. Figure 9.11 shows how multiple sequence tracks can be created for one media source.

Using indexes for analysis and postprocessing

It is possible to create tools for both the analysis of the media streams and the postprocessing of the media streams in order to create new, modified streams. For video it is envisaged that the media streams are postprocessed to generate periodic full intra-frames in order to provide multiple entry points into the inter-coded original stream. This will enable playback from arbitrary places in the stream.

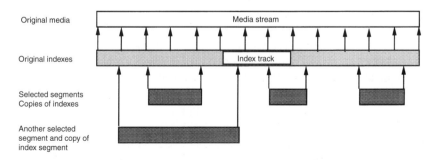

Figure 9.11   Multiple edits of a medium.

With analogue video a new whole frame is sent to the display every 0.04 seconds. Owing to the way digital video is compressed using intra-frames and inter-frames, whole new frames are rarely (if ever) sent to the display. These intra- and inter-frames are the differences from the previous image. A whole frame is reconstructed from the differences of the image contained in the intra- and inter-frames. Our technique will have the benefit of having a full image at all times during playback. Without these full inter-frames it will be possible to replay the video from an arbitrary place but only a few flickering blocks of changing inter-coded video will be seen. Furthermore, as this technique will generate whole images at a regular frequency it will be possible to view a video sequence in a fast-forward mode.

When using video data compression, such as the H.261 encoding, the encoded data stream contains changes from the previous image. The changes take the form of inter-frames and intra-frames. Inter frames are used for small, local changes, and intra-frames are used for large changes.

By doing an analysis on the intra-frames it is possible to determine when large changes have occurred within a video sequence because a large change in the motion or a scene change will cause the encoder to generate intra-frames. The analysis could determine where intra-frames occur within a compressed video stream and automatically create a new index into that video.

For fast perusal video, the compressed domain again provides some benefits. As it is known where scene changes or major motion events occur, then an indexing mechanism could be devised based on this information which will create a new index with references only to the specified points. When such an index is created, the playback mechanism could go to each indexed point in the video and play back a few seconds to the user, and then skip to the next index point. In this way the user will see all of the main events of the original video without the need to do a random search. The user could then choose to go back to any point and start playing the video in full.

To aid searching a continuous media stream such as video, we plan to do automatic scene-change analysis to determine when a scene has changed to a new one and do motion analysis to determine if there has been a lot of motion within one scene. It is in these points that the user will be interested.

Index references as data

It is possible that the data referenced by an index are not a packet collected from the network, but are a reference to an element of another index: that is, a level of indirection is allowed. Once index references are available it is possible to build arbitrary structures of indexes, including hierarchies and networks of interconnected indexed material.

There are two components that constitute an index reference. First, the name of index being referenced, and second, an offset into that index. The offset is the number of index elements from the start of the referenced index. Using this name/offset pair as the data, new indexes can be built that reference other indexes.

For example, one may want an index that has entries only when there are intra-frames in a piece of video so that playback of video happens only when there is a whole screenful of data. As intra-frames occur only occasionally, a smaller index can be built that references the original index elements which point to the intra-frame packets. The two indexes are shown in Figure 9.12. Index0 is the original primary

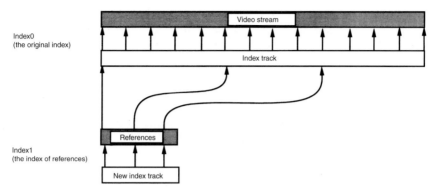

Figure 9.12   An index of index references.

index for the video media, and index1 is the index of the index references. Index1 has only three elements as there are only three packets with intra-frames in the original data.

In the new index the value for the milliseconds since start field is application specific and may be a copy of the time from the index element being referenced, or it may be set to some other value. However, the annotations field will not be copied as the annotations are specific to the original index. The new index can have its own, independent annotations. It is the responsibility of a player to determine the cause and effect of these values.

Lists of index references

By allowing the data field to an index reference rather than a packet, different structures of indexes can be built. However, there is often a requirement to have one index element refer to multiple indexes. That is, the data field is a list of index references rather than a single index reference. This allows one index to reference a whole conference for example, have playback via that index, and have all the conference-specific annotations attached to that index.

Using indexes for time synchronisation

Once lists of index references are available then time-based indexes can be built. These have an entry every *n* seconds, with the references to all of the media and the sources for those elements. If there were, say, twelve sources then each new index element would have a list of twelve index references. Each of the twelve references would be for a time closest to the second boundary in the original indexes.

In Figure 9.13 there is an example showing a time-based index referencing three other indexes. There are three index references for each element of the time-based index. The time-based index has an element for each second of elapsed time, and the references associated with each element point to the index element whose time is closest to the number of elapsed seconds.

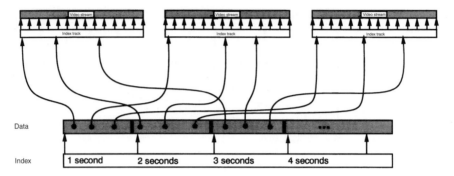

Figure 9.13   A time-based index referencing three other indexes.

Using indexes for sender timestamps

Instead of relying on receiver-based timestamps, which are in the main index for a medium, it is possible to create an index where the timing is based on sender timestamps. A mechanism is required which analyses each source packet for the sender timestamp and creates an index entry based on that.

Using indexes for joining segments

We have to consider how separate segments from different media can be combined using the index. This process needs extra information in the index header. Also, because the segments may come from arbitrary conferences, the timestamps in the indexes may not allow for synchronisation. Therefore, some normalising process is required for all the timestamps within the joined segments.

Enhanced use of indexes

Researchers are investigating enhanced uses of index tracks to aid both replay and search of media streams. When playback access to digitised audio streams is done from an arbitrary point, the resulting sound is a comprehensible signal. However, this approach is not suitable for compressed digitised video.

With video, it is difficult to go to exact places, as one can in a book for instance. Video is a continuous medium without obvious demarcation points for the information; at present it is not possible to peruse a video in the same way as a book. There is no alternative but to watch large parts of the video by using the fast-forward and rewind buttons to skip to a certain place and then watching a section to determine if it is the correct one.

Researchers are designing some techniques that may be developed to improve the ability to find information in continuous media such as video. Existing work in this area uses just digitised video to extract information. Our approach is novel in that it uses compressed digitised video which has been stored in a multimedia storage system, such as the video conference recorder, to extract the indexing information. We believe that it is possible to devise techniques for video that are equivalent to flicking through a book. This technique constructs a thumbnail video with just key frames presented. For example, one could show 1 second's worth of frames for every 20 seconds or minute of real video. This will give a fast-forward view of the video.

Techniques for encoding indexes into video have been devised at many places including MIT and Berkeley. These access digital video to create index information. Because multimedia conferencing and distance learning generally use data compression, it is pertinent to devise these new techniques which use the compressed video directly.

The techniques which will be developed here will help users to search and peruse the online archives. If we compare finding information in a book with finding information in a video we see there are significant differences. A book is structured by separating information into chapters, sections and paragraphs; a structuring which aids human comprehension and allows non-sequential access to the data. The book can be accessed one page at a time, or by going directly to a page which is the start of a chapter or a section. This is because a book is a collection of discrete sections. Further information about the book can be created by building indexes into the book which can be used to go to parts of the book which are about a subject in the index.

Once one can build indexes for the video, then the perusal of the stored video material can be readily used in various applications. One of the main applications for this kind of storage and indexing is in distance education in which compressed video and audio are heavily used. In distance education most of the remote classrooms and students do not have access to the raw video of the main classroom, they receive a compressed video stream which is stored for later use. It is expected that the students use the indexing information to scan existing video recordings in order to play back relevant parts of lectures and seminars. The indexes allow the student to access and peruse many hours of video rapidly in a similar way to perusing a book.

9.4.9 Strategies for recording and playing

This section describes the strategies that are needed in both the recorders and players to record and play back different kinds of media, each possibly using a different protocol.

The recorder

The recorder must deal, firstly, with multiple media within each conference and, secondly, with multiple sources for each of the media.

Each medium will be received on a different multicast address and port pair. It is the responsibility of the recorder to collect data from the multicast address for each medium and determine the source of the sender. The utilisation of the multicast address is in effect a multiplexing process by the senders. Each source sends packets to the same multicast address, and the underlying virtual network delivers those packets to all the members of that multicast address. There is neither a guarantee of delivery nor a guarantee of ordering for packets so each receiver may see the data arriving differently. The recorder, which has to join the multicast address

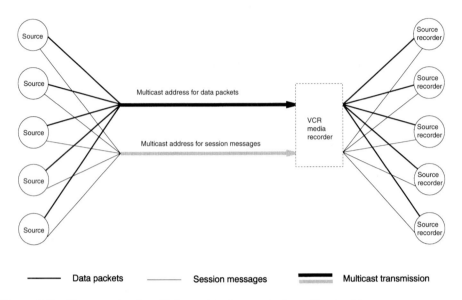

Figure 9.14   The recorder demultiplexes data from a single multicast address.

to receive the data and is therefore a member, has to demultiplex information from the multicast address in order to determine the original source. This process is shown in Figure 9.14.

When the recorder receives packets for media they are demultiplexed from the media's multicast address, the source is determined, and the packet data are then stored unmodified using an index for each of the sources. This is the simplest approach to recording and can be used for data on any multicast address. The data do not need to be a traditional medium, but can be any multicast data.

Many media applications use two (and occasionally more) multicast addresses; one for data and another for session messages. If two multicast addresses are used, the recorder needs to be able to accommodate them. Given the different kinds of media and their associated session messages, it is pertinent to have specialised per-media recorders that can deal with this.

Once the issue of multiple multicast addresses is dealt with, some recorders may need to look at the contents of the packets before doing the indexing process. Of particular interest are sender timestamps, which are contained in the packet header for a medium. Much of the RTP specification deals with sender timestamps and how to process them. It is expected that a specialised RTP recorder can utilise this functionality.

A further enhancement of the recorders is to deal with cross-media synchronis-ation signals. These will probably contain sender timestamps for multiple media in order to allow receivers to calibrate themselves and to facilitate lip synchronisation. Without media tool support, lip synchronisation is not possible. Furthermore, any recorder of such media must also cope with these calibration signals.

The player

The player needs a mechanism for media selection and source selection. It must also deal with the problem of address allocation, particularly with respect to uniqueness. The player must deal with merging multiple media and multiple sources of each media, and try to address the problem of multiple sources coming from a single host.

The player has to play each of the sources in a synchronised way. It has to cope with the fact that the recorder may have started before any data arrived for a particular source. We observe that there is a different delay between when the recording started and when data arrived for each source, and for each media. This delay is shown in Figure 9.15. The delay between the recording start time and the arrival of the first packet may be very significant, running into hours. To avoid players replicating this huge delay it is possible for the player to determine the minimum

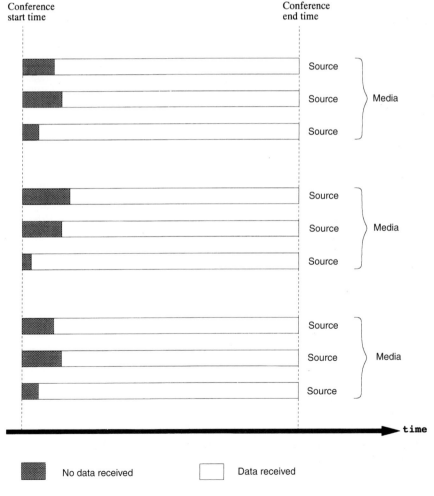

Figure 9.15 The delay between record start time and source data arrival.

time between the recording start time and the arrival of the first packet for all the sources, and then to skip this amount of time during playback. Using this mechanism at least one source would start to play immediately.

For a simple playback, a player can join a multicast address, read data from an index and send packets onto the network with the same inter-packet gap as when they were recorded. If there is more than one index then the data from each of the indexes has to be multiplexed onto the same multicast address. It is the responsibility of the receiving tool to determine the source stream, but this can be problematic as all data seem to come from one IP source.

When a recording has session messages, a specialised player is needed to accommodate these. Whilst this special player is sending data packets to one port, the session messages, or a modified form of them, should be played back onto the session message port. With the addition of session messages in the player, the receiving tool has a better chance to determine the source as extra information is available.

As some media use RTP for transmission, special recorders can utilise the sender timestamps in the RTP packets. Similarly, special players can be made to do the same. In this way, a special RTP recorder/player pair can be devised which can send data back to the network independently of the way it arrived at the recorder, but with respect to the timestamps at the sender. Also, RTP has source identification that is independent of the IP source so there is no reliance on where data came from. This is beneficial for a system as each RTP source will have a different RTP source identifier even though all the packets come from the one player. However, not all tools currently utilise the RTP source identification correctly which undermines its usefulness.

If recorders can deal with RTP together with cross-media calibration, then the players also need to deal with it. This too will involve even more specialisation in the player. It is of particular note that cross-media calibration requires the media tools to participate in the scheme as well as recorders and players.

Because the user can create new indexes after the recording has finished, it is necessary to have special players that accommodate this feature too. This type of player has to know how to player indexes that contain index references rather than just data packets. Once these players have been devised then it will be possible to have playback via time-synchronised indexes. Such indexes have elements for regular time intervals rather than having elements for when packets arrive. These players will be able to skip backwards and forwards in time across every medium and every source because each index element will address a constant time interval as opposed to the raw indexes which are recorded at irregular intervals.

Command propagation Each object in the hierarchy communicates by sending messages from one object to another. In Figure 9.16 we see how the play command to the conference object is duplicated and propagated to both the media objects and source objects in turn. Each source object is responsible for playing each source, and does this by doing operations on the index objects and by using timer events in the event handler.

A similar approach is used when determining the minimum time between the conference recording start time and the arrival of the first packet. The conference object needs to know the minimum for all sources. The method used is as follows:

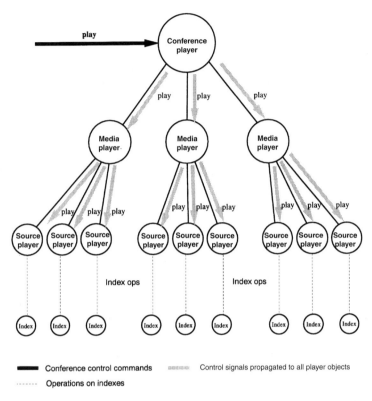

Figure 9.16 The propagation of commands through the object hierarchy.

1 The conference object requests the minimum delay time from all of the media objects.

2 Each media object requests the minimum delay time from all of its associated source objects.

3 Each source object will report to its associated media object the time between the record start time and the arrival of the first packet for that source.

4 Each media object evaluates the minimum delay from the set of delays reported by its sources. This per-media minimum is then reported back to the conference object.

5 The conference object evaluates the minimum delay from the set of delays reported by each media object. This is the minimum for all of the sources. This minimum value is sent to all the media objects.

6 The minimum value is then reported by the media objects to the source objects. Each source subtracts this minimum delay from the time to play its first packet.

After this process is completed, at least one source will have no delay on start-up, and the media for that source will be sent to the user immediately.

9.4.10 Reliable multicast

The recording and playback of most media involves the recorder collecting packets from the network, and the player sending the packets back to the network. However, for media that use a reliable multicast mechanism this approach is not possible. It is necessary for the recorder and player to have an implementation of the reliable multicast code within themselves.

Consider the case where a recorder notices that some of the shared workspace data have not arrived. It is the recorder's responsibility to request that the lost data be retransmitted, but without full knowledge of the details of the retransmission scheme this cannot be done. Therefore, the data stay lost within the recording. At playback time, when the player sends out the recorded data this loss will be observed by the current receivers. They will send a retransmission request. However, a player without a retransmission scheme implementation will be in a poor situation. Firstly, it will not have the data to retransmit because the recorder never recorded it and, secondly, it cannot reply to the requests because it does not have the relevant implementation.

This area of recording and playback is particularly tricky, and further work needs to be applied to this. It also requires the tool writers to have standalone implementations of their reliability and retransmission code, which can be slipped into servers as required.

9.4.11 Address allocation

One of the problems when playing back media to a single user or small group of users is choosing a multicast address for the playback. This problem does not arise when doing playback to a conference because conferences are usually on well known or well defined addresses. In choosing an address for a user there must be no clash with existing, in-use multicast addresses.

As well as uniqueness of the address, it has to be decided who makes that decision. There seems to be four options:

- The user
- A client
- The server
- An external service

For the first three options it is hard to determine how they can guarantee uniqueness given that they have no mechanism for deciding which addresses are already in use, and therefore which are free to use. The most appealing choice is for some external service to make the decision. This service can be used by all systems that require a new multicast address for their purposes. Although such a service does not currently exist, it is in the design phase. The session directory tool (Handley and Jacobson, 1996) already has an intelligent mechanism for choosing new addresses for conferences started under its auspices, but is not usable by other systems as it is standalone. The ongoing work described in Chapter 7 will culminate in the definition of a session description protocol, and should lead to the implementation of a server that does allocate new multicast addresses on demand. Once this server has been implemented, any program can get unique multicast addresses.

9.4.12   Source identification on replay

When data are replayed by the server, the receivers of these data observe that all packets come from one host. Many media tools have been designed to expect that each source comes from a different host. If multiple sources for each medium are being replayed then all the sources seem to be one host, which can confuse some media tools. As there are some mechanisms available to overcome this problem, other media tools are more tolerant.

There are currently two approaches to this problem:

1   In the vat protocol it is possible to add an IP address to the packet header to signify that the original source of the packet is not the sender but is that put in the packet.

2   In the RTP protocol there is a field for a host-independent channel identifier. This allows streams of media to be recognised by their channel ID rather than their source address. As these data are in the packet they will be recorded and, when replayed, will be used by the new receivers.

For problem-free source identification on replay, media tools need to be designed with media recording and playback in mind. Using RTP is a good approach for this as it allows host-independent channel identification; however, not all media tools are compliant with this mechanism.

9.5   REMOTE CONTROL OF PLAYBACK

We are now used to being in control of the boxes which generate our media. Hi-fi equipment has controls which allow us to start, stop and pause prerecorded audio playing from CDs, tapes or records. We can even use the controls to select which parts of the recording we wish to listen to. Alternatively, we can tune into live sounds from radio stations, and switch channels. If we have a spare tape, we can record the live broadcast for posterity, or perhaps to listen to it at a more convenient time as we drive home. Similar controls are available on our video devices, allowing movies to be recorded from TV broadcasts, and giving us the opportunity to see our favourite sporting events time after time.

If our audio and video streams come to us over a network, and are available in the computer's memory, then at the very least we should expect to be able to control the streams in the same fashion as we control traditional media. We should be able to start the program playing, pause the stream if we wish, skip further along the stream to locate the interesting bits, and slow or speed up the program as required. Since the medium for the stream is a network connected to a computer, then building the controls is simply a matter of designing a program and the associated techniques for talking to other programs.

Earlier in the book we talked about how the streams of data can be compressed audio, video or even data intended for updating some application, such as stock market figures, or a sequence of polygons to be rendered in a virtual reality environment. The stream is generated by a node on the network which we will term the *media server*, and is sent as a stream of packets over the network to the receiver(s), which process and pass the data up to the application.

We have two ways of controlling the media streams: we could send messages back over the network to the source of the stream to ask the source to play, stop, pause etc., or we could allow the stream to come to us, and simply manipulate the media in memory, keeping control within the receiving computer. Both techniques are possible, but each is suitable in a different environment.

When the stream of data coming over the network is shared by many different users, such as in a multicast event, it becomes more appropriate to keep the controls local to the receiver. Since the source has many different receivers, there is a potential implosion problem if all the receivers sent control messages to the source. The source may then be overwhelmed by messages. Alternatively, if there are many receivers and no floor control, the source may have difficulty in resolving the conflicting demands from the receivers: what to do if one asks to stop, whilst the other asks to play? If authority over the view is delegated equally amongst all the receivers, then each receiver should manipulate the stream locally. If they decide to start the stream, then they should join the group and let the routing take care of bringing the data to the computer. If they decide to pause, they should simply stop displaying any more stream and buffer incoming data, and if they decide to stop the stream, then they should leave the multicast group, allowing the routing to prune their branch from the multicast tree (see also Chapter 3).

When the stream of data coming over the network is owned by just one user, then the network and server resources are more efficiently used if the media stream is manipulated at source. Note that even though the media streams are multicast, floor control within the session may have designated an owner who has control over the streams.

9.5.1   Remote invocation of stream controls

Stream control requires the receiver to send a message to the media server, asking it to perform some action. There may or may not be some response. This paradigm of request/response over a network has been well known for many years and has been formulated as a *remote procedure call* or RPC.

In a remote procedure call, the remote server offers a selection of procedures that the local machine can call. These calls are labelled in a unique fashion across the server. When the local machine wishes to make a call, the calling program constructs a packet which references the label on the remote server, adds any arguments to the call encoded in a machine-independent format, and sends the packet to the server. The server receives the packet, routes the request to the appropriate bit of code, unpacks the arguments so that they can be understood and executes the request. If there are any return values or any error responses, these are packed into a packet and sent back to the sender. The strength of RPC mechanisms lays in the fact that the code to construct the packets at the local machine, and demultiplex and deconstruct the arguments at the server, can be generated automatically from descriptions of the procedures that are similar to programming languages with which programmers are familiar, such as C. The canonical reference for RPC is the work by Birrell and Nelson from Xerox PARC. The most widely used RPC system has probably been the Sun RPC system, whilst every vendor with an interest in providing network solutions has some variation upon RPC, such as DCOM from Microsoft, the Java RMI system and the DCE RPC system.

Most projects which have designed networked multimedia systems have used an RPC system to build the stream controls. An influential project was Pandora out of Cambridge. This work pioneered the use of ATM-type systems to deliver real time media such as audio and video, but also used RPC mechanisms to implement the network controls.

RPC systems make life very simple for the applications programmer, and for the conceptually simple controls for a media stream, they would seem to provide an ideal solution. However, as ever, there are a few problems.

RPC mechanisms are intended to support the networking of heterogeneous machines, but there is no widespread RPC system available across all platforms. CORBA provides a generic object-oriented technology for integrating operating systems, and is seen by many to be the key integrating technology. Currently, CORBA technology is costly, but increasing use should see its adoption by more than major corporations.

Using RPC mechanisms makes defining the control interfaces easy. However, there remain some subtleties in interpreting the precedence of control requests. What happens if a number of play requests are sent – should they be queued? How then should the streams be interrupted if the requests are queued? How should the server track the current state of the stream? There is the need for a small 'stateful' protocol at the server to deal with the ordering of play and pause requests. Inherent in controlling streams of data remotely is the necessity to keep state at the server about the requests that have been made. Requests must have an associated sequence number, so that the server can service the incoming requests in the correct order, despite any reordering that may occur.

If a client requests the transmission of a stream, the server has to return some identifier to the client so that this stream can be distinguished from others. The mapping between this identifier and the stream is held both on the server and on the client and can be the source of major difficulties in designing a complete solution. The problem comes in deciding what happens when the state is lost at either the client or the server. If the state is lost at the server, then the server can no longer associate control requests with the outgoing stream. If the client loses state, then it will not be able to generate control requests for the stream. If the stream consumes many resources, then this may be disastrous, since a long-lived stream which no one is using and which is uncontrolled is just a resource hog and may block other legitimate uses.

Solutions to the problem rely either on being able to recreate the state (see the introduction to Part Two) or on ensuring that the protocol is failsafe, whereby unless control is continuously asserted, the stream stops.

9.5.2 An aside – the hypertext transfer protocol as a universal RPC mechanism

Underlying the World Wide Web is the hypertext transfer protocol, HTTP. This was originally designed purely to serve HTML documents, so provided a simple 'get' of a document URL, which received a response from the receiver consisting of the HTML in plain ASCII. But it is in the nature of all good ideas to become more complicated. Why should documents simply be ASCII? Why not allow other character sets? Documents do not consist entirely of words – why not allow pictures and other forms of media? And so it came to pass that HTTP used the MIME standard to encode the documents transferred from server to browser, allowing a range of media types and encodings. Since HTTP was now passing generic objects around, identified using the URI and typed by MIME, the current set of designers thought to themselves, 'Hey, we have the basis of a generic request response protocol which we can use for RPC, but encoded in ASCII. Let's turn the next generation of HTTP into an RPC protocol.'

So, the hypertext transfer protocol in its current formulation of version 1.1 has extended its capabilities beyond a simple protocol to transfer HTML documents to becoming a generic request/response protocol for the Internet. Its authors describe it as an 'application-level protocol' which is a 'generic, stateless object-oriented protocol which can be used for many tasks, such as name servers and distributed object management systems through extension of its request methods.'

Like many other protocols emerging from the IETF, the protocol is based around ASCII header fields.[1] The model is that the client sends a request to a server, possibly via one or more proxies. If the request is not serviced by any of the intermediate proxies, then it eventually reaches the server. The server responds to the request with a response which returns via the proxies. The fields of the messages are split into four separate headers which relate to different parts of the protocol (see Figure 9.17). We give a brief overview below, which is sufficient to understand the structure of the RTSP protocol; for full details the reader should go to the HTTP standard itself.

The HTTP messages have a first line which contains the type of request or the response, followed by a general header, a request or response header, and an entity header. If appropriate, there is also a message body.

The first line of any request indicates the type of method: 'get', 'head', 'options', 'post', 'put', 'delete', 'trace' are currently defined. After the type of request comes the uniform resource identifier (generally a URL) upon which the request is to act, followed by the version of the protocol. The first line of any response gives the status of the request, which has the version of the protocol, a numeric code and a textual description of the response, for example, numeric code 200 is 'OK', whilst 404 is 'Not Found'.

The general header applies to both request and responses, but not to the body. They include the fields *cache-control, connection, date, pragma, transfer-encoding, upgrade* and *via*.

The request header includes additional information for the request, such as the range of encodings that the client can accept, the most recent entity the client has, and the client software. Response headers give information about the age of the response, when to retry on failure and the type of server.

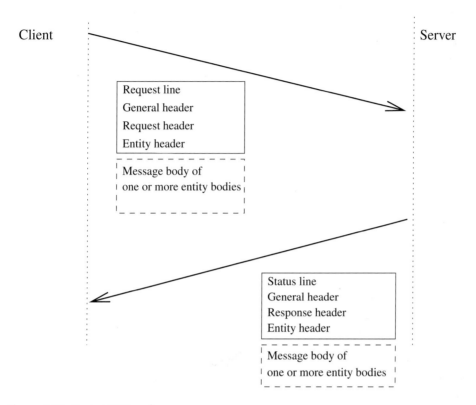

Figure 9.17 Basic HTTP exchange.

The entity header gives optional information about the body of the message, such as the length (*content-length*), the type of the entity (*content-type*), when it expires (*expires*) and when it was last modified (*last-modified*). There may be an entity header for each of the entity bodies present.

Finally, the bodies contain the actual data associated with the request and the resource, such as the HTML page, the image or the audio file.

9.5.3 The real time stream protocol (RTSP)

The real time streaming protocol (RTSP) establishes and controls either a single or several time-synchronised streams of continuous media such as audio or video...In other words, RTSP acts as a 'network remote control' for multimedia servers.

As we have already discussed, the interactions of a client with a server using a network remote control is best modelled by the use of an RPC mechanism. However, rather than using an RPC mechanism directly, the designers of RTSP decided to use a variation on HTTP, since in its current incarnation of version 1.1, it approximates an application-level RPC mechanism. The designers felt that they could lever the work already done in producing HTTP to produce production code for RTSP clients and servers, and, in particular, use the technology developed for proxies and security.

Multimedia presentations are identified by URLs, using a protocol scheme of 'rtsp'. The hostname is the server containing the presentation, whilst the port indicates which port the RTSP control requests should be sent to. Presentations may consist of one or more separate streams. The presentation URL provides a means of identifying and controlling the whole presentation rather than co-ordinating the control of each individual steam. So,

rtsp://media.example.com:554/twister/audiotrack

identifies the audio stream within the presentation *twister*, which can be controlled on its own. If the user would rather stop and start the whole presentation, including the video, then they would use the URL:

rtsp://media.example.com:554/twister/

RTSP add a number of new requests to the existing HTTP requests. These are

- *Describe*: Causes a server to return a description of the protocol using the session description protocol.
- *Announce*: Allows a client or server to register a description of a presentation.
- *Options*: Causes a server to return the list of supported methods.
- *Setup*: Causes a server to allocate resources for a stream and starts an RTSP session. This manipulates state.
- *Play*: Starts data transmission on a stream allocated by 'setup'. This manipulates state.
- *Record*: Starts a server recording an allocated stream. This manipulates state.
- *Pause*: Temporarily halts transmission of a stream without freeing server resources. This manipulates state.
- *Teardown*: Frees resources associate with a stream, so that the RTSP session ceases to exist. This manipulates state.
- *Get Parameter and Set Parameter*: Placeholder methods to allow parameters of presentations and sessions to be manipulated.
- *Redirect*: Causes a client to go to another server for parts of a presentation.

Putting all this together: to send a control request, the client constructs a line consisting of the method, the request URL and the protocol version number. Then it includes a general header, a request header and possibly an entity header, as for the HTTP protocol. This is sent to the server, who executes the request if possible. It then returns a response containing a status line and general response and entity headers. The status line contains the protocol version, the numeric status code and a textual description.

The media streams are left unspecified by RTSP. These could be RTP streams or any other form of media transmission. RTSP specifies only the control and it is up to the client and server software to maintain the mapping between the control channel and the media streams.

A key concept in RTSP is that of a *session*. RTSP works by first requesting a presentation to be started by a server, receiving in return a session identifier which it then uses in all subsequent controls. Eventually, the client can request the teardown of session, which releases the associated resources. The session identifier represents the shared state between the client and server. If the state is lost – for example through one of the machines being rebooted – then the protocol relies on the transport of the media stopping automatically, for example through not receiving RTCP messages if using RTP or the implementation using the 'get parameter' method below as a keep-alive.

The control requests and responses may be sent over either TCP or UDP. Since the order of the requests matters, the requests are sequenced, so if any requests are lost, they must be retransmitted. Using UDP thus requires the construction of retransmission mechanisms, so there are very few occasions when the application can get away with using UDP.

The most obvious additions to the request header fields are a *Cseq* field to contain the sequence numbers of requests generated by the client, and a *session* field to both request and response headers to identify the session. Session identifiers are generated in response to a Setup request, and must be used in all stateful methods. The *transport* field allows the client and server to negotiate and set parameters for the sending of the media stream. In particular, it allows the client and server to set ports and multicast addresses for the RTP streams. There are a number of other header fields, such as the time range of the presentation upon which the method executes (*Range*), and various fields which interact with caches and other proxies.

Descriptions of session use the session description protocol (described in Chapter 6), which provides a generic technique for describing the details of the presentation, such as transport and media types of the stream, and the presentation content. Importantly, it also provides the start and end times of the presentation, so that the client can play from and to any point in the presentation they wish.

Media streams are referenced through specification of their times, either relative to the start time of the presentation, or in real time. RTSP allows the use of the standard time codes used in industry such as SMTPE or Normal Play Time, or by specifying an absolute time for presentations in real time.

To display a presentation, the client software first requires the RTSP URL of the presentation. If it has this URL, it can then display the presentation by following these steps:

1   The client first requests the description of the presentation using the Describe method. This supplies details of the media streams so that the client can start the appropriate media applications.

2   The client then requests that the session is set up, receiving a session identifier in return. The server would allocate state, such as the sockets through which the media will be sent, plus any reservations for bandwidth.

3   The client requests that the media streams of the session are played, by specifying the URL, the session identifier, and the times at which to start and finish playing.

4   At any point the client may pause the presentation, and continue from any other point in the presentation by specifying a new time range in the Play request.

5   When finished, the client issues a Teardown request to destroy the session and deallocate any resources.

RTSP is intended to be a generic protocol for manipulation of continuous media over the Internet. For a given presentation or server, there may be limitations upon the controls the client can use. For instance, if a company has created a media presentation, it may well desire that a session is not recorded. Since the controls may sometimes be present and at other times not, this presents a problem in the design of a user interface. If a control is represented in the user interface but is not available for a particular presentation, then the user may attempt to use the control and be confused by the subsequent interactions.

Fortunately, the Options command allows the client to interrogate the server to determine the available methods, and the component streams. Once these have been determined, the client software can then build an appropriate interface, representing only the available control, and presenting an indication of the components of the stream.

9.5.4   Movies-on-demand

To show how RTSP is used, we shall demonstrate the implementation of a media-on-demand service, borrowed from the standard itself. The client wants to receive audio and video streams from two different media servers A and V respectively. The actual description of the movie is held on a Web server W, which contains sufficient information to allow the client to set up the appropriate receiving applications. We assume that the reader is familiar with the session description protocol from Chapter 6.

```
C->W: DESCRIBE rtsp://foo/twister RTSP/1.0
      CSeq: 1

W->C: RTSP/1.0 200 OK
      CSeq: 1
      Content-Type: application/sdp
      Content-Length: 164

      v=0
      o=- 2890844526 2890842807 IN IP4 192.16.24.202
      s=RTSP Session
      m=audio 0 RTP/AVP 0
      a=control:rtsp://audio.example.com/twister/audio.en
      m=video 0 RTP/AVP 31
      a=control:rtsp://video.example.com/twister/video
```

The client first requests the description of the protocol. Notice that the request has a sequence number CSeq associated. The response returns with the numeric status code of 200, indicating 'OK'. It returns the sequence number, along with entity headers describing the body of the message. The description of the presentation is held within the message body using the session description protocol. The session consists of two streams, an audio and a video stream.

```
C->A: SETUP rtsp://audio.example.com/twister/audio.en RTSP/1.0
      CSeq: 1
      Transport: RTP/AVP/UDP;unicast;client_port=3056-3057
```

```
A->C: RTSP/1.0 200 OK
      CSeq: 1
      Session: 12345678
      Transport: RTP/AVP/UDP;unicast;client_port=3056-3057;
                 server_port=5000-5001

C->V: SETUP rtsp://video.example.com/twister/video RTSP/1.0
      CSeq: 1
      Transport: RTP/AVP/UDP;unicast;client_port=3058-3059

V->C: RTSP/1.0 200 OK
      CSeq: 1
      Session: 23456789
      Transport: RTP/AVP/UDP;unicast;client_port=3058-3059;
                 server_port=5002-5003
```

The client then requests the set up of the audio and the video streams, using the *transport* header field to indicate the preferred parameters for the RTP streams. The responses confirm that these are acceptable, adding the necessary ports to receive from the server. Importantly, the Setup responses return *session* identifiers to be used in associated commands with the appropriate streams in all subsequent messages.

```
C->V: PLAY rtsp://video.example.com/twister/video RTSP/1.0
      CSeq: 2
      Session: 23456789
      Range: smpte=0:10:00-

V->C: RTSP/1.0 200 OK
      CSeq: 2
      Session: 23456789
      Range: smpte=0:10:00-0:20:00
      RTP-Info: url=rtsp://video.example.com/twister/video;
        seq=12312232;rtptime=78712811

C->A: PLAY rtsp://audio.example.com/twister/audio.en RTSP/1.0
      CSeq: 2
      Session: 12345678
      Range: smpte=0:10:00-

A->C: RTSP/1.0 200 OK
      CSeq: 2
      Session: 12345678
      Range: smpte=0:10:00-0:20:00
      RTP-Info: url=rtsp://audio.example.com/twister/audio.en;
        seq=876655;rtptime=1032181
```

The client then requests that each of the streams is played, specifying the range using SMTPE timestamps. The start times of each of the streams is actually specified as 10 minutes into the stream. The servers respond 'OK', returning the end of the time range that will be played.

```
C->A: TEARDOWN rtsp://audio.example.com/twister/audio.en RTSP/1.0
      CSeq: 3
      Session: 12345678

A->C: RTSP/1.0 200 OK
      CSeq: 3

C->V: TEARDOWN rtsp://video.example.com/twister/video RTSP/1.0
      CSeq: 3
      Session: 23456789

V->C: RTSP/1.0 200 OK
      CSeq: 3
```

Finally the client requests that the session be ended, tearing down the state associated with the media streams.

9.5.5 RTSP criticisms

RTSP suffers from attempting to produce a lowest common denominator standard, using extensions of a stateless protocol. Since the ordering of Play requests matters, the sequence numbers must be used to order the Play requests. In addition, the sending of a Pause request stops the stream and places the server into a state where it must remember where the current position in the stream is. Allowing the control requests to be sent using UDP in which messages can be lost allows the possibility of the server and client locking when the stream is paused and the server loses a Play message. It is to be hoped that these problems can be overcome by the user thinking their way around and repeating requests, but this is not satisfactory. When packets can be lost, there is no real substitute for building a reliable transport protocol such as TCP.

More importantly, the protocol says nothing about the problems of recovering state over machine or software failure. Imagine the situation where a user is listening to a presentation at home on their PC, and some unlikely event occurs requiring the PC to be rebooted. The client software has now lost state and can no longer send any control messages to turn off the media streams. The media streams are high bandwidth and continue to occupy most of the incoming bandwidth into the user's home. What can they do? The current protocol does not describe how a session identifier can be recovered after state loss as in the soft state approach described in the introduction to Part Two. The authors of the standard hope that implementations use a failsafe mechanism, relying on the media stream to remain live, or using dummy Get Parameter messages to probe the liveness of the client.

9.5.6 Conclusion

The real time stream protocol is an Internet standard, defined in RFC 2326. It provides a base set of control messages for controlling media streams, such as Setup, Play and Pause. With these simple controls it is possible to control many complex multimedia presentations, but at the cost of fairly complex logic in the client and servers.

9.6 SUMMARY

In this chapter we presented emerging Internet multimedia recording and playback technologies.

The main requirements for a video conference recorder are the following: when recording, multiple media streams need to be archived, with the possibility of having stream synchronisation; the record mechanism should allow a selection of the streams to be specified; the retrieval of recorded material needs to be easy for users to access, either for direct playback to the user or for inclusion in another multicast multimedia conference; users need to see which conferences have been recorded and are online for access in order to select streams for playback; and the recording system must be fully equipped with large storage capabilities.

To meet those requirements, the following objectives were set:

1 The ability to record multicast conference data whose source may be any of the conferees.

2 The ability to play back recorded material either directly to one user or into another multicast conference.

3 To provide synchronisation between streams from each source.

4 To allow users to create their own segments of recorded material and their own material for playback.

5 To provide a single point of contact for recording and playback.

6 To supply a large repository of archive space which is accessible to authorised network users who wish to record or play back multimedia data.

9.6.1 Synchronisation support

As stated, the system does support the synchronisation of different media. For the three kinds described earlier (9.4.3), the following type of support is provided:

1 For inter-packet synchronisation there is support in each player. This means that data is sent to the network either with the same order and inter-packet gap as the recorder saw by using the recorder timestamps, or with the same order and inter-packet gap as the original sender intended by using sender timestamps.

2 For time synchronisation there is support via the indexes. It is possible to have an index entry at a specified regular time interval with references to each media stream. By following these references it is possible to access the media streams in a time-synchronised way.

3 For lip synchronisation there is little support that the server can provide. It relies on cross-media control messages plus support in the receiving media tool. Without this support, lip synchronisation can never be achieved.

9.6.2   An index architecture

Indexes form the basis for a general set of applications based on multimedia. They provide the general facilities required for real time media interaction and presentation. These facilities can be viewed as an architecture for operating on real time media. In Figure 9.18 an architecture for indexes is presented. At the two lowest levels are the data and the indexes themselves. For server purposes, the data are either video, audio or whiteboard packets, with index entries for each packet. The next layer has the operations on the indexes. These operations include such things as creating an index element, selecting regions of an index and adding an annotation to an index element. The top level of the architecture has applications. These perform operations on indexes to achieve media recording or media playback.

9.6.3   Control of playback

Clearly, a multimedia recording and playback server is a small part of a much larger architecture. It is possible to design and build a large set of applications on top of real time multimedia indexes. For future reference, there are at least two major efforts

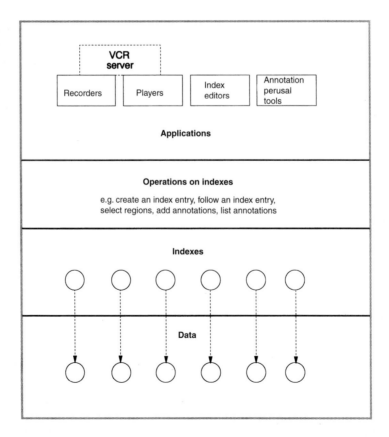

Figure 9.18   The index architecture.

under way to define protocols for retrieving multimedia from Web servers, and even organising collections of Web servers to function as a type of application-level multicast delivery network. These are the RealAudio effort from Progressive Networks, and the RTSP (real time stream protocol) currently under discussion in the IETF working group on multimedia. More details are available from `http://cgi.realaudio.com/` and the relevant draft standards.

RTSP is designed to operate over TCP, and over RTP/UDP, and is aimed largely at controlling the play-out of media, much in the way that a (typical infrared-based digital wireless transmission) remote control is used to control a domestic VCR. The actual delivery of the media itself, if VoD, near VoD, or real time, would be accomplished typically using techniques described in this book.

An interesting exception to this design approach is one of the proposals in DAVIC, designed for delivery of digital TV over cable TV networks. Here audiovisual information is the only first-class citizen, and other data types are layered *on top of* the media stream, which, it has been proposed, would be carried in an MPEG systems stream over an ATM layer modulated on the raw cable signal.

Whether this takes off remains to be seen, but it seems more likely that a pervasive IP-based approach offers more flexibility and management, as well as immediate availability of a range of other Internet-based applications.

Note

1 The use of text-based protocols is still controversial. The proponents claim that they provide easier design, the assumption of least common denominator, the ability to use powerful tokenising tools, debugging capabilities and easy extension via self-describing fields, against slightly more complex specifications and a less efficient protocol.

CHAPTER TEN

Security and Policy in Multicast Multimedia

10.1 INTRODUCTION

This book is about using computer networks to enable people to communicate with each other. Whilst there will no doubt be different forms of interaction, we will generally talk about the same subjects – work, play and the other parts of the rich fabric of our lives – as we do in face-to-face situations. Because we live in an imperfect world, we can thus expect the problems that come with communication to be the same as they have always been, such as fraud, eavesdropping and prevention of communication, along with new problems from using new technology, and changing relationships between people and technology. In this chapter, we focus upon the problems of security and of ensuring that the human goals of communication cannot be subverted by other people.

10.2 ROADMAP

We first motivate the need for security by examining a number of scenarios and extract the major security requirements for multicast multimedia. We then give a brief overview of a very useful weapon in keeping streams secure – cryptography. We then discuss techniques to keep the media streams secure, ranging from solutions at the network level and at the transport level to the application level, and finally we discuss the infrastructure problems in distributing keys.

10.2.1 Formal distributed conference

Imagine the situation: a global teleconference has been convened by the UN to discuss how to regulate the global Internet. Each participant is geographically separate from all others and uses the Internet to communicate with the other participants. Meanwhile there are myriad observers who wish to discover how their favourite communication medium is going to evolve. Because such weighty matters hang upon the utterances of each speaker, the participants need to be sure that each speaker is

actually who she purports to be. Indeed, there is a band of rogue hackers who dis-
agree with the direction that Internet evolution is proceeding in, and wish to subvert
the conference. The hackers intend to imitate speakers and thus drag the conference
to a more anarchic decision.

For the technology described previously, the hackers need only create the speech
packets, and then send to the multicast group, using the same identifiers as the real
participant.[1] If they wish to be really sneaky they could forge group leave packets
for the participant they are imitating, and then feed the imitated person sufficient
of the conference so that their suspicions are not aroused.

It is obvious that the technology in the above scenario needs to be extended:

1 It is necessary to prove the identity of the speakers to the participants, and to a
   lesser extent the observers.

2 The routing of the traffic must be protected to ensure that listeners cannot be
   denied service.

How is the identity of the speakers proven? Through authenticating that the
packets came from the purported source, generally by attaching some data explicitly,
or implicitly in the stream, which can be generated only by the source. In talking to
people, this comes in voice patterns, in the patterns of speech such as mannerisms,
in the subjects and things they know, and most importantly, by checking that their
physical appearance corresponds to the person we believe. However, there are times
when we do not know enough about the individual to use these techniques; instead
we trust to some token which only the individual could possess – a letter of introduction from a trusted friend, or the policeman's badge.

In the networked domain, we use the same techniques – if we are talking to people
we know, then it is sufficient to trust to the past history to give us clues that they are
who they say they are. However, this is more difficult in the electronic domain, and so
we can expect the growth of new urban myths where students embarrass teachers by
pretending to be someone else. In the plenary session above, the technique used
would be to attach to the packets a token which can only have been generated
by the individual. How can we generate these tokens? We shall discuss this below
in the use of cryptography.

Our hackers above could deny service to the participant because the network is
open. There are many good reasons to design open networks,[2] but there are times
when it is necessary to protect the network. This can be achieved through the
use of features of the routing protocols, the judicious use of filters and firewalls,
and careful design of network topology.

10.2.2 Pay per view distribution of Rolling Stones

One of the first times the Mbone gained exposure on TV and in newspapers was when
the Rolling Stones provided an Mbone feed of a concert on the Voodoo Lounge tour.
Mick and Keith strutted and posed over the nascent multicast network, and the
audience whooped in appreciation. The next time the Stones appear on the Internet,
they may be selling a pay per view distribution of the event. In a similar fashion to
cable or satellite TV pay per view events, only the punters who have paid the
fee should be able to see this event. For satellite and cable, this is achieved by

encrypting the TV signal, and handing out the decryption key in exchange for money. In a similar fashion, the multicast multimedia extravaganza would be encrypted and could only be decrypted by those who had paid for the decryption key.

What are the requirements here? Obviously, we need to be able to encrypt and decrypt the stream. A subtler requirement is the need to distribute keys in a scalable manner – in a world of information, it is unlikely that the key would be contained in a physical medium such as a smart card for a large consumer event, since the physical distribution costs would be large. Instead, the keys would be distributed to the millions using the same Internet. Since the distributors would be encouraging people to sign up at any time, the key distribution mechanisms would need to scale and not melt down upon receiving too many requests.[3]

10.2.3 Inter-company brainstorm

Two companies have organised an informal teleconference in which they intend to brainstorm a new product. This is a tentative meeting in which options for co-operation will be investigated. To ensure the maximum creativity and imagination, the participants want guarantees that nothing they say can be used against them later and that no commitments can be made inside of the conference. In a competitive marketplace, the ideas discussed are valuable commodities, and so the media streams should be protected against eavesdroppers. Indeed, the fact that the two companies are talking to each other may be valuable, since it may affect the share prices of the company.

The need to ensure that participants can repudiate what they have said is a contradictory requirement from ensuring that the members are authenticated. It can be achieved by sending the data through a trusted third party who acts as an anonymiser. Authentication is provided to the third party on both input streams and output streams. Going further, the third party can help to prevent connectivity leakage by aggregating many traffic streams and ensuring that there is no mapping between input and output streams.

10.2.4 Global traffic disasters

We can distinguish two (unfortunately common) further types of attack: general denial of service by flooding (all too easy with multicast or reflectors) and traffic flow (source destination matrix) analysis. Defences against these range from the introduction of inter-router authentication, to the generation of uniform random traffic *noise* that is reduced as real traffic is added. Charging for traffic also helps to deter the former problem. A scenario that represents an extreme case of potential paranoia where we would be concerned with these attacks is that of an Mbone-based share auction.

10.2.5 Pulling the requirements together

In the scenarios above, the requirements have built upon each other.

1   *Service protection*: If the connectivity is crucial to the mission, then sufficient security must be built into the system such that the probability of a denial of service attack being mounted and succeeding is less than or equal to the probability of connectivity being broken through faulty equipment or human error in configuration or maintenance.

2   *Data integrity*: Obviously, if data can be removed, substituted or appended, then things can go wrong. For video and audio streams, the results could be anything from embarrassing through to disastrous – imagine insertion of manipulated images into a video stream to show someone with rabbit ears.

3   *Authentication*: It is often required that the sender of a stream must be authenticated and, additionally, the receivers of a stream must be authorised to view the media. This requires authentication.

4   *Confidentiality*: The stream should be protected from prying eyes, depending upon what is in the stream.

5   *Key distribution*: Key distribution should be only to the authorised users, and on some occasions must scale both in the number of users and in the rate at which keys change.

6   *Specialist requirements*: There are many other security requirements depending upon particular circumstances, such as the ability to repudiate transmissions in the brainstorming scenario above. Other possible requirements include access control to the equipment in a video conference such as the cameras and microphones, and non-repudiation of transmission.

For the individual requirements, the best approach is to separate the actors within the application and construct their security requirements. However, in all cases, one must make the engineering trade-off of the cost of meeting the security requirement against the cost of not meeting the requirement and being insecure. There may be occasions when a different means of transmission, such as delivery by trusted human courier may be preferable.

10.3   A BRIEF INTRODUCTION TO CRYPTOGRAPHIC TECHNOLOGY

10.3.1   What is cryptography?

Cryptography, according to Schneier (1994), is 'the art of keeping messages secure'. There are two choices for communication over networks: prevent unauthorised people gaining access to the network, as described in section 10.4; or scrambling the data so that they cannot be understood. If the latter root is taken, then cryptographic technology will be used. For multimedia streams this generally requires the use of fast encryption using shared keys on the media streams, and public key cryptography to distribute the shared keys for the media streams.

Remember that our information is just bits in memory and on the wire. If these data are viewed as the representation of large numbers, then we can apply mathematical functions to them, i.e. if our input text, known as cleartext, is x, our cryptographic function is $f()$ and we have a key k, the output of $f(k, x)$ is the encrypted text y or cyphertext. Now, if we choose our mathematical function $f()$

so that there is no easily discovered inverse mapping, i.e. given y, it is extremely difficult to calculate x without knowing k, but it is possible if k is known, then we have a means of encrypting our data.

10.3.2 Symmetric cryptography

If the key for encryption and decryption is the same shared secret, then the cryptographic algorithm is termed a *symmetric* algorithm. As in Figure 10.1, the key must be shared by both the sender and the receiver. The sender applies the encryption function using the key to the cleartext to produce the cyphertext. The cyphertext is sent to the receiver who then applies the decryption function using the same shared key. Since the cleartext cannot be derived from the cyphertext without knowledge of the key, the cyphertext can be sent over public networks such as the Internet.

The US standard for symmetric cryptography, in which the same key is used for both encryption and decryption is the Data Encryption Standard (DES). This is based upon a combination and permutation of shifts and exclusive ORs (XORs) and so can be very fast when implemented directly on hardware (1 GBps throughput or better) or on general purpose processors. The current key size of 56 bits (plus 8 parity bits) is now starting to seem small, but the use of larger keys with triple DES can generate much greater security. Since the implementation of DES is fast, it can easily be pipelined with software codecs and not affect the performance.

IDEA is an alternative and stronger form of symmetric block encryption. Its security is based upon combining XORs with addition and multiplication in modulo 16 arithmetic. This is also fast on general-purpose processors and is comparable in speed to DES implementations. The major advantage of IDEA is that the keys are 128 bits and thus much stronger (harder to break) than standard 56 bit DES.

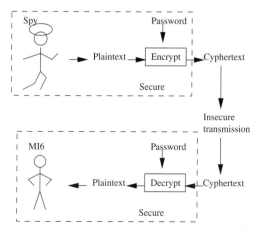

Figure 10.1 Encrypting to provide confidentiality.

What size keys?

The larger the key, the more security one gets. Since most attempts to decrypt rely on searching through the key space, adding another bit to the key doubles the size of the search space. One can see that large keys will generate large search spaces: 64 bit keys can probably be broken in under 245 hours, 128 bit keys need the development of faster computers to be breakable in a realistic time. However, large keys do slow the speed at which encryption can take place, but not very much – if speed is essential, one can always buy a faster computer. More importantly, large keys are frowned upon by governments, since it then becomes difficult for government agencies to decrypt all the encrypted traffic flowing over the Internet which is generated by criminals – at least, that is the excuse that governments offer for refusing to allow good encryption.

Instead, one can use key escrow, where a part of your key is held in a secure registry which only a trusted member of the security agencies can get at it. Thus, when you encrypt, anyone who is not a member of the government has to decode using the full length of key, but government agencies get a head-start by knowing a large portion of your key. In this way, only the government agencies can read your email and listen to your audio calls!

10.3.3 Public key cryptography

Public key encryption is a much slower alternative to symmetric cryptography. It is based upon mathematical functions of two pairs of numbers. For the well known RSA algorithm, the security comes from the difficulty of factoring large numbers in Galois fields.[4]

Each key is a pair of keys K and $K - 1$. If a message is encrypted using K then it can only be decrypted using $K - 1$. If $\wedge$ means the application of the encryption function and *text* is the cleartext, then the following hold true:

$$(text) \wedge K \wedge K - 1 = text$$

$$(text) \wedge K \wedge K \neq text$$

$$(text) \wedge K - 1 \wedge K = text$$

$$(text) \wedge K - 1 \wedge K - 1 \neq text$$

Importantly, one cannot derive K from knowledge of $K - 1$ or vice versa. This allows the primary use of public key technology, where one key is made public and the other remains secret. This provides a much larger degree of functionality, extending the use of cryptography to supply authentication and integrity as well as confidentiality.

Authentication is provided by taking a piece of text and encrypting it using the private key which is known only to you. If it can be decrypted using your public key, then it is known to be encrypted by you. This then functions to authenticate the text.

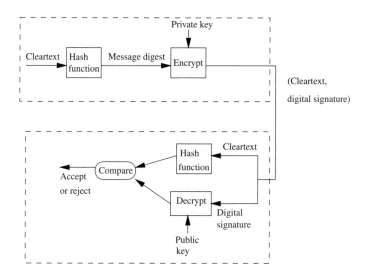

Figure 10.2   Authentication and integrity with digital signatures.

Encryption is slow, so what is used is another mathematical function which takes text in and produces a pseudorandom fixed-size number that can only have come from the original input text. This is known as a *hash function*. The hash function takes in the whole of the cleartext and generates a 128 byte message digest which is then encrypted using the public key. This is known as a *digital signature*. When the receiver receives the message, they run the hash function over the data to regenerate the message digest. They decrypt using the public key, and if the digests match, then they know that the message was sent by the purported sender, and that the message was not interfered with – the integrity of the message has been protected. This process is illustrated in Figure 10.2.

In the original Diffie–Hellman proposal, the two parties, Alice and Bob, choose two large integers, n and g, such that g is less than n. Then the following occurs:

1   Alice chooses a random large integer x and calculates

$$X = g^x \bmod n \tag{1}$$

2   Bob also chooses a random large integer y and calculates

$$Y = g^y \bmod n \tag{2}$$

3   Alice sends Bob X and Bob sends Alice Y. x and y are both kept secret.
4   Alice computes

$$k = Y^x \bmod n \tag{3}$$

5   Bob computes

$$k' = X^y \bmod n \tag{4}$$

Both k and k' equal g^{xy} mod n. However, it is very unlikely that anyone else listening on the channel can calculate the key, since the calculation of discrete logarithms under field arithmetic is very hard (see Galois fields).

Whilst RSA is the normal set of algorithms used in public key cryptography, Diffie–Hellman is still used in such places as the SKIP protocol.

10.4 NETWORK-LEVEL SOLUTIONS

If the goal of security is to prevent the unauthorised discovery of information or use of resources, then one way of meeting this goal is to prevent intruders being able to read or access the protected information. If the intruder cannot copy the communication data, then they cannot read it. So the first level of security is to implement network-level solutions to prevent the traffic being visible to potential miscreants.

At the lowest level, networks are physical communications links and lines joined by packet switches. If these lines, links and switches are physically secured by locking them up in bombproof rooms and guarding the passage of the communication link with razor wire and armed guards, then the administrator can be fairly certain that the lines will not be physically tapped. Not every enterprise has the resources to implement military security, so isolating the network within the headquarters may be sufficient, where the wires run through the dry risers, and switches are kept in locked cupboards and machine rooms.

If communication occurs only between those people in the building, then the administrator may feel fairly happy – they need only worry about the trustworthiness of the employees. But if the network connects with the outside world, the network administrator has to ensure that any valuable information does not inadvertently leak outside. For this, the administrator has to keep a careful rein on the routing of packets within the network, and to carefully configure what is known as a firewall. Whilst this is not the place to discuss in detail securing an enterprise network, we shall discuss the implications of the multicast multimedia for controlling the routing and implementation of firewalls.

The problem with multicast for the conscientious network administrator is that the IP multicast model allows open and unknown receiver groups. For security purposes, this is anathema, and so the security-minded administrator must work at controlling the routing of multicast groups, so that they do not leak outside the protected domain to unknown receivers. One can filter at the boundaries of a network based on known sets of multicast addresses, a technique known as *administrative scoping*. Having set up known groups of addresses, one needs to dynamically grow the boundaries of the enterprise, according to the communication requirements, so one *tunnels* through the Internet to connect bounded domains. Tunnelling is made more difficult through the use of *firewalls*, which need to be carefully configured. In order to disguise communication patterns, e.g. that IBM and Digital executives are talking to each other, the traffic may go through *redistribution centres*. Finally, the eventual goal is for the inter-domain routing of multicast to be amenable to configuring the *policy* of the domains explicitly.

10.4.1 Administrative address scoping

One way of preventing groups leaking is to set up filters on the group addresses at the border routers of the region. This is implemented inside of the mrouted release, but is not terribly well known. A group of addresses is defined as being administratively scoped, and when the addresses reach the borders of the region they are blocked from going outside. Similarly, packets using the same group address in the outside world cannot penetrate inside.

10.4.2 Tunnels

Tunnels, in which packets are encapsulated inside other packets, are a feature of today's Internet since they provide a way of creating a virtual private network (VPN) over the Internet. Two machines are set up as the tunnel end-points, and when traffic is to be sent to the sites from inside one of the other sites, it is redirected to the tunnel end-point, encapsulated inside IP (protocol version 4) or inside a UDP packet, possibly encrypted and sent to the other machine over the Internet.

However, although tunnels provide the VPN, managing them within the framework of multicast IP routing prevents some complex problems. The Mbone has grown as a virtual network using tunnels, but there have been a number of problems related to the fact that all the tunnels have to be manually administered. If a metric is badly set then a site can disappear and seem unreachable. If tunnels are used to connect sites together as a single domain for multicast, then a lot of work must be done to ensure that the domain remains *convex*, i.e. there is no better route to the sites than through the tunnels.[5] If there is, then administratively scoped traffic will not be able to reach the other site. If the traffic does not reach the site then it is useless.

10.4.3 Firewalls

Firewalls are used to prevent traffic entering a site (and sometimes to prevent traffic leaving a site). They work on assuming that the services that people use are fixed and well known and can be configured in a filtering table. However, multicast uses dynamically assigned addresses, and to allow users access to traffic requires a programmable filter.

The safest way of achieving dynamic programming is to use a pair of multicast relay machines either side of the firewall. The machine on the unfriendly side of the firewall receives all the multicast traffic and allows through only groups which it has been programmed to accept. It then encapsulates the traffic and sends it through to the other side of the relay, which checks the origin of the traffic (to prevent spoofing), unwraps it and sends it out. The dynamic programming can be achieved through authenticated RPC control and sensible policy in recognising which sessions should be allowed.

10.4.4   Redistribution centres

Traffic analysis is a potential problem. If both company A and company B are in the same encrypted multicast session, the fact that they are talking to each other may leak valuable information. To prevent this, trusted service providers may provide anonymous redistribution, using address mappings to prevent eavesdroppers from easily determining origin. In order to make traffic analysis more difficult, extra bogus traffic can be generated from the redistribution centre to hide the actual traffic patterns.

10.4.5   Policy routing of multicast

Administrative scoping, tunnels and redistribution centres all have a common aim: to control the routing of multicast traffic so that the receiver and sender groups are constrained. This should really be controlled by the routing protocol, in the same way that the border gateway protocol controls the placement of unicast routes. However, as yet, none of the multicast routing protocols appears to have properly addressed the question of policy (although PIM is doing better than any of the others).

One can expect to see a multicast policy and QoS routing protocol from the IETF within the next year or two.

10.5   MEDIA ENCRYPTION

For the media streams, the processor should be concerned with generating and processing the media, not with encryption. Thus the encryption should be low cost. Fortunately, both DES and IDEA are fast encryption technologies, and data, audio and video can be encrypted in real time on an ordinary processor.

Session keys have to be human readable to allow people to type them in. However, the entropy of the session keys (the randomness) is then badly compromised since the keys tend to come from real words. To increase the distribution of keys over the space of possible keys, most applications generate the actual session key from the input string by running a hash function over the key such as the MD5 digest function. Whilst this does not increase security, it requires attackers to compute an MD5 of every string they want to try.

At which point in the protocol stack to encrypt is yet to be determined. Until the IP security architecture described is in place, the current Mbone applications will use the *ad hoc* approach to encryption discussed in RTP.

10.5.1   IP security architecture

The IP security architecture (Atkinson, 1995a) uses the concept of a security association as the basis for building security functions into IP. A security association is simply the bundle of algorithms and parameters (such as keys) that is being used to encrypt a particular flow. The choice of algorithm is left up to the users. A security parameter index (SPI) is provided along with the destination address to allow the security association for a packet to be looked up. For multicast, therefore, a security association is provided for the group and is duplicated across all authorised receivers of the group. There may be more than one security association for a group, using different SPIs, so allowing multiple levels and sets of security within a group. Indeed, each sender can have multiple security associations, allowing authentication, since a receiver can know only that someone who knows the keys sent the data. Note that the standard does not describe how the association is chosen and duplicated across the group; it is assumed that a responsible party will make the choice.

Two headers have been designed to provide security for both IPv4 and IPv6:

1 The IP authentication header (Atkinson, 1995b) provides integrity and authentication and non-repudiation, if the appropriate choice of cryptographic algorithms is made.

2 The IP encapsulating payload (Atkinson, 1995c) provides confidentiality, along with authentication and integrity.

As usual, the default algorithms used are keyed MD5 for integrity in the AH and DES-CBC (cypher block chaining) for confidentiality in IPEP.

10.5.2 RTP security

Eventually all low-layer security services will be provided by the IP security architecture. However, since deployment of security is never speedy, owing to government intervention and export problems, RTP (Schulzrinne *et al.*, 1996) has defined how streams can be encrypted at the RTP layer to provide confidentiality.

The base encryption algorithm used is DES in CBC mode, with the initialisation vector chosen to be zero. RTP packets have pseudorandom headers from the timestamp, but since RTCP has known plaintext at the start of each packet, a random 32 bit number is prepended to the RTCP header before encryption. Each packet is padded to multiples of 64 bits before encryption. Validity checks on each header are used to ensure that the data have been decrypted properly, such as checking that the payload types are known, and the SSRC ID has been seen before.

Key munging techniques are outside the scope of the specification but are agreed between the implementors of tools which desire to be interoperable.

10.6 KEY DISTRIBUTION

Here we look at the key distribution problems, including aspects of the following:

- Problems of scalability
- SKIP and Photuris
- Core-based trees
- Email – PEM and PGP
- X.509
- Session invitation protocol

The easiest way to distribute a key for a session is by hand (or telephone, or any other out-of-bounds technique), so that the channel is out of bounds from the network, and the user puts the key in by hand. There are a number of problems with this approach though:

- The user may make a mistake in entering the key.
- The key must be secured on its passage.
- It is not very timely.
- It is labour intensive.
- It does not scale.

To reduce the amount of manual work, encrypted email can be used to deliver the key, and the key can be processed automatically by the local environment.

10.6.1 Email invitations

Encrypted email is becoming widespread. The PGP package (Zimmermann, 1995) is widely used, and provides encryption capabilities that are strong enough to satisfy all except the most paranoid. PGP has not acquired the stamp of the IETF, though – the IETF has produced its own secure mail standards in privacy enhanced mail (PEM) and MIME object security services (MOSS). However, given the head-start that PGP has been given, the IETF standards may not be used in the wider world.

With the use of MIME objects encapsulated in secure mail, it is possible to send mail to individuals that will enable the receiver to start the conference applications automatically and securely. If someone wants to start a secure conference, she first collects the names and email addresses of everybody who will be invited. She then constructs the message, adding a specially delineated section that can be used to start the media receivers using the selected address(es) and the keys needed to decrypt the media. She sends the mail out to everybody through her secure email agent, which encrypts, authenticates and adds integrity checks. The receivers get the email and pass it through their secure email agent to discover that it is really from whom they thought, and has not been tampered with. They then have the option of starting the session by using the supplied key and address, or, if their user agent has been enhanced, by simply clicking a button.

However, although secure email improves the scalability of issuing invitations, it still suffers from scalability problems, since a separate email must be sent to each user. In sending the email, the public keys for the receivers must be found, and used, whilst at the receivers, the public key for the sender must be used to decrypt and authenticate the message. If these public keys are cached locally, then this is not too much of a performance problem, but if they must be obtained through the use of a public directory such as X.500, then the overhead in processing the message may be very high. In the case of a pay per view scenario, it is unlikely that the customers would be happy about receiving their keys so slowly.

10.6.2 Certification hierarchies

In using a public system, there has to be a way of obtaining the public key. The obvious way is to store public keys on a server and then request the keys as required from the server. But this presents problems, since if an imposter were able to intercept the request to the server and substitute a different public key, then they would be able to read all mail sent with that key and the intended recipient would not be able to. So, there must be a way of ensuring that public keys are really the intended public key.

One way of doing this is to have a trusted third party authenticate and sign the keys, so that the public key can be believed. This approach is embodied in the X.509 certification standard. This standard defines the format of certificates which are authenticated by trusted third parties, such as the government agency responsible for telecommunications. The authentication of the certificates can be delegated to other agencies, such as Internet service providers, so creating a hierarchy of certifiers. Thus when one receives a certificate, as long as one can trace a path up and down the hierarchy to a certifier one trusts, then one can trust that the public key within the certificate is really the public key of whom it purports to be.

10.6.3 Problems of scalability

The basic problem with using cryptographic techniques is that each person to whom a key must be distributed has to be authenticated. This is not a great way to scale. Alternative solutions which are based on shared secrets are not as secure.

10.6.4 SKIP and Photuris

At the time of writing, the default key management protocol for the IP security architecture has not been chosen. The choice appears to be between Photuris, a connection-oriented session protocol, and SKIP, a stateless connectionless key management scheme. SKIP appears to be the better choice for multicast, so this will be described.

SKIP is based on the Diffie–Hellman transformation, where to construct a key for communication, each of the participants combines their private part with the other's public part to create a shared secret key. This is then used to send a session-specific key to the other which is used from then on. This is completed in message exchange and so requires very little overhead. The construction of the shared secret key can include a time component so that the shared key does not remain constant over time, and since it is used only to pass the session key, there is very little text to attempt to break the secret key of the users.

The public part of the key is assumed to come from a directory of some sort, such as from the X.509 certification hierarchy or secure DNS. To this end, the name space identifying whose public key should be used is flexible and so can use IPv4 or IPv6 address space, domain names or X.500-distinguished names. Keys can also be manually configured for machines, so that the public keys for each of the machines in a trusted network can be stored in a file on each machine.

For multicast, the above approach is generalised by assuming that there is a group owner identified with the group. To get the session-specific keys, the group members contact the group owner using the normal SKIP protocol, and thus the SKIP protocol introduces membership control based on the authentication involved in SKIP.

10.6.5 Core-based trees

As described in Chapter 3, CBT sets up hard state in the routers that are part of the delivery tree. Since a lot of work goes into establishing this tree, it is possible to complement the tree construction with security services such as authentication. In particular, the tree lends itself to scalable key distribution, since the tree can be seen as a hierarchy of routers, with the core at the top of the hierarchy. Key distribution can then be performed by sending the key from the core on demand to the authenticated routers, using encrypted exchanges.

10.6.6 Session announcement protocol

In the session announcement protocols described in Chapter 6, announcements that are multicast out can include a session key for each media stream. Obviously, the announcement packets must themselves be encrypted. It is intended that the receivers will be supplied with keys which are used to receive session announcements. When an encrypted announcement is received, the receiver will go through the set of keys trying to decrypt the message using each of its keys. If it succeeds, then the announcement is displayed and cached, or else it is discarded, and only the ID of the announcement is retained to discard duplicates.

10.7 CONCLUSION

Security in the Internet is improving. The increasing use of the Internet for commerce is improving the deployed technology to protect the financial transactions. Extension of the basic technologies to protect multicast communications is possible and can be expected to be deployed as multicast becomes more widespread.

Control over routing remains the basic tool for controlling access to streams. Implementing particular policies will be possible as multicast routing protocols improve. Cryptography is a tool which may alleviate many of the perceived problems of using the Internet for communications. However, cryptography requires the safe implementation of complex mathematical equations and protocols, and there are always worries about bad implementations. A further worry is that users are integral to securing communications, since they must provide appropriate keys. As the founders of First Virtual point out:

> a safe application of cryptographic technology will pay close attention to how public keys are associated with user identities, how stolen keys are detected and revoked and how long a stolen key is useful to a criminal. (Borenstein, 1996)

Cryptography may be groovy technology, but since security is a human issue, cryptography is only as good as the practices of the people who use it. Users leave keys lying around, choose easily remembered keys, do not change keys for years. The complexity of cryptography puts it outside the understanding of most people and so motivation for the practices of cryptographic security is not available (Anderson *et al.*, 1992).

Notes

1 Since the voice characteristics which make voices unique are removed in compressing speech, it becomes easier to produce good copies of someone else's speech – how many times have you been mistaken for someone else on the 3 kHz telephone?

2 Ponder the irony that the US Department of Defense funded the design of the very open Internet...

3 Of course, it is a lot easier to design a scalable key distribution protocol in a symmetric capacity network such as the current-day Internet, than in an asymmetric system such as the current-day cable TV network or proposed IP on ADSL and cable modem networks.

4 Knowing what a Galois field is represents another convenient barrier to breaking such systems.

5 Recent work is addressing this problem.

Afterword

The future is very hard to predict. Sometimes, technology is selected by the market which is severely suboptimal; but at a large enough production scale, the difference becomes marginal. One can cite CD and VHS video as multimedia examples of just this. In other cases, such as TV standards, the market permits multiple standards to exist.

In the future, the firmament of network technologies will no doubt expand. We can see some interesting transmission technology for expansion of reach and capacity for the Internet in the emergence of cable modems, ADSL and satellite, as well as in mobile/wireless access through GSM, LEO and Wavelan and IrDA access networks.

These will no doubt lead to certain interesting problems. Amongst those that we already know we have to solve are the following:

- Routing and QoS for mobile
- Routing and QoS for asymmetry (cable, ADSL, satellite)
- Quality of service for multicast sessions
- Quantitative scaling for very large groups and very large numbers of groups potentially with high receiver and sender change rates
- Simplicity/management of new services
- Integration of legacy TV/telephone services
- Possible Web/Mbone unification

Glossary

A2D analogue to digital

AAL ATM adaption layer – a framing protocol to enhance cell switched networks

AAL5 framing protocol to turn a cell switched network into a packet switched network

ABR available bit rate – an ATM bearer service class for adaptive applications to be given, dynamically, a fair share of the network

ADSL asymmetric digital subscriber loop – a recent way to provide Mbps over standard telephone lines

ADU application data unit – the program's view of the packet

ALF application-layer framing – a technique for designing protocols around the synchronisation unit that is most convenient for the application

APCM adaptive pulse code modulation

API application programming interface – a standard set of calls for the user

ARP address resolution protocol

ARQ automatic repeat request

ATM asyncronous transfer mode – another name for cell switched networks

AVT audio video transport – the IETF's working group that devised RTP

BCD binary coded decimal

BCH Bose, Chaudhurie and Hocquemham signalling technique

BONDing a technique for turning seperate B-ISDN channels into a higher bandwidth aggregate serial channel

broadband as opposed to narrowband – use of higher capacity, generally. (Specifically, used to refer to use of multiple frequencies on the same transmission medium)

CBQ class-based queuing – an architecture for supporting IP QoS

CBR constant bit rate – ATM bearer service class that emulates leased digital circuits

CBT core-based trees – a multicast routing algorithm

CCCP conference control channel protocol

CD compact disk

Cell B sun video compression scheme

CELP code excited linear predictor – a high compression standard for audio

CEO chief executive officer

CGBT core group based trees, an hierarchical variant of CBT

Chrominance colour content

CIDR classless inter-domain routing – hierarchical aggregation of Internet addresses

CIF common interchange format, as per H.261 video input

CLNP connectionless network protocol

CLNS connectionless network service

CMMC communications multimedia multiplexing centre

CMY cyan, magenta, yellow

CNAME canonical name

codec coder/decoder

CSCW computer-supported collaborative work

CUSeeMe Cornell University's Mac and PC video conferencing tool

DAVIC digital audio video interactive council

DCT discrete cosine transform – basic building block for H.261 and MPEG video compression

DEC LAT Digital Equipment Corporation local area terminals

DES data encryption standard

DHCP dynamic host configuration protocol – an Internet standard for configuring nomadic and mobile hosts

DNS domain name system

DR designated router

DTS digital time service – DEC service similar to NTP

DVB digital video broadcast

DVI digital video interactive

DVMRP distance vector multicast routing protocol

FDCT forward discrete cosine transform protocol

FDDI fibre dual distributed interface – 100 Mbps LAN standard

FEC forward error correction

FTP file transfer protocol

GCC generic conference control

GIF graphic interface format

GSM Groupe Spatiale mobile

GUI graphical user interface

HDTV high definition television

HPIM hierarchical protocol independant multicast

HSV hue, saturation, value

HTML hypertext markup language

HTTP hypertext transfer protocol

IETF Internet engineering task force

IGMP Internet group management protocol

ILP integrated layer processing

imm image multicast

INRIA Institut National de Recherche en Informatique et en Automatique

IP Internet protocol

IPEP IP encapsulating payload

IPv4 version 4 (current) of the Internet protocol

IPv6 version 6 (being developed) of the Internet protocol

ISDN integrated services digital network

ISI Information Sciences Institute

ISSL integrated services over specific link layers

ITU International Telecommunications Union
ivs INRIA videoconferencing system
JPEG Joint Picture Expert Group
LAN local area network
LAT local area terminals
LBL Lawrence Berkeley Laboratories
LPC linear predective coding
LSA link state advertisement
Mbone multicast backbone
MCR minimum cell rate
MCS multipoint communications service
MCU multipoint control unit
MD5 message digest algorithm number 5
MIME multipurpose Internet mail extension
MMCC multimedia conference control
MOSPF multicast open shortest path first
MPEG Motion Picture Expert Group
MTU maximum transfer unit
NACK negative acknowledgement
NBMA non-broadcast multiple access
NFS network file system
nte network text editor
NTP network time protocol
NTSC North American Television Standards Committee
nv network video
OPWA one pass with advertising
OSPF open shortest path first
PCM pulse code modulation
PDA personal digital assistant
PEM privacy enhanced mail
PES packetised elementary stream
PGP pretty good privacy
PIM protocol independent multicast
PNNI private network network interface
PNO public network operator
POTS plain old telephone system
POV point of view
PSDN packet switched digital network
PST Pacific Standard Time
PTT post, telegraph and telephone
PVP packet voice protocol
QCIF quarter common interchange format
QoS quality of service
RDBMS relational database management system
RF radio frequency
RFC request for comments
RGB red, green, blue
RLJMP remote leave and join multicast protocol
RMP reliable multicast protocol

RP rendezvous point
RPC remote procedure call
RSA Rivest Shamir Adelman
RSVP resource reservation protocol
RTCP real time control protocol
RTP real time transport protocol
RTT round-trip time
SCIF super common interchange format
SDAP session directory advertisement protocol
SDP session description protocol
SECAM sequential couleur à memoire
SMDS switched multi-megabit data service
SMTP simple mail transfer protocol
SNA systems network architecture
SNR signal-to-noise ratio
SPF shortest path first
SPI security parameter index
SRM scalable reliable multicast
SSRC synchronisation source
TCP transmission control protocol
TIFF tagged image file format
ToS type of service
UBR unspecified bit rate
UCL University College London
UDP user datagram protocol
UI user interface
UNI4 user network interface 4
URI uniform resource identifier
URL uniform resource locator
UTC universal co-ordinated time
VBR variable bit rate
VC virtual circuit
VCI virtual channel identifier
VCR video cassette recorder
VJCC Van Jacobson congestion control
VoD video-on-demand
VPI virtual path identifier
VPN virtual private network
VR virtual reality
VRAM video random access memory
VRML virtual reality markup language
WAN wide area network
wb whiteboard
WFQ weighted fair queuing
WWW World Wide Web

Bibliography

ALMEROTH K., AMMAR M., (1995) The role of multicast communication in the provision of scalable and interactive video-on-demand service. *Proc. International Workshop on Network and Operating System Support for Digital Audio and Video (NOSSDAV)*, Lecture Notes in Computer Science. Durham, NH: Springer-Verlag, pp. 267–270.

ALTENHOFEN M., DITTRICH J., HAMMERSCHMIDT R., KUPPNER T., KRUSCHEL C., KCKES A., STEINIG T., (1993) The BERKOM multimedia collaboration service. *Proc. ACM Multimedia*, Anaheim, CA, pp. 457–463.

AMIR E., MCCANNE S., ZHANG H., (1994) An application level video gateway. *Proc. ACM Multimedia*, San Francisco.

ANDERSON D. P., OSAWA Y., GOVINDAN R., (1992) A file system for continuous media. *ACM Transactions on Computer Systems*, **10**(4).

ANDERSON R., (1995) Why crypto systems fail. *Communications of the ACM*.

ARANGO M., BATES P., FISH R., GOPAL R., GRIFFETH N., HERMAN G., HICKEY T., LELAND W., LOVERY C., MAK V. *et al.*, (1992a) Touring Machine: a software platform for distributed multimedia applications. *IFIP'92*, Vancouver, p. 11.

ARANGO M., BATES P., GOPAL G., GRIFFETH N., HERMAN G., HICKEY T., LELAND W., MAK V., RUSTON L., SEGAL M. *et al.*, (1992b) Touring Machine: a software infrastructure to support multimedia communications. *ACM Computer Communication Review*, **22**, 53–54.

ARANGO M., KRAMER M., ROHALL S. L., RUSTON L., WEINRIB A., (1992c) Enhancing the Touring Machine API to support integrated digital transport. *Third International Workshop on Network and Operating System Support for Digital Audio and Video*, San Diego, CA. IEEE Communications Society, pp. 166–172.

ARMITAGE G. J., (1995) Multicast and multiprotocol support for ATM based internets. *ACM Computer Communication Review*, **25**, April.

ARMSTRONG S., FREIER A., MARZULLO K., (1992) Multicast transport protocol. RFC 1301.

ATKINSON R. (1995a) Security architecture for the internet protocol. IETF, RFC 1825.

ATKINSON R., (1995b) IP authentication header. RFC 1826.

ATKINSON R., (1995c) IP encapsulating payload. RFC 1827.

AWERBUCH B., AZAR Y., (1995) Competitive multicast routing in virtual circuit environments. *Wireless Networks*, **1**, January.

BAKER F., GUERIN R., KANDLUR D., (1996) Specification of committed rate quality of service. Internet draft. (Work in progess.)

BALLARDIE T., CROWCROFT J., (1995) Multicast-specific security threats and counter-measures. *Proc. ISOC Symposium on Network and Distributed System Security*.

BALLARDIE A., FRANCIS P., CROWCROFT J., (1993) An architecture for scalable inter-domain multicast routing. *Proc. ACM SIGCOMM*, pp. 85–95.

BATES J., BACON J., (1995) Supporting interactive presentation for distributed multimedia applications. *Multimedia Tools and Applications*, **1**, 47–78.

BAUER F., VARMA A., (1995) Degree-constrained multicasting in point-to-point networks. *Proc. Conference on Computer Communications (IEEE Infocom)*, Boston, MA.

BENNETT J. C. R., ZHANG H., (1996) WF2Q: worst-case fair weighted fair queuing. *Proc. Infocom*, March.

BERRA P. B., CHEM C. Y., GHAFOOR A., LIN C. C., LITTLE T., SHIN D., (1990) Architecture for distributed multimedia database systems. *Computer Communications*, **13**(4).

BETTATI R., FERRARI D., GUPTA A., HOWE W., HEFFNER W., MORAN M., NGUYEN Q., YAVATKAR R., (1995) Connection establishment for multi-party real-time communication. *Proc. International Workshop on Network and Operating System Support for Digital Audio and Video (NOSSDAV)*, Lecture Notes in Computer Science. Durham, NH: Springer-Verlag, pp. 255–266.

BIERSACK E., NONNENMACHER J., (1995) WAVE: a new multicast routing algorithm for static and dynamic multicast groups. *Proc. International Workshop on Network and Operating System Support for Digital Audio and Video (NOSSDAV)*, Lecture Notes in Computer Science. Durham, NH: Springer-Verlag, pp. 243–254.

BIRMAN K. P., (1991) The process group approach to reliable distributed computing. Technical Report, Cornell University.

BOLOT J., WAKEMAN I., TURLETTI T., (1994) Scalable feedback control for multicast video distribution in the Internet. *Proc. ACM SIGCOMM*, London.

BORENSTEIN N., (1996) Perils and pitfalls of practical cyber-commerce. *Communications of the ACM*, **39**(6), 36–45.

BRADEN R., CLARK D., SHENKER S., (1994) Integrated services in the Internet architecture: an overview. RFC 1633. ftp://ds.internic.net/rfc/rfc1633.txt

BRADEN R., ZHANG L., BERSON S., HERZOG S., JAMIN S., (1996) Resource reservation protocol (RSVP) – version 1 functional specification. http://www.ietf.org/html.charters/intserv-charter.html.

BRODNIK A., CARLSON S., DEGERMARK M., PINK S., (1997) Small forwarding tables for fast routing lookups. *Proc. ACM SIGCOMM*, Cannes, France. http://www.inria.fr/rodeo/sigcomm97/papers/p192.html.

BUDDHIKOT M. M., PARULKAR G. M., COX J. R., JR, (1994) Design of a large scale multimedia server. *Proc. INET*.

BUSSE I., DEFFNER B., SCHULZRINNE H., (1995) Dynamic QoS control of multimedia applications based on RTP. *First International Workshop on High Speed Networks and Open Distributed Platforms*, St Petersburg.

CAMPBELL A., HUTCHINSON D., AURRECOECHEA C., (1995) Dynamic QoS management for scalable video flows. *Proc. International Workshop on Network and Operating System Support for Digital Audio and Video (NOSSDAV)*, Lecture Notes in Computer Science. Durham, NH: Springer-Verlag, pp. 107–118.

CASNER S., (1993) Frequently asked questions (FAQ) on the multicast backbone (MBone).

CASNER S., (1994) Are you on the MBone? *IEEE MultiMedia*, Summer, pp. 76–79.

CASNER S., DEERING S., (1992) First IETF Internet audiocast. *Computer Communications Review*, **22**(3).

CASNER S., JACOBSON V., (1998) Compressing IPUDPRTP Headers for Low-speed Serial Links. (Work in progress.)

CCITT (1990) *H.261, Video codec for Audiovisual Services*, CCITT/H.261, Geneva.

CHANG Y-C., SHAE Z-Y., WILLEBEEK-LEMAIR H., (1996) Multiparty videoconferencing using IP multicast. *Multimedia Computing and Networking*.

CHERVENAK A. L., (1994) Tertiary storage: an evaluation of new applications. PhD thesis, Dept of Computer Science, University of California at Berkeley.

CLARK D. D., (1988) The design philosophy of the DARPA Internet protocols. *SIGCOMM Symposium on Communications Architectures and Protocols*, Stanford, CA, pp. 106–114.

CLARK D. D., DAVIE B. S., FARBER D. J., GOPAL I. S., KADABA B. K., SMITH J. M., SINCOSKIE D. W., TENNENHOUSE D. L., (1993) The AURORA gigabit testbed. *Computer Networks and ISDN Systems*, **25**, 599–621.

CLARK D. D., TENNENHOUSE D. L., (1990) Architectural considerations for a new generation of protocols. *Proc. ACM SIGCOMM*, Philadelphia.

COLE E., (1981) PVP – a packet video protocol. USC-ISI Technical Report, USC-ISI, LA, August.

CONSULTATIVE COMMITTEE ON INTERNATIONAL TELEGRAPHY AND TELEPHONY (1988) *The Directory: Authentication Framework*, Recommendation X.509. CCITT.

CROWLEY A., (1990) MMConf: an infrastructure for building shared multimedia applications. *Proc. CSCW '90*, Los Angeles.

DABBOUS W., KISS B., (1997) A reliable multicast protocol for a white board application. Research Report, INRIA.

DEERING S., (1988a) Multicast routing. PhD thesis, Stanford University, California.

DEERING S., (1988b) Multicast routing in internetworks and extended LANs. *ACM SIGCOMM*, August, pp. 55–64.

DEERING S., (1989) Host extensions for IP multicasting. RFC 1112.

DEERING S., CHERITON D., (1990) Multicast routing in datagram internetworks and extended LANs. *ACM Transactions on Computer Systems*, May, pp. 85–111.

DEERING S., ESTRIN D., FARINACCI D., JACOBSON V., LIU C-G., WEI L., (1994) An architecture for wide area multicast routing. *ACM CCR*, **24**(4), 126–135.

DEERING S., PARTRIDGE C., WAITZMAN D., (1988) Distance vector multicast routing protocol. RFC 1075, November.

DELGROSSI L., BERGER L., (1995) Internet stream protocol version 2 (ST2) protocol specification – version ST2+. RFC 1819. ftp://ds.internic.net/rfc/rfc1190.txt.

DOAR M., LESLIE I., (1993) How bad is naive multicast routing? *Proc. IEEE Infocom*.

DONNELLEY J., (1994) WWW page distribution using multicast. Technical memorandum, November.

DREYFUS S. E., WAGNER R. A., (1972) The Steiner problem in graphs. *Networks*, **1**, 195–207.

DROMS R. (1993) Dynamic host configuration protocol. RFC 1541, October.

DUVAL E., OLIVIE H., (1993) A distributed multimedia information resource. Dept of Computer Science, Catholic University, Leuven.

ELEFTHERIADIS A., PEJHAN S., ANASTASSIOU D., (1995) Address management and connection control for multicast communication applications. *Proc. Conference on Computer Communications (IEEE Infocom)*, Boston, MA.

ELLIOT C., (1993) High-quality multimedia conferencing through a long-haul packet network. *Proc. ACM Multimedia*, Anaheim, CA, pp. 91–98.

ELLIOT C., (1994) A 'sticky' conference control protocol. *Internetworking: Research and Experience*, **5**, 97–119.

ERIKSSON H., (1993) MBone – the multicast backbone. *Proc. International Networking Conference (INET)*, San Francisco, pp. CCC1–CCC5.

ERIKSSON H., (1994) MBONE: the multicast backbone. *Comm. ACM*, **37**, 54–60.

FALL K., PASQUALE J., MCCANNE S., (1995) Workstation video playback performance with competitive process load. *Proc. International Workshop on Network and Operating System Support for Digital Audio and Video (NOSSDAV)*, Lecture Notes in Computer Science. Durham, NH: Springer-Verlag, pp. 179–182.

FIELDING R., FRYSTYK H., BERNERS-LEE T., (1996) Hypertext transfer protocol HTTP/1.1. RFC 1945.

FIROIU V., TOWSLEY D., (1995) Call admission and resource reservation for multicast sessions. Technical Report TR 95-17, Department of Computer Science, University of Massachusetts.

FLOYD S., JACOBSON V., (1993a) Random early detection gateways for congestion avoidance, *IEEE/ACM Transactions on Networking*, **1**(4) 397–413.

FLOYD S., JACOBSON V., (1993b) On the synchronisation of periodic routing messages. *Proc. ACM SIGCOMM*, San Francisco.

FLOYD S., JACOBSON V., MCCANNE S., LIU C-G., ZHANG L., (1995) A reliable multicast framework for lightweight sessions and application level framing. *Proc. ACM SIGCOMM*, Cambridge, MA.

FREDERICK R., (1994) Experiences with real-time software video compression. *Sixth International Workshop on Packet Video*, July.

GAUTHIER E., LE BOUDEC J-Y., OECHSLIN PH., (1996) Many-to-Many ATM Multicast. Report no. 96/168, EPFL.

Generic Conference Control, (1996) ITU Recommendation T.124.

GULBRANDSEN A., VIXIE P., (1996) A DNS RR for specifying the location of services. Internet draft: draft-gulbrandsen-dns-rr-srvcs-02.txt. (Work in progress.)

HAMPAPUR A., JAIN R., WEYMOUTH T. E., (1995) Production model based digital video segmentation. *Multimedia Tools and Applications*, **1**, 9–46.

HANDLEY M., (1995) The use of plain text keys for encryption of multimedia conferences. Draft V1.4.

HANDLEY M., (1995) Network Text (nt) – A scalable shared text editor for the Mbone. Dept of Computer Science, University College London.

HANDLEY M., (1996) SAP: session directory announcement protocol. Internet draft: draft-ietf-mmusic-sap-00.txt. (Work in progress.)

HANDLEY M., JACOBSON V., (1996) SDP: session description protocol. Internet draft: draft-ietf-mmusic-sdp-02.txt.

HANDLEY M., WAKEMAN I., CROWCROFT J., (1995) The conference control channel protocol. *Proc. ACM SIGCOMM*, Cambridge, MA.

HARDMAN V., SASSE A., WATSON A., (1995) Reliable audio for use over the Internet. *Proc. INET*.

HEDRICK C., (1988) Routing information protocol. RFC 1058, June.

HEINANEN J., (1996) Protected best effort service. Internet draft: ftp://ds.internic.net/internet-drafts/draft-heinanen-pbe-svc-01.txt.

HOFFMAN D., FERNANDO G., LYON T., (1994) RTP encapsulation of MPEG1/MPEG2. Internet draft.

HOFFMAN D., SPEER M., FERNANDO G., (1993) Network support for dynamically scaled multimedia data streams. *Proc. 4th International Workshop on Network and Operating System Support for Digital Audio and Video*, Lancaster, UK, pp. 251–262.

HOLBROOK H., SINGHAL S., CHERITON D., (1995) Log-based receiver-reliable multicast for distributed interactive simulation. *ACM SIGCOMM*, **25**(4), 328–341.

HUITEMA C., (1992) Software codecs and work-station video conferences. *Proc. INET92*, Kobe, Japan.

IEEE (1993) Protocols for distributed interactive simulation applications. IEEE Standard for Information Technology, pp. 1278–1993.

IETF (n.d.) home page, http://www.ietf.cnri.reston.va.us.

INTEGRATED SERVICES (n.d.) Charter. http://www.ietf.org/html.charters/intserv-charter.html.

INTEGRATED SERVICES OVER SPECIFIC LINK LAYERS (n.d.) Charter. http://www.ietf.org/html.charters/issll-charter.html.

ISAACS E. A., MORRIS T., RODRIGUEZ T. K., TANG J. C., (1995) A comparison of face-to-face and distributed presentations. *Proc. Conference on Computer Human Interaction (CHI)*, Denver, CO, pp. 354–361.

ITU Recommendation H.320. Available from http://www.itu.int/.

JACOBSON V., (1988) Congestion avoidance and control. *ACM SIGCOMM*, **18**(4), 314–329.

JACOBSON V., (1990) Compressing TCP IP headers for low-speed serial links. RFC 1144, January.

JACOBSON V., (1994a) Internet multimedia tutorial. ACM SIGCOMM Conference, London. http://www.cs.ucl.ac.uk/mice/van/.

JACOBSON V., (1994b) Multimedia conferencing on the Internet. *SIGCOMM Symposium on Communications Architectures and Protocols*, London. (Tutorial slides.)

JACOBSON V., MCCANNE S., (1992) The LBL audio tool vat. Unix manual.

KADIRIRE J., (1994) Minimising packet copies in multicast routing by exploiting geographic spread. *ACM CCR*, **24**(3), 47–62.

KADIRIRE J., (1995) Comparison of wide-area dynamic multicast routing algorithms. *Proc. Conference on Computer Communications (IEEE Infocom)*, Boston, MA.

KATO T., MIZUTORI T., (1989) Multimedia data model for advanced image information system. *ADSS*, Kyoto.

KELLY F. P.,(1994) Tariffs and effective bandwidths in multiservice networks. *Proc. 14th Int. Teletraffic Cong.*, Amsterdam: North-Holland/Elsevier Science. **1**, 387–410.

KELLY F. P., (1996) Charging and accounting for bursty connections. In L. W. McKnight and J. P. Bailey (eds), *Internet Economics*. Reading, MA: MIT Press.

KIRSTEIN P. T., HANDLEY M. J., SASSE M. A., (1993) Piloting of multimedia integrated communications for European researchers (MICE). *Proc. International Networking Conference (INET)*, San Francisco, pp. DCA1 – DCA12.

KUMAR V., (1995) *MBone: Interactive Multimedia on the Internet*. London: Macmillan.

LEINER B. M., COLE R. H., POSTEL J. B., MILLS D., (1985) The DARPA Internet protocol suite. *Proc. IEEE Infocom*.

LIDL K., OSBORNE J., MALCOLM J., (1994) Drinking from the firehose: multicast USENET news. *Proc. Usenix Winter Conference*, San Francisco, pp. 33–45.

LINN J., (1993) Privacy enhancement for Internet electronic mail. Part I: Message encryption and authentication procedures. RFC 1421, February.

LITTLE T. D. C., GHAFOOR A., (1991) Spacio-temporal composition of distributed multimedia objects for value-added networks. *IEEE Computer*, no. 10, 42–50.

LUN K., LAW E., LEONGARCIA A., (1995) Multicast and self-routing in ATM radix trees and banyan networks. *Proc. Conference on Computer Communications (IEEE Infocom)*, Boston, MA.

MACEDONIA M. R., BRUTZMAN D. P., (1994) Mbone provides audio and video across the Internet. *IEEE Computer*, **27**(4), 30–36.

MACKIE-MASON J., VARIAN H., (1993) Some economics of the Internet. *Networks, Infrastructure and the New Task of Regulation*. Cambridge, MA: MIT Press.

MCCANNE S., (1996) Scalable compression and transmission of Internet multicast video. Report no. UCB/CSD 96-928 (PhD thesis).

MCCANNE S., JACOBSON V.,(1995) vic: a flexible framework for packet video. *Proc. ACM Multimedia*.

MCCANNE S., JACOBSON V., VETTERLI M., (1996) Receiver-driven layered multicast. *ACM SIGCOMM*, August.

MILLS D., (1990) Network time protocol version 2 specification and implementation. RFC 1305.

MITZEL D., ESTRIN D., SHENKER S., ZHANG L., (1994) An architectural comparison of ST-II and RSVP. *Proc. Infocom*. http://www.isi.edu/div7/rsvp/pub.html.

MONTGOMERY T., (1997) RMP: http://research.ivv.nasa.gov/projects/RMP/RMP.html. NASA/Berkeley, Concurrent Engineering Research Center. !tmont@cerc.wvu.edu¿

MOY J., (1993) Multicast routing extensions for OSPF. *Proc. International Networking Conference (INET)*, San Francisco, pp. BCC1 – BCC7.

MOY J., (1994) Multicast extensions to OSPF. RFC 1584, March.

NATIONAL INSTITUTE OF STANDARDS AND TECHNOLOGY (1988) *FIPS Publication 46-1: Data Encryption Standard*. NIST.

NIBLACK W., BARBER R., (1993) The QBIC project: querying images by content using color, texture, and shape. *IS&T/SPIE Symposium on Electronic Imaging: Science and Technology*.

PALIWODA K., CROWCROFT J., (1988) A reliable multicast transport protocol, *ACM SIGCOMM*.

PAREKH A., GALLAGHER R., (1993) A generalized processor sharing approach to flow control – the single node case. *IEEE / ACM Transactions on Networking*, **1**(3), 366–357.

PAREKH A., GALLAGHER R., (1996) A generalized processor sharing approach to flow control – the multiple node case. *IEEE/ACM Transactions on Networking*, **2**(2), 137–150.

PARNES P., (1997) RTP extension for scalable reliable multicast. LuTH/CDT draft-parnes-avt-srm-00.txt. (Work in progress.)

PARTRIDGE C., (1993) *Gigabit Networking*. Reading, MA: Addison-Wesley.

PARTRIDGE C., MENDEZ T., MILLIKEN W., (1993) Host anycasting service. RFC 1546, November.

PEJHAN S., ELEFTHERIADIS A., ANASTASSIOU D., (1995) Distributed multicast address management in the global internet. *IEEE Journal on Selected Areas in Communications*, **13**, 1445–1456.

PERKINS C., HARDMAN V., SASSE A., (1997) The robust audio tool. *Communications of the ACM*, **41**(5), 74–80.

PLUMMER D. C., (1982) An ethernet address resolution protocol. RFC 826, November.

POSTEL J., ed. (1981a) Internet protocol. RFC 791, September.

POSTEL J., ed. (1981b) Transmission control protocol. RFC 793, September.

RANGAN P. V., VIN H. M., RAMANATHAN S., (1992) Designing an on-demand multimedia service. *IEEE Communications Magazine*, **30**(7).

RATHKE B. K., (1995) Evaluation of a distance-vector based multicast-routing protocol for datagram internetworks. Diplomarbeit, Department of Telecommunications, TU Berlin, Berlin.

RAVINDRAN K., (1995) A flexible network architecture for data multicasting in 'multiservice networks'. *IEEE Journal on Selected Areas in Communications*, **13**, 1426–1444.

RIVEST R., (1992) The MD5 message-digest algorithm, RFC 1321, MIT Laboratory for Computer Science and RSA Data Security, Inc., April.

ROWE L., BORECZKY J. S., EADS C. A., (1994) Indexes for user access to large video databases. Computer Science Division, University of California at Berkeley.

ROWE L., SMITH B. C., (1992) A continuous media player. Computer Science Division, University of California at Berkeley.

SALTZER J. H., REED D. P., CLARK D. D., (1984) End-to-end arguments in system design, *ACM Transactions on Computer Systems*, **2**(4), 277–288.

SASSE A., BILTING U., SCHULTZ C-D., TURLETTI T., (1994) Remote seminars through multimedia conferencing: experiences from the MICE project. *Proc. INET*.

SCHNEIER B., (1994) *Applied Cryptography*. New York: Wiley.

SCHOOLER E. M., (1991) A distributed architecture for multimedia conference control. Technical Report ISI/RR-91-289, University of Southern California/Information Sciences Institute.

SCHOOLER E. (1992) The impact of scaling on a multimedia connection architecture. *Proc. Third International Workshop on Network and Operating System Support for Digital Audio and Video*, San Diego, CA.

SCHOOLER E. M., (1993) Case study: multimedia conference control in a packet-switched teleconferencing system. *Journal of Internetworking: Research and Experience*, **4**(2), 99–120. Also available as an ISI technical report ISI/RS-93-359 (August 1993). ftp://ftp.isi.edu/pub/hpccpapers/mmc/joi.ps.

SCHULZRINNE H., (1995) Dynamic configuration of conferencing applications using pattern-matching multicast. *Proc. International Workshop on Network and Operating System Support for Digital Audio and Video (NOSSDAV)*, Lecture Notes in Computer Science (LNCS). Durham, NH: Springer-Verlag, pp. 231–242.

SCHULZRINNE H., (1996) Personal mobility for multimedia services in the Internet. *IMDS'96*, 4–6 March. ftp://ftp.fokus.gmd.de/pub/step/papers/Schu9603: Personal.ps.gz.

SCHULZRINNE H., CASNER S., FREDERICK R., JACOBSON V., (1996) RTP: a transport protocol for real-time applications. RFC 1889.

SHENKER S., CLARK D., ESTRIN D., HERZOG S., (1996a) Pricing in computer networks: reshaping the research agenda. In L. W. McKnight and J. P. Bailey (eds), *Internet Economics*. Reading, MA: MIT Press.

SHENKER S., PARTRIDGE C., GUERIN R., (1996b) Specification of guaranteed quality of service. Internet draft: ftp://ds.internic.net/internet-drafts/draft-ietf-intserv-guaranteed-svc-06.txt.

SHENKER S., WEINRIB A., SCHOOLER E., (1994) Managing shared ephemeral state: policy and mechanism. *Proc. International Workshop on Multimedia Transport and Teleservices (COST237)*, Vienna.

STEVENS W. R., (1992) *TCP/IP Illustrated*, Vol. 1, Reading, MA: Addison-Wesley. Also Vol. 2, 1994; Vol. 3, 1996.

STUBBLEBINE S., (1993) Security services for multimedia conferencing. *Proc. 16th National Computer Security Conference*, Baltimore, MD, pp. 391–395.

SUN MICROSYSTEMS COMPUTER CORP., (1993) Cell image-compression bytestream descriptions. (Unpublished memorandum.)

TALPADE R., AMMAR M. H., (1995) Single connection emulation (SCE): an architecture for providing a reliable multicast transport service. Technical Report GIT-CC-94-47, Georgia Institute of Technology, Atlanta, GA.

TANG J. C., ISAACS E., (1993) Why do users like video? Studies of multimedia-supported collaboration. *Computer Supported Cooperative Work (CSCW)*, **1**, 163–196.

TENNENHOUSE D. L., (1989) Layered multiplexing considered harmful. In H. Rudin and R. Williamson (eds), *Protocols for High Speed Networks*. Amsterdam: Elsevier.

THYAGARAJAN A. S., CASNER S. L., DEERING S. E., (1995) Making the MBone real. *Proc. International Networking Conference (INET)*, San Francisco, p. 9.

THYAGARAJAN A. S., DEERING S., (1995) Hierarchical distance vector multicast routing for the Mbone. *ACM CCR*, **25**(4), 60–67.

TIERNEY B. L., JOHNSON W. E., (1994) The image server system: a high speed parallel distributed data server. LBL-36002, Lawrence Berkeley Laboratory.

TOPOLCIC C., (1990) Experimental Internet stream protocol, version 2 (ST-II). RFC 1190. ftp://ds.internic.net/rfc/rfc1190.txt.

VIN H. M., RANGAN P. V., (1993) Designing a multiuser HDTV storage server. *IEEE Journal on Selected Areas In Communications*, **11**(1).

WAKEMAN I., (1993) Multimedia application requirements for multicast communications services. *Proc. International Networking Conference (INET)*, San Francisco, pp. BFB1–BFB9.

WAKEMAN I., GHOSH A., CROWCROFT J., JACOBSON V., FLOYD S., (1995) Implementing real time packet forwarding policies using streams. *Proc. Usenix Conference*, New Orleans.

WALL D. W., (1980) Mechanisms for broadcast and selective broadcast. PhD thesis, Dept of Electrical Engineering, Stanford University.

WATERS G., (1994) A new heuristic for ATM multicast routing. 2nd IFIP Conference on Performance Modelling, Bradford, 4–7 July.

WAXMAN B. M., (1995) Models for multipoint connections in gigabit networks. *Proc. of Gigabit Networking Workshop*, Boston, MA.

WEI L., ESTRIN D., (1994) A comparison of multicast trees and algorithms. *Infocom.*

WHITE P., CROWCROFT J., (1997) The integrated service internet – state of the art. *Proc. IEEE*, **85**(12), 1934–1946.

WROCLAWSKI J., (1996a) Specification of the controlled-load network element service. Internet draft: ftp://ds.internic.net/internet-drafts/draft-ietf-intserv-ctrl-load-svc-03.txt.

WROCLAWSKI J., (1996b) The use of RSVP with IETF integrated services. Internet draft. (Work in progress.)

ZHANG H., STEPHEN D., (1998) Implementing distributed packet fair queueing. *A Scalable Switch Architecture.*

ZHANG L., DEERING S., ESTRIN D., SHENKER S., ZAPPALA D., (1993) Rsvp: a new resource ReSerVation protocol. *IEEE Network*, **7**, 8–18.

ZHANG L., SHENKER S., CLARK D., HUITEMA C., DEERING S., FERRARI D., (1995) Reservations or no reservations. *Proc. Conference on Computer Communications (IEEE Infocom)*, Boston, MA. (Panel-discussion slides.)

ZIMMERMANN P., (1995) *The Official PGP User's Guide*. Reading, MA: MIT Press.

Index

Entries of the form *x.y.z*, which refer to Section numbers, and Ch. *X*, which refer to Chapter numbers are immediately followed by the page number on which that Section or Chapter begins